D1069390

# From Crisis to Crisis

Debates on why architecture criticism matters today

Editors:
Nasrin Seraji
Sony Devabhaktuni
Xiaoxuan Lu

Department of Architecture
University of Hong Kong

# Contents

# Preface

'Just what polemical position do you write from Madame?' a French journalist asks
of Ada Louise Huxtable. To which she answers, 'From crisis to crisis…'
–Ada Louise Huxtable, *On Architecture* (2008)

*Prelude*
On a beautiful, clear and crisp October afternoon in 2016 in Hong Kong, while
re-reading the twelfth book in the well-known and colourful AA Words series –
this one on Lina Bo Bardi and marked by a bright pink cover – an idea sparked: a
symposium on criticism and architecture.

Bo Bardi's essays may seem out of date to some. They are mostly about the
social duties of architecture and about how architects are not achieving much if
they are unaware of their socio-political context. At that moment, I thought as
well of architecture critic Ada Louise Huxtable, who had died a few years earlier.

My *esprit d'escalier* took me to other questions: why was there so little interest
among students to engage in debate? Why weren't there any radical movements
in architecture these days, as in the 1960s and 1970s? Why is architecture being
confused with object design? Why is architecture no longer political?

Would architecture students from the University of Hong Kong head to the
streets to save a building as students had done for the Sydney Opera House?
Remembering things past: the energy of the New South Wales student protests
backed by young architects such as Harry Seidler, sparked when the conservative
government forced Jørn Utzon to resign and refused to pay him, arguing that he
was late with deliverables and had gone over budget. Times have changed.

*Intermezzo*
Taking the reins of a department of architecture with only 60 years of history
was an exciting but also challenging perspective. Exciting, for it could be a true
laboratory for questioning architectural education after having toured some of

the best schools in Europe and the United States: the new chapter in Asia would complete the 'Grand Tour'. Challenging because the department was set in its habits. It had its own 'ways to do things'. Lectures and lecture series were put together based on who was going to be 'in town' or, at best, a loose theme that brought some sort of continuity. Architecture was not treated as culture, but rather mostly as a profession.

Perhaps most schools still function in this very conservative, old-hat way: preparing students for a profession that no longer exists. Architectural education has never been so in need of criticism as a means to find a way forward.

Pedagogical programmes are currently often modelled on curricula that date from when a generation of late-boomers were themselves students in the late 1970s and early 1980s. This was a time when drawing was debated as a form of description – as architectural writing – and when utopias were real and crucial. It was a time when the Architectural Association, Cornell and the Cooper Union were the most difficult schools to get into because of the radical productions of their students. Today, these schools don't appear on the QS (Quacquarelli Symonds) rankings; they are not universities and do not produce 'academic research'.

I had these thoughts about criticism and architectural education at a moment when the world was in crisis: Donald Trump had just been elected president of the United States, Europe was steering to the extreme right, the left was in a mode of intellectual deficit. This crisis has not abated. Through it all, criticism is suffering.

China is seemingly ever closer to economic parity with the US. Its global influence has equalled that of any other nation. Yet, it is still difficult to publish and write freely, let alone critically. If architecture is losing ground because of economic changes and technological breakthroughs, how do we debate and teach the humanistic core that is the basis of its existence?

Around the globe, architectural periodicals serve as the advertising agencies and portfolios of architects. Magazines such as *l'Architecture D'aujourd'hui* live on the fumes of early myth, though very much in despair: no budget, hence no real editorial line. Every issue is guest edited and fragmented. Freelance writers work not knowing whether they will contribute, and be paid, from one issue to the next.

*Dezeen* and *ArchDaily* ('broadcasting architecture worldwide') have usurped the role of the printed page, replacing it with a single, continuous stream of advertising, architectural objects, 'daily-design' paraphernalia and interviews. All within an infinite database of content, saturated images and the possibility to click as you please, or as you 'like'; this information is read by a global community of architects as the whole truth.

The few magazines that discuss architecture as a socio-political urgency are most-often run by teaching staff, researchers and architects discontent with the state of practice. They are sometimes non-profit organisations: *Log, Criticat, OASE, Manifest* and *AA Files*[1] are among the best.

But, if most students (and some faculty) don't read (as a mark of pride), if they don't go to lectures, if they don't like to be present in debates, then why should the production of critical thinking matter? Criticism has been reduced to 'good or bad', 'like or don't like'. Notions of a discursive, nuanced understanding of the societies in which we operate have been lost. Criticism is now synonymous with aggressive views, as 'not being nice'. How can we still be optimistic about education?

*Finale*
If we don't re-invent 'the education of an architect', the discipline will look more and more like the corporate system dominating the world much the same way advertising in the 1960s moulded a society of spectacle and consumerism.

*From Crisis to Crisis: Reading, Writing and Criticism in Architecture*[2] was offered as a platform to discuss and investigate the state of architectural criticism and its future role in the formation of young architects. In the contributions gathered in this collection, we partake in the generosity and pertinence of ideas

1    Since our symposium in April 2017, *AA Files* has disappeared in spite of a global uproar on social media. Its discontinuation has been explained through the unacceptable excuse of financial deficit
2    The title of the symposium has metamorphosed, hence the book's title insists on the necessity of debate and criticism in architecture.

from an international cohort of architects who have mostly chosen not to design buildings. They have crafted alternatives to the traditional practice of architecture. They have created journals, books, blogs and forums for a critical debate. They teach, write and craft architecture as an intellectual and cultural discipline.

Together, we reflected on how to situate architectural criticism in a global, neoliberal market. We passed through history as a marker of positions on contemporary criticism. We explored the art of criticism in China where methods, discourse and 'being modern' have specific histories and meanings. This also enabled us to discuss pedagogy in a postmodern, post-liberal society and to draw hypothetical conclusions as to where the education of architects may be leading. We explored the recurring mandate in universities around the world to exclude the architectural discipline, and consequently design, as non-academic 'research'. Over three days of discussion, the optimism that seems at this moment to be evanescent was confronted by the possibility that the architect still has the capacity to be an intellect with the tools to transform the world.

I would like to thank all the speakers and participants, the faculty who introduced each session, and especially Sony and Lu who have, for the past year and a half, tirelessly put their energy, trust and good will in carrying forward this *chantier*.

I wish the University of Hong Kong's department of architecture many more symposia and publications of this quality and calibre.

Nasrin Seraji AA dipl FRIBA
Professor and Head of the Department of Architecture
June 2018 Hong Kong

# Criticism Today

## Criticism Today
Eunice Seng

What are the forms and spaces of contemporary architectural criticism? How does one pursue architecture, not least architectural inquiry, in this milieu? The turn towards the marginal, the ordinary and the vernacular, which once occupied the postwar avant-garde and challenged universal modernism, have today been normalised, giving way to nostalgia. What and where are the sites, old and new, in which discourses are produced, cultivated and disseminated? With the emergence of global networks of commentators, there is a pressing need for informed local inquiry.

The past two decades have witnessed a crucial shift in commentary on contemporary building construction. Until 2000, the dominant architectural discourses coming out of the East Coast academic scene could be traced through the journals *Oppositions* (1973–84), *Assemblage* (1986–2000) and *Any* (1993–2000). These three publications provided a counterpoint to *Architectural Record*, founded in 1981 and still in print, which was aimed at architecture, engineering and design professionals. Yet the voices cultivated within these journals are still heard today, and they have collectively elicited a post-critical response.

The 2000s then saw notable efforts to rethink and update the status of the magazine/journal as a discourse-maker through the peer reviewed *Grey Room* (2000) by MIT Press, the student-run *306090* (2002–13) by Princeton Architectural Press, and *Log* (2003), also published by the ANY Corporation. No longer claiming to be the prime bearers of discourse and acknowledging that architecture was moving towards a 'pure image', editors of *Log* asserted that, from the start, their project created a space for 'recording observations of the present through writing in time'.[1] Now available both in print and in a downloadable digital format, *Log* represents an attempt to relocate a space for reflection and critical inquiry in architecture against a backdrop of image and rhetoric.

Fed by the postwar discourses of the North American Ivy League and compelled by the anxieties of postcolonial and national ethnic subjectivities, my attempts to locate the sources and spaces of criticality have consisted

1 Cynthia Davidson, 'What's in a Log?', *Log* 1 (Fall 2003) pp5–8.

of a discovery and recovery of suppressed, latent histories; and the re-encounter with other narratives, mostly stemming from critiques of neoliberal globalisation that flattens the diversity and cogency of relations and local histories.

In her essay 'What Is Critical about Chinese Architectural History?' Swati Chattopadhyay highlights that the crisis of history is viewed differently by different constituencies, though for some, this has launched 'a myriad of profitable enterprises'.[2] This demands new analytical modes and creates possibilities for a historical imagination distinct from the one that has been articulated in Europe and the US. Chattopadhyay's essay resonates with Stanislaus Fung's observation that the information-poor context among Chinese architects and educators means that the most effective way to engage Chinese audiences is through a close reading of buildings with multiple images. Ideas are sharpened through contrasts between positions. Referring to the study of strategies of meaning in China and Greece developed by French philosopher Francois Jullien, he believes that for Chinese people, 'to be critical is to be performative rather than constative'.[3]

In 'Slashed', published in *e-flux*, Joan Ockman attributes the demise of criticism to the 'managerial revolution' that has overtaken architectural academia: 'Instead of history/theory today', she writes, 'what we now have is research … As for criticism: arguably, we now have something like curation. History/theory has turned into research/curation.'[4] That Ockman used an online platform to comment on the contemporary status of history, theory and criticism is a tacit acknowledgement of certain transformations in architectural production: the dispersal of architectural discourse, the predominance of the architectural project as pure image, and the media socialisation of architecture.

The emergence of online platforms such as *Design Boom* (1999) *Dezeen* (2006), *Archdaily* (2008) and *The Architect's Newspaper* (first introduced in print in 2003), print-on-demand journals and blogs have seen far greater readership than print publications. The globalised architectural practice

2  Swati Chattopadhyay, 'What Is Critical about Chinese Architectural History?', *Journal of the Society of Architectural Historians* vol 73, no 1 (March 2014) pp5–7.
3  Stanislaus Fung, 'Orientation: Notes on Architectural Criticism and Contemporary China', *JSAH* vol 62, no 3 (2009) pp16–17, 96.
4  Joan Ockman, 'Slashed', *e-flux architecture, History/Theory* (2018).

ushered in by starchitects has seen the proliferation of a visual architectural culture marked by impatience and distraction, as online platforms respond at increasingly rapid speeds with more information. As Sarah Whiting candidly explains, 'Labour has become measured in the quantity of opinions produced … Simultaneity has replaced singularity.'[5] With distraction a universal marker, everyone is now a critic.[6] Like/dislike is the main operative mode.

The line between theory, criticism and building has always been highly tenuous. As Manfredo Tafuri noted, these connections remain problematic because the making and writing of architecture in the age of (global) capital negates any operative possibility of criticism. With architectural criticism now fully socialised by the media, any exegesis on architectural production confronts the problem of how to reach diffuse publics and how to cultivate forums where ideas can be applied to local issues.

The authors in this section – publishing architectural criticism in French, Farsi and English – highlight the challenges of writing simultaneously for specialist and general publics. Françoise Fromonot, cofounder and editor of *Criticat*, foregrounds tendencies and processes in contemporary urbanism and recuperates the architectural project as a production of theory and criticism. Kamran Afshar Naderi cultivates *Memar* as an incubator for architectural criticism and a place to advocate for urban design and architecture in post-revolution Iran. Graham Brenton McKay situates his blog *Misfits' Architecture* as an 'online research laboratory' to raise questions on the relevance of the 'architectural avant-garde and glitterati', and also to discover those who make meaningful contributions to 'better performing buildings'. Differing contexts notwithstanding, they insist that making space for criticism is imperative.

5  Sarah Whiting, 'Possibilitarianism', *Log* 29 (Fall 2013) p53.
6  Joshua Rothman, 'A New Theory of Distraction', *The New Yorker* (2015).

# Out of Control – From Crises to *Krisis*

Françoise Fromonot

If we listen to economists, sociologists, climatologists, political scientists and, more widely, to the numerous experts that scrutinise, evaluate and even predict the state of our world, the dramatic crises generated by the developments of unfettered global capitalism are only beginning. Among them, or perhaps encapsulating all of them, the environmental crisis with its potentially devastating consequences – rarefaction of resources, climatic disasters, population displacements – could and probably will be the crisis of all crises: an endless series of uncontrolled catastrophes as powerful as our uncontrolled thirst for wealth, comfort and status.

As part of a major segment of the world economy, architecture and its related fields – urbanism, urban design and even product design – have a responsibility within this threatening state of things. Altogether, building activities account for more than half of greenhouse gas emissions, and perhaps more if you also include the resources and energy needed to produce, maintain and recycle buildings and the substances from which they are made.

Indeed, the building professions are dependent on this situation, whose features largely escape their scope of influence. Cycles of growth and recession generate both cuts in public funding and the rampant privatisation of public space, social services and housing (itself once a collective ideal is now a mere speculative commodity). Wealthy societies attempt to compensate for the decline of their industries by imposing new technologies, new materials and new regulations to stimulate their building economy under the rarely questioned imperative for 'innovation' or 'sustainability'.

All of these dynamics affect the way architecture is commissioned, designed, calculated, built, perceived and used. The seductive forms of celebrated contemporary buildings are more often than not a dressing-up of this seemingly inescapable condition. The more spectacular the envelope, the more powerless the architect. The paradox becomes apparent as a whole profession is increasingly deprived of fully exercising its capacities to translate the concerns of *project* into design beyond the required *imagineering* of a given commission.

If one of the roles of criticism is to clarify what is at stake in order to enlighten judgment, then in this situation the urge for criticism has never been more pressing. For architecture, this means that inquiry into selected problematic designs has the potential to generate an intelligence that can possibly be folded back into practice. However architectural criticism is often reduced either to a specialised branch of cultural journalism or to an academic – theoretical or research-based – exercise. Both are of course absolutely necessary, but do they really count as *criticism*?

In the first instance, journalism, whether in daily newspapers, weekly magazines, professional journals or online, is at best an informed commentary on a selection of singular formal achievements. The problem is, of course, that these buildings are published because they are remarkable, and they are remarkable because they are published. In this vortex, articles about recent buildings are based on, and illustrated with, information and images provided, directly or not, by the architects themselves, often in press kits sent by public relations agents or distributed during visits. Sometimes this information is even 'borrowed' from other journals or blogs. The same facts and pictures circulate endlessly to the point of creating a kind of surrogate reality. Commentary on these spectacular achievements is destined for a broad public mainly interested in trends and lifestyle, and for architects eager to see these works as mirrors of their profession at its best.

In academic work, research is meant to be more independent, thorough and informed. It claims scientific value in so far as its base material is properly sourced and its information can be traced. Arguments are demonstrated; hypotheses and conclusions are problematised. Academic work is aimed at widening disciplinary knowledge, constantly laying new grounds on which to build new research. It is therefore mainly directed towards specialists – architectural academia and its insiders – generating little or no debate beyond its walls.

I certainly do not intend to dismiss either of these activities. I practise them myself – by writing on contemporary architecture in various journals, by researching architectural history to produce books and essays and by running academic seminars. But as far as criticism goes, neither journalism nor research fundamentally challenge the broad reality that architecture both contributes to and depends upon, particularly in regard to the politics that account for our current state.

*Five points, four 'tools'*

How then to escape these dilemmas? Perhaps by trying to build an architectural criticism that is as accessible, readable and enjoyable as cultural journalism – with the rigour that this genre sustains in other fields – and as informed, reliable, articulate and reflexive as academic research, leaving aside its rigid codes. In other words, a *demanding* criticism that aims at elucidating both the contemporary condition and its expression in our built environments in order to transform thinking and to re-generate debate in architectural circles and beyond.

I have pursued this somewhat ambitious goal or philosophy through a journal called *Criticat*, started from scratch in 2008 with a small group of friends, both architects and academics. The editorial content and voice of *Criticat* have been built up from a series of simple principles. First, consider *architecture as a vantage point*. Architecture stands by definition at the crossroads of many fields – economics, social issues, aesthetics, technology, industry, material culture – that make it an ideal platform to observe, discuss and evaluate one and the other, or one through the others. Rather than explain and justify architecture with an elaborate set of cultural and social considerations, *Criticat* strives to examine society and culture through the lens, or magnifying glass, to reintegrate it into everyday issues and discussions.

A second principle was to treat criticism as a dissection of artefacts – a deconstruction of evidence that leads to the *de-naturalisation of cultural reality*. In the late 1970s, in the European context, the neoliberal turn replaced the ideological supremacy of the social model embodied by the welfare state – a model that had sustained architectural modernism and its values. This led to the pluralistic stance of so-called postmodernism, summarised in the famous maxim 'anything goes' (as long as it sells). In the wake of globalisation, the triumph of economics over politics has resulted in increasing and successful attempts to naturalise these dominant economic forces under the guise of the ubiquitous, invisible hand of the market personified as a wilful, benevolent genius. Events shaping contemporary societies, we are told, are somehow beyond human control: inevitable. Criticism could be a possible means of intellectual empowerment against this imposed fate.

Another imperative for *Criticat* was to establish a means to *critical autonomy*. If as critics we are tired of being kindly advised what to write by omnipresent public relations blurbs, let's construct our own judgment by doing research ourselves. This entails in-depth investigation into all of the subjects related to a project under consideration, including the source of the commission, the programme and the political issues and economical stakes that provide a context for, or even determine, the work. However, to maintain a level of autonomy, this mode of investigation requires breaking with standard press procedures, shunning professional visits – including the requisite lunch with the architect – and the use of commissioned professional pictures and official graphic documents. It also means relinquishing a certain idea related to the social status of the critic whose reputation is tied to the fame of those he or she interviews. Only by doing so is it possible to construct another, different, position. The unconditional celebration of architects and their buildings, great or small, can be counterproductive, and this approach does nothing to assist practitioners with their dilemmas. At the same time, it sterilises debate, killing autonomous thinking and its expression: in the profession, in architecture schools and ultimately in the public.

In order to achieve this autonomy, *Criticat* has built an *alternative editorial economy* at a small, experimental scale. (figs. 1, 2) Most journals are funded by publicity, by sponsors or by institutions – sometimes even by all three. We believe that intellectual freedom is inseparable from financial sovereignty. *Criticat* is therefore an independent body reliant only on its readers and subscribers, structured as a non-profit association, with everyone – authors, editors, graphic designers – working on a volunteer basis. The only expenses are the copyeditor, the printer and postage. Of course, this demands that everyone has other sources of income. If we consider that there can be no fair financial reward for intellectual work, other kinds of gratification should be found to compensate for this effort. One of them is having created a room of our own – to borrow the much-quoted phrase by Virginia Woolf on the necessary autonomy of women in a man's world. Another is the prospect of being read, discussed or even criticised, triggering further reflection and action.

Economy was also a key factor in shaping the journal. Its format maximises the area available on standard printing paper and the journal is printed in black and white – to reduce the mesmerising power of images and enhance the importance of text. The decision to publish it in a physical, rather than dematerialised – or digital – form comes from our engrained faith in the autonomy and pleasure inherent to the handling of printed matter.

A fifth principle was to attempt a *reconstruction of collective critical thinking*. Our increasing dissatisfaction with mass individualism led us to gather as a small collective of equals, where group reflection could develop in dialogue with the more solitary exercise of investigating and writing the articles themselves. Not so long ago such an assembly of content producers was called an editorial committee – albeit with its hierarchies – and every commercial journal had one. Stimulated by new technologies and the reconfiguration, concentration and 'uberisation' of the media world, most journals have shed this *modus operandi* to cut expenses. Contributors now work as freelancers, with tight deadlines, limited formats and a fee-per-page often so low that true investigation and critical elaboration are made impossible. Our editorial committee is conceived as a regular forum, a meeting place where potential subjects are put

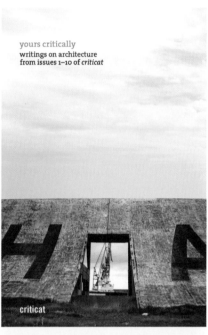

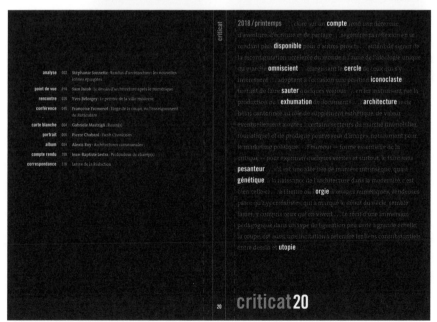

1 *Yours Critically: Writings on Architecture from issues 1-10 of Criticat*
was self published by *Criticat* in 2015.

2 The text of the cover is a *cadavre exquis* made out of one sentence of each article,
mirroring the table of contents printed on the back cover.

The children's playground looks like a contemporary sculpture garden. Curious smooth and refined objects are cleverly arranged on a coloured carpet. The design imperative leaves no room for a slide or a sandbox. One admires the installation but little playing takes place there.

The pavements are wide but congested with countless street lamps, poles, bollards, traffic lights and signs of all kinds. The entire street furniture supplier catalogue is on show. Added to this, the logic of "each to his lane" transforms simple intersections into genuine labyrinths.

Office buildings flank a large tree-lined boulevard, named "Cours de l'Île Seguin". At the end of this avenue, a new bridge leads to the aforementioned island. Because of its size and shape, one building stands out, the Horizons Tower. Its design was entrusted to a famous architect.

The overall composition is simple, the streets rectilinear, urban templates dead straight. All the characteristics of the ZACs built in France for the last 20 years or so are gathered together here. And yet, the developers are boasting everywhere about the originality of this new 'sustainable' quality of life.

3, 4  Drawing as critical tool: Martin Etienne, excerpts of a 'drawn visit' of the new urban developments in Boulogne Billancourt, a close suburb of Paris. (*Criticat* #8, 2012) on the table and ideas are discussed, sometimes hotly, anticipating the debate we are hoping to provoke among readers.

*Investigation* is paramount to the criticism we advocate and try to practise. It entails gathering first-hand facts through research, interviews and visits, publicising forgotten texts and essays that have never been translated, assembling anthologies on a given subject and occasionally designing graphs from specific data in order to visualise evidence. Criticism is understood as a production of knowledge aimed at increasing public understanding of a given condition, seen through the prism of architectural concerns.

In order to counteract the sensation of an eternal present generated by the so-called information society in which we are living – what historian François Hartog calls *presentism* – it seems necessary to weave into the picture the longer, more relative perspective of *history*, where architectural culture has built up its ideas and inventions. And because the mass circulation of images that tend to replace reality is both overwhelming and frustrating, we try to find alternative ways to *represent* buildings and the built environment, using our own photographs and occasionally drawings, collages and comics, in addition to careful *writing* to describe and to depict: for re-presenting reality is already a critical act. **(figs. 3, 4)**

*Case studies*

> *Criticat* has equally been attracted to documenting issues revealed by public polemics, to stripping bare the claims of some prominent practices and to revisiting the architectural icons offered for universal admiration by various media.

Our first issue opened with the unravelling of the fierce controversy surrounding the resumption of high-rise construction in Paris. The article listed and analysed the arguments behind the pros and cons, discussing their origins and nature and eventually underlining their contradictions. In the process, it exposed the challenges this issue posed for the new municipal administration and the strategic use of architecture by politicians and architects. It also showed the paucity of rational arguments on both sides, revealing the flaws of a debate generated by the paradoxes of an urban politics that is based on an obsession with the 'renewal' of the city's image at a global scale.

There are many sacred cows in architecture that *Criticat* has been eager to scrutinise. For instance, in France and elsewhere, Lacaton & Vassal are considered the most successful representatives of an alternative attitude towards the relationship between space, programme and budget – heralds of a virtuous shift from an emphasis on form to a concern for use. The well known principle underpinning their work is to build cheaper in order to build larger and in order to offer un-programmed, free spaces capable of welcoming any activity, releasing the creativity of users or increasing the comfort of inhabitants. But beyond the generosity and seduction of this discourse, does it work? What really happens in these spaces? 'Flexibility' is not a new concept. Is it relevant today, and if so, how, what and whom does it serve? (fig. 5)

The hype around spectacular design often masks the deeper or more complex reasons and effects of a given project. When it opened, the reconversion of the former, disused railway known as the High Line was widely praised for its elaborate, elegant landscape design and for the new public space it created in a former industrial neighbourhood of Manhattan. Architectural publications considered it only from this angle. In an essay for *Criticat,* a local resident – a former diplomat – analysed this conversion both as a real estate phenomenon and as an instrument of gentrification, touching upon the role of design in the process.

In the same vein, another essay considered Metropol Parasol, the huge, waffled mushrooms built between 2004 and 2011 by Jurgen Mayer H above Seville's Encarnacion Plaza. Looking beyond the problematic hiatus between architectural form and constructional logic that had been conveniently overlooked by most commentators, or the pretext of turning the roof into an uncomfortable promenade to give an appearance of usefulness, Pierre Chabard related the project to the 2008 real estate bubble, which bankrupted the city and the country, revealing the absurdity of this ultimate emblem of economic hubris and blindness. An exhaustive site visit and discussions with the various project actors included meetings with the representatives of the political movement Indignados who ironically used the Plaza as a site for demonstrating against the politics of the Spanish government's austerity measures after 2008. (fig. 6)

The opening of the Pompidou Centre in Metz in eastern France was an opportunity to write something I had been wanting to do for a long time: take a prestigious new icon as to check on all the other buildings that have been built during that year in the same city – the banal commissions that are built year after year to house ordinary programmes by architects that are never featured in journals. The idea was to gauge the extraordinary against the ordinary, and the other way around, in order to try to evaluate the relative performance of each. Thus measured, the Pompidou Centre was not doing so well considering the ideal conditions of the project: a prestigious client, an exceptional programme, a large budget, special urban derogations, a design by a then rising star of Japanese architecture, Shigeru Ban working with the international engineering firm Arup. Why was the building so problematic then, as testified by the pictures taken during a visit by a local photogra-

5  (Above) The paradoxes of well-meaning architecture: Valery Didelon on Lacaton & Vassal's architecture school in Nantes. (*Criticat* #8, photograph by the author)

6  (Below) Behind the cool icon: Pierre Chabard on Jurgen Mayer H.'s Seville waffles. (*Criticat* #9, photograph by the author)

7, 8  A tree can hide a forest: Françoise Fromonot on the Pompidou Center in Metz.
(*Criticat* #7, photographs by Jacqueline Trichard)

pher friend? Conversely, some of the less spectacular buildings seen in the surrounding city – a sport ground, a parking garage, semi-detached housing – appeared as remarkable achievements if one factored in the ordinary conditions faced by their designers. This simple displacement of the criteria of critical assessment showed that, in this respect, and contrary to the new Pompidou Centre, their architectural, social, expense ratio was quite high. Food for thought? **(figs. 7, 8)**.

Articles on architecture seldom discuss certain programmes. For instance, office space, where millions of people spend time every day amounting to one third of their life, is often overlooked as an issue. The new campus of the Novartis pharmaceutical labs in Basel, Switzerland where dozens of *starchitects* have been asked to build at the turn of the century is impossible to visit without an appointment and the guidance of two dedicated public relations agents. The article in *Criticat* tells this story before discussing the icy design of the buildings and the role of the campus' compositional urbanism from the point of view of contemporary evolution of workspaces – and of the ideology of work – as planned and implemented by these huge global firms.

The hard-won freedom to criticise has made us all the more confidant to bring attention to some minute, fragile or radical alternatives to the prevalent order of things: a small house in the Paris suburbs whose unassuming design by Eva Samuel encapsulates a vision of contemporary metropolitan Paris; the extraordinary experience of Kraftwerk, the now famous communal housing project in Zurich; or the daring modesty and methods devised by the architect Pierre Bernard to reform one of the most underprivileged neighbourhoods of Roubaix, in northern France, where all previous solutions had failed. **(figs. 9, 10)**

*As a tentative conclusion*
*Investigations in contemporary reality and in history, articulated through writing and drawing – Criticat* is based upon this open definition of architectural criticism. This mode of criticism can be practised in many ways: in articles and in books, but also in teaching, lectures, courses and even in design studios, where the positions gained from critical examinations can be turned into proposals.

Criticism is linked by its very etymology with the notion of crisis – not a depressing one but a generative *krisis* that overturns a sorry state and opens up new perspectives. Let's destabilise the *status quo*, question the obvious, risk interpretation, disagree, debate, dare to say. Let's reaffirm the importance of a committed critique of our world as it is being built. Then perhaps the state of things will not seem as inescapable as *fate*, and we will, in the process, gain a grasp on another future.

9, 10  (Previous page and above) Discovering cooperative housing in Zurich.
(*Critica*t #11, drawings by Martin Etienne)

While we await the advent of true 3D representation, how can we film architecture and, in particular, capture its spatiality on screen? This question arises whenever a building plays a starring role in a film. The analysis of three films shot in the OMA-designed "Bordeaux house", one of the world's most famous contemporary villas, provides us with an opportunity to identify ways of dealing with this challenge.

## Striptease
### Félix Mulle
### Drawings by Diane Berg

In combining the space of the image with narrative or musical time, cinema, or the moving image in general, is *a priori* the medium best equipped today to accurately render the experience of architecture. Of course, the flatness of the screen cancels out the third dimension, and the effect of central perspective specific to the optical lens constrains the view in a frame and a given format. Furthermore, the absence of peripheral vision means that there is a lack of fluidity between two focal points. Our perception of space and the movement within it is inevitably poorer as a result. And yet, we feel, intuitively, that compared to other modes of representing architecture — such as the plan and its codifications, the still frame of the photograph or the textual description, which, however evocative it may be, cannot avoid a certain degree of abstraction — audiovisual techniques can achieve something very similar to what we really feel when we wander through a space. Compared with other mediums, the movie camera's representation of an architectural object projects us more completely and more immediately into space. However, if we try to verify this intuition, a number of questions arise. Indeed, in what way and to what extent do the specific qualities of film enable it to capture new facets of space? What particular perspective on architecture is this medium then likely to produce?

### Three films

Three relatively recent films will serve as a basis for this reflection on the potential of film language in relation to the representation of space. The

Mulle & Berg: Striptease                                                                                     215

world, and which thereby forges a link between the inner world and outer world. Compared to abstraction, which characterises Western art before the Renaissance and which stems from instinct and therefore a form of archaic anxiety and fear in relation to the reality of the world, *Einfühlung* is considered to stem from understanding, and as such a much more real way of engaging with the world. For Worringer, as an artistic approach, abstraction is in no way "inferior" to empathy; rather he considers them as two distinct ways of approaching the world. Thus he states: "Whereas the urge to empathy is a happy pantheistic relationship of confidence between man and the phenomena of the external world, the urge to abstraction is the outcome of a great inner unrest inspired in a man by the phenomena of the outside world."

This distinction would seem to be relevant for the three films briefly examined here. Indeed, in Copans' film, the goal is to understand the building, to make it less strange by analysing it and putting it into readily understandable words and images. The urge to abstraction is at work, indeed as it is in Claerbout's film, in which, at least partially, the house tends to lose its reality and to appear as a series of evocative references. In the Lemoine Béka film, we see a radically different urge at work, driven by the desire to experience the building, to experience it with one's entire body, despite its flaws and despite the absurdity of certain situations. This is *Einfühlung*. Breaking with the conventional language of representation, orienting its commentary in a radically different direction — in keeping with Worringer's definition of empathy — the film emphasises the experienced dimension of space. Here, the cinematic medium shows its ability to capture and show, disseminate and share a dimension so volatile and elusive that it is almost entirely absent from architectural representation. By affirming that dimension's existence, film may succeed in making a new place for it among the many other facets of our understanding of space.

P.S. At the time of writing, Ila Béka and Louise Lemoine are continuing to develop their *Living Architectures* series, applying the same process of discovering an iconic building through the people who use it. Yet none of their other films have reached the grace and depth of the film devoted to the Lemoine house. Why? We could assume that it is because the buildings, such as Richard Meier's Jubilee Church in Rome or Renzo Piano's IRCAM in Paris, are less explicit in their relationship to the body, whereas the Koolhaas house makes Mr Lemoine's disabled body its primary dimension. On the other hand, the fact that Louise Lemoine lived in the house when she was younger would seem to suggest that extensive, first-hand experience is required to achieve such an accurate study of a space. Yet if this highly delicate dimension of architecture can only be understood by familiarity built over time, how can it be communicated? How do we go about representing it so it can be shared? F.M.

Mulle & Berg: Striptease                                                                                     251

**11,12  Re-visiting architecture movies.**
(*Criticat #7*, drawings by Diane Berg)

13  'No comment'. A postcard made by Martin Etienne
in 2013 for *Criticat*'s 5th anniversary.

# The Role of Architectural Criticism in Post-Revolution Iran

Kamran Afshar Naderi

In his 1435 book, *On Painting*, Leon Battista Alberti writes that in artwork he does not appreciate ornaments made of gold, but rather colours that imitate gold because they are the invention of the artist.[1]

At the Galleries of the Academy of Venice there is a huge painting that belongs to Paolo Veronese, one of the most important Venetian painters of the sixteenth century. The painting is called *The Feast in the House of Levi*. It was executed in 1573 and was supposed to share an appellation with Leonardo da Vinci's *The Last Supper*. Apparently, there is nothing spiritual in Veronese's representation. Even Christ can hardly be distinguished among the vast number of people and animals present at the party. The liberties that Veronese took in interpreting one of the fundamental moments of the Christian faith displeased the city's holy tribunal, and he was called to the court to answer the charge of heresy. The inquisitors criticised Veronese for making a representation full of absurdities that ridiculed those things held scared by the Catholic church. I believe the words of these inquisitors represented a very crude and primitive form of art criticism. Veronese responded to the charges, saying we 'painters take the same license as the poets and madmen to express our ideas in the way we consider more appropriate'. The inquisitors asked the artist to modify the painting, but he agreed only to change the title to *The Feast in the House of Levi*. This example reveals how much, by the Renaissance, artists were starting to think critically about the content of their work, claiming both authorship of their ideas and a status equal to that of poets.

---

1 'Truovasi chi adopera molto in sue storie oro, che stima porga maestà. Non lo lodo. E benché dipignesse quella Didone di Virgilio, a cui era la faretra d'oro, i capelli aurei nodati in oro, e la veste purpurea cinta pur d'oro, i freni al cavallo e ogni cosa d'oro, non però ivi vorrei punto adoperassi oro, però che nei colori imitando i razzi dell'oro sta più ammirazione e lode all'artefice', Leon Battista Alberti, 'De pictura' 1435.

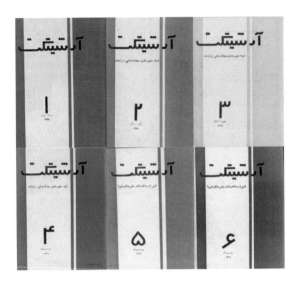

Until the Renaissance, artists were mostly considered craftsmen. In the Middle Ages, painters were associated with the guild of doctors and druggists. The materials they used, as opposed to ideas and creativity, determined their identities. And while guilds in Europe experienced improved status by the fifteenth- and sixteenth-centuries, in Iran this was not the case.[2] During the post-Islamic period, guilds were not publicly governed, and until the beginning of the twentieth century in Iran, the social status of the architect was no greater than the status a medieval tradesman.

In Iran each guild and town had its own style. Individual creativity and changes were not tolerated. Transformations of style occurred after important socio-political events and the resulting cultural contamination between populations such as Romans, central Asians, Arabs and Mongols. Iranian architects have not left significant written documents or other traces that provide insight into their ideas. Their names rarely appear on buildings or in records. No form of architectural literature, including criticism, existed. Poets, philosophers, scientists and theologians expressed their ideas and opinions, but architects were considered to be only practising professionals.

The beginning of the modern era in Iran is associated with the Persian Constitutional Revolution of 1905–11 in which people and intellectuals demanded liberty along western paradigms. Later, Reza Shah, the founder of the Pahlavi

2 Hasan Shahpari and Tahereh Alavi Hojjat, *Islamic Economy and Social Mobility, Cultural and Religious Considerations* (Hershey, PA: IGI Global, 2016) p199.

1 Covers of *Architect,* the first architectural magazine in Iran,
published between 1946-48.

dynasty, focused his attempts on the modernisation and westernisation of the country. Nikolai Markov, an Iranian architect of Russian descent, introduced the Russian classical style to Iran. By the 1930s, the Iranian-Armenian architect Vartan Hovanesian introduced the art-deco style throughout the country. In 1946, he founded the first architectural magazine in Persian and declared his views against traditional Iranian building styles. (fig. 1) From the 1940s–70s the 1970s, International Style residential buildings proliferated in large cities. With the introduction of modernism, the social status of the architect also changed. People began to consider architects to be intellectuals as well as professionals.

However, the *role* of the architect was not so clear. In fact, until 20 years ago, when Tahmineh Milani, an architect and director, made a film in which one of the characters was an architect, no Iranian writer or filmmaker had used an architect as a character in a story.

Until the 1960s, architecture schools accepted modernism as the dominant mode of design. In universities, professors taught using the studio method, using trial and error to develop projects. Both in the university and the profession, competence and taste determined quality. Neither professionals nor professors had a critical approach to their era, or towards design.

In his 1961 book *Return to the Self*, Ali Shariati, a theoretician of modern Islam, criticised Iranians for entirely accepting western paradigms of civilisation. He also disapproved of those who showed an interest in their culture but imitated Europeans – pointing out that many from the west considered Iran to simply be a traditional society of poets and carpet weavers.

In fact, in Iranian houses that belonged to the nouveau riche and aristocratic families, one could see many Iranian decorations and objects that would never appear in a traditional house: donkey saddles as sofa-coverings, horse ornaments as drapery, painted bathroom tiles applied to dining room walls, old dishes and pots as decorative objects, old decorated doors removed from their original locations and hung on blank walls. In my own home I enthusiastically did the same.

By the 1970s, architects such as Kamran Diba and Nader Ardalan questioned the International Style and instead took inspiration from historical buildings. The Museum of Contemporary Art by Diba and the Iran Center for Management Studies by Ardalan are two well-known examples of this trend. (fig. 2)

2  Museum of Contemporary Arts in Tehran by Kamran Diba.

3  Iranian Academies of Culture design proposal by Hadi Mirmiran.

In 1973, Nader Ardalan and Laleh Bakhtiar wrote *The Sense of Unity*, the first original book of architectural theory in Iran. The text proposed a conceptual and symbolic reading of Iranian art and architecture and had a great impact on architects of the next generations.

The Iranian Revolution was a populist, nationalist and Islamic insurgency that replaced the dictatorial monarchy of the Pahlavi dynasty with a theocratic system. Demonstrations against the Shah commenced in October 1977, developing into a campaign of civil resistance. In the period between 1977 and the victory of the revolution in 1979, architecture was the last concern of the people. In the same years, I was studying architecture at Tehran University. During that time, universities were battlefields for the revolution – there was no time for study.

In 1980, authorities decided to close universities in order to revise the nation's educational programme. There were many disputes regarding the restoration of tradition and the teaching of Islamic principles. From the beginning of the Iranian Revolution, there was a reaction to the formalist architecture and aesthetics of the upper class, which were considered to be unacceptable signs of luxury and caprice. The new academic programme sought to focus on functionality and the integration of Islamic architectural heritage into design.

By the beginning of the 1990s, following the end of the war with Iraq, the economy picked up. At that time, after a decade during which Tehran University was often closed, people started to think about architecture from a new point of view. In 1994, a year after returning to my country, I visited the exhibition of the winning projects of the first important post-revolution competition: Iranian Academies of Culture. There were several models and panels displayed in a large hall. Among them, I noticed a work that was clearly different from the others. The project, by Hadi Mirmiran, was based on a clear and bold formal idea. It was modern and had elements of historical Iranian architecture. I had the impression that something was really changing. Mirmiran would go on to influence an entire generation of architects in Iran. **(fig. 3)**

Although the jury voted for Mirmiran's project, the client later decided to build the third-prize project – an eclectic and mediocre work. **(fig. 4)** But I had been so excited by the project that I asked my boss to make an introduction so that I could write an article on Mirmiran's work. After three weeks spent trying to secure an interview, we finally met and I was able to begin writing my first piece of criticism. My article was dedicated mostly to the design process and an analysis of style.

Before the revolution, there were a few architectural periodicals published for short periods in Iran. *Art and Architecture* was the most popular magazine, dedicated mostly to modern architecture and the cultural events associated with the monarchy. After the revolution, only two, black and white, poor quality architec-

4  Iranian Academies of Culture by Asar Consultant Engineering.

tural magazines survived: *Abadi* and *A&U*.

I first sent my article to *Abadi*, the official architectural quarterly of the Ministry of Housing and Urban Development. Receiving no answer, I tried the second magazine, which accepted and published my article. Mr Khosroshahi, editor of *A&U* told me, 'Mr. Afshar Naderi, you know this is the first architectural criticism ever published in Iran.' Not taking much stock in his assessment, it was only years later that I discovered the article was the first work of criticism on an Iranian architect by another Iranian.

A few days after the article was released, Soheila Beski, editor of *Abadi* – who later played an important role in my life – called me and said their magazine was looking for someone who could write architectural criticism. Beski was not an architect but a talented writer. I accepted her offer to collaborate and we began a relationship that lasted 20 years.

In 1997, Beski, Ex-Deputy Minister Hashemi and I founded the magazine *Memar* ('architect' in Persian). The graphic design and paper of *Memar* were of higher quality than the existing, black and white publications. *Memar* had colour pictures, published fresh articles about new trends and took on young and capable collaborators. Many new magazines followed. All were to some extent influenced by *Memar*, and the period led to a wave of energy in architectural publication. (fig. 5)

In 2001, the magazine founded the first annual award for architectural realisations, mostly bestowed on young architects for small and cheap creations. Both magazine and award became the main validating mechanisms for new architecture in Iran. The impact of the prize was so great that some people started to question whether architects worked for their clients or for the prize. There were probably some architects that first conceived photogenic views and then carried out their projects.

The *Memar* Award has been always a cultural event, accompanied by criticism and discussion. A number of international architects took part in jury sessions and brought with them fresh ideas and new ways of looking at the projects. Fumihiko Maki, Nasrin Seraji, Han Tumertekin, Chris Bosse, Hariri & Hariri, Francisco Mangado, Mehrdad Yazdani and Vincente Guallart were among these jury members. Most of the well- known, young architects in Iran – among them Alireza Taghaboni, Abbas Riahifard, Rambod Ilkhani and Kamran Heirati – owe part of their reputation to the prize.

In the 1990s, following years of partial isolation, Iranians used every means available to extend contact with the world. Travel abroad became easier and more frequent. International books could be imported and sold to students and professors at subsidised prices. Satellite dishes, despite being prohibited, were installed in many houses allowing people to start using internet.

After 2000, important international architects began to visit Iran: Mario

Botta, Charles Jencks, Philip Jodidio, Michele De Lucchi, Michael Sorkin, Patrik Schumacher, Arata Isozaki and many others participated in meetings and seminars. Some Iranian architects collaborated with international architects on projects in Iran.

The younger generation was not interested in local traditions and history but concerned with showing that they were part of a world community. Architectural critics, professors and journalists referred to international magazines and books. In the first decade of the new millennium, we observed many works that drew inspiration directly from international works and trends: Fluid Motion Architects are among the first architects to have radically detached themselves from the past.

The positive impact of the Islamic revolution was that people started to think critically about every aspect of life – from religion to politics, from habits to aesthetics. At the same time, schools and universities increased in size. Today, literacy has reached 96 per cent – close to European standards. Despite this improvement, challenging subjects such as philosophy, art history and the social sciences are not part of the educational programme of students who enter schools of architecture.

According to a 2015 World Economic Forum report, Iran has the second-highest number of engineers per capita globally. Students who go to foreign universities prefer entering engineering, medicine and science faculties, which are considered more economically rewarding fields of study. In recent years, due to increasing numbers of architecture students – now more than 65,000 – some graduates with an aptitude for writing have moved toward criticism or journalism.

Besides numerous monographs and articles, many private organisations and groups have held public discussions on the work of Iranian architects. Iman Raisi's *Architecture and Critical Thinking* has become a reference for universities. With these developments, a new generation has begun to appreciate Iranian contemporary architecture instead of limiting themselves to the works of international *starchitects*.

Concurrent to this interest in architecture, Iranian cinema, theatre, music, painting and poetry have also flourished. Criticism in these fields is more common and popular. Motivated by the possibility of a creative, renewed Iranian architecture with a global place and recognising the unique possibilities for doing something useful for the country, some architects are looking to local culture for inspiration, experimenting with technology, crafts and materials and exploring history and society.

In 2016, three Iranian projects were among the finalists for the Aga Khan Award for Architecture. The winner – Nature Bridge – is the largest pedestrian overpass built in Iran. The tradition of the bridge as a place for leisure dates back to seventeenth-century Isfahan, and the architects, Leila Araghian and Alireza Behzadi, conceived the bridge as a passageway and destination, a multilevel

6  Tabiat Bridge by L. Araghian and A. Behzadi, winner of Aghakhan Awards 2016.

7  40 Knots House in Tehran by H. Madjdabadi and A. Mashhadimirza.

structure that connects two large parks. **(fig. 6)**

The other outstanding project shortlisted by the Aga Khan Award was the 40 Knots House, a small apartment building with a facade that drew inspiration from carpet weaving for its texture and construction method. Habibeh Majdabadi, one of the two authors of the project, believes that architecture has shifted from the formal to the conceptual. Her concern is to grasp and transform traditional concepts and methods, rather than using historical forms. **(fig. 7)**

Other talented architects include Pouya Khazaeli, who is exploring local low-tech architecture from both technical and expressive points of view. **(fig. 8)** And in their recent works, Sara Kalantari and Reza Sayadian explore the dualism of rigid geometry and free forms as it had been used in the millenary tradition of decorative arts and architecture. **(fig. 9)**

Critics and critical thinking in architecture do not have a long history in Iran. The new generation has made a radical change. Today critical discussions are common, and hundreds of architects and students participate actively in numerous cultural events. There are many courses supported by private organisations such as the Iranian Architecture Center on theoretical and practical subjects, including architectural criticism. Iranian architects have much more international

8 Observatory, an experimental construction in Esfahak by Pouya Khazaeli.

9  Saba apartment building in Teran by Sara Kalantari and Reza Sayadian.

1  Poster for the 1929 Soviet movie, *Fragment of an Empire*.

# The Blog as Online Research Laboratory

Graham Brenton McKay

I teach at a university in the United Arab Emirates, but I am here today because I run a blog called Misfits' Architecture.

The title doesn't always translate. In Russian, 'misfits' means something closer to 'outcast'. In Chinese I imagine it could easily translate into a word such as 'dissident', or into words such as 'nonconformist' or 'eccentric' in Japanese. Even in English, the word 'misfit' is almost never used to describe people excluded from the mainstream. Much like this title, blogs themselves are somewhat inscrutable. They are usually thought of as online magazines, publishing self-generated content on some topic of personal interest. Like any platform involving text and image, blogs involve reading, writing and comment, which sometimes become a form of criticism. And yet the platform has more potential – it can function as part of a process of architectural research and production.

The logo for Misfits' Architecture comes from a poster for a 1920s Soviet film called *Fragment of an Empire* in which a man wakes up after a long sleep to find himself in a perfect world. I liked its optimism and how it suggested buildings were a part of that perfect world. (fig. 1) The 1920s was one of the most creative decades the world has ever seen. Artists and thinkers across Europe and the Soviet Union communicated through small print journals – arguably proto-blogs in terms of content. While Ozenfant's and Le Corbusier's *L'Esprit Nouveau* and the de Stijl movement's *De Stijl* are the most well known, they were just two of the many journals that disseminated new thinking.

These journals were small and specialised, but they linked people in the same field who wanted to share knowledge and ideas. They were the internet of their time, but this model wasn't fast. Collecting photographs and information, translating it and then editing everything for publication, which was then printed and distributed across Europe by post meant the cycle of architectural research, production and dissemination had a long feedback loop. This wasn't such a bad thing because it gave people time to read and discuss the journal's ideas before deciding if or how to apply them. For one short decade, reading, writing and criticism were an integral part of the cycle of architectural research and production, and Europe and the Soviet Union became one large research laboratory.

Initially I thought the blog itself might be a source of ideas and thus a kind of online research laboratory, but it can't do this any more than a system of printed journals and letter-writing can. A blog is only a medium for the delivery of ideas. The real work happens in the research laboratories both outside and as a result of it. Blogging has taught me to never leave the conclusion until the end, and so my conclusion here is that the blog stimulates, rather than simulates.

'Www.misfitsarchitecture.com' began with architectural research and simulated architectural production intersecting as they do at universities. In 2010, a final-year student named Bashar asked me to supervise his graduation project. Disenchanted with the notion of architectural aesthetics, or at least how he had been taught to perceive them, he wanted to engineer a building using only energy-performance criteria and without any regard for notions of architectural beauty. This resonated with my own misgivings about architectural aesthetics.

For one of our early meetings, Bashar produced two comparisons to illustrate his thinking. He first compared the ungainly Sukhoi SU-35 fighter plane with the sleeker looking Typhoon Eurofighter. And yet the Sukhoi has better performance according to all criteria by which a fighter plane is measured. His second example concerned assault rifles. We don't need to know anything about assault rifles to think the American M-16 a more handsome rifle than the Russian AK-47, but it is the comprehensive performance of the AK-47 that makes it the world's weapon of choice. It is of course a pity that both examples relate to military technologies, but not all that surprising given that the military is a field where aesthetics is secondary to performance.

Bashar's building had a unique section that integrated apartment access with ventilation and the water cycle, rooms with depths optimised for daylight penetration, and so on. If it had been a real project, it would have easily scored Platinum according to LEED Core and Shell 2009. His final presentation consisted of three A0 sheets and a book of data.

Bashar wasn't the first person to see beauty in terms of comprehensive building performance. Hannes Meyer, the second head of the Bauhaus, aspired to do exactly the same, and one of the blog's first entries – 'Architecture Misfit #1' (of 28 misfits and counting) – was a tribute to him, and I am immensely pleased the Hannes Meyer Foundation links back to the post.

Another aspect of the main theme of performance beauty is to draw attention to useful things that are not trying to be beautiful. My first-ever post was

'The Tree is not Trying to Look Beautiful'. Others followed – on microprocessors, the incremental development of fighter planes, the intelligence of seashells [14] and the development of the Shinkansen. These posts all attempted to show how real improvements in performance are possible when aesthetics are no longer a concern. The blog thus began as a platform to think through ideas and articulate them, and this initial theme of performance beauty has remained. When I checked last week, 125 out of 351 posts were related to it in some way.

One recurring theme is our cognitive bias to see beauty in terms of representation. For example, we tend to think of the cheetah and jaguar as the fastest animals on earth – and they are if we think of speed in terms of acceleration and top speed. The top speed of the pronghorn antelope is not as high, but its huge heart and lungs give it superior endurance. These animals were made to run, and with a two-second head start, a pronghorn antelope can easily outrun a cheetah. This lesson from the natural world tells us that what represents speed is not always the speed that matters. (fig. 2)

Energy performance deals with the same theme. A series of posts from last year considered cruise liners as closed environmental systems designed to keep people alive and comfortable in a hostile environment. In that respect they are not much different from castles, Antarctic research centres, the International Space Station and many other high-performance structures. (fig. 3)

Over the years, the blog has become a repository for information on architects, buildings and ideas that are not covered in conventional histories of architecture. It is all very interesting but based on this alone a blog is no more than an online magazine for me and anyone else happens to read it. In order to be

2 The pronghorn antelope is the world's fastest land animal,
depending on how the speed is measured.
(Photo by USFWS Mountain-Prairie)

something more it requires interaction. To facilitate and support the work of an architectural research laboratory, a blog needs to connect people with similar concerns who are motivated to produce solutions to real problems and share their knowledge and solutions with others. Misfits' Architecture contains three necessary conditions for an architectural research laboratory.

*A research laboratory can't exist in isolation.*
This eliminates most corporate architectural production. What is good for the company or brand is not necessarily good for architecture.

*The focus must be on architectural production.*
My definition of architectural research is quite narrow because I think it should be concerned with how to make better buildings for more people. This excludes a substantial amount of academic production.

*The knowledge a research laboratory generates must be capable of being shared for possible wider application.*
This eliminates much of what is produced in the name of architecture and shared in the name of architecture.

Rural Studio at the University of Auburn perhaps fits this description most closely, but these three conditions are not often met. It is little wonder that for the first few years the majority of the blog's visitors and followers were students who had expected architectural education to be more than gratuitous shape-making.

3 Cruise liners such as The Royal Princess are self-contained machines for living. (Photo by Barry Skeates)

In early 2015, Victor, a student in Yekaterinburg in central Russia contacted me about the importance my posts placed on the geometry and the spatial efficiency of building plans. I don't see this as anything special – it is just a fundamental skill of architects that enables a more efficient use of resources. It was also one of the things Victor had admired about constructivist architect Moisei Ginzburg, whom he suggested as a potential *misfit architect*. Victor and I ended up collaborating on a series of posts about Ginzburg and the work of the Stroykom architectural research laboratory he led. Formed by a group called the Organization of Contemporary Architects, Stroykom tasked itself with finding architectural solutions to the very real and urgent problem of inadequate and insufficient housing in the Soviet Union at the time. It explored the relationships between plans and sections to make the best use of enclosed building volume, devised prototypes and offered them as solutions. **(figs. 4a, 4b)**

The group also published a journal called *Modern Architecture*, which aimed to show how *the functional method in architecture* could be applied to social and industrial problems. It also reported on new thinking across Russia and in other countries. A subscription was 15 roubles (about 50 cents), and it was published six times a year, suggesting that two months was the minimum production time for the journal to be an effective indicator of contemporary thought. The work of Moisei Ginzburg and Stroykom continues to inspire because the problem of inadequate housing and insufficient resources for its construction has not gone away. It continues to manifest itself in various ways around the world and needs to be continually restated as one of the topics that applied architectural intelligence might solve.

Ginzburg and the Stroykom team weren't just a model for our informal research laboratory; their actual work was also what we thought the work of an architectural research laboratory should be. One current problem concerns co-living or co-housing in which unrelated people inhabit the same dwelling – a type of living that is increasingly common in Europe and America. One post from last summer gave a brief overview of various co-housing developments around the world and, to summarise, I attempted to improve upon the Stroykom team's Type F apartment, devising an economical housing prototype more suited to co-living – and prompting a reply from Marc Macy, the architect of one of the developments mentioned in the post. Another post on the same topic commented on the trend for circulation space to be used both as social and living space. Marco Giacometti, an architect dealing with co-housing issues in Zurich, contacted me and offered some useful information and perspective on recent co-housing projects in Switzerland. **(figs. 5, 6)**

In a post called 'The Expansible Home', I thought a useful housing product might result from combining the structural integrity of Rafael Viñoly's 432 Park Avenue with the spatial and structural clarity of Yemeni houses to produce

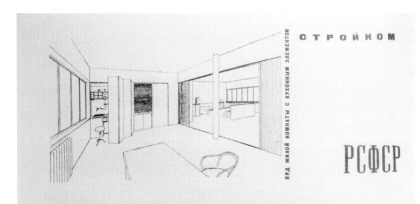

СТРОЙКОМ

ВИД ЖИЛОЙ КОМНАТЫ С КУХОННЫМ ЭЛЕМЕНТОМ

РСФСР

# РАЦИОНАЛИЗАЦИЯ КУХНИ

RATIONALISIERUG DER KÜCHE

При рациональном усовершенствовании любой машины все устремлено на получение максимальной компактности. Утилизирование объема—задача нашего времени не только от нашей сегодняшней бедности. Но эта аксиома как будто не затрагивает вопроса планировки кухни — у нас последняя торжествует в своей неприкосновенности.

Когда кухня, как изолированная комната, оказывается слишком большим накладным расходом, ее переводят в разряд так называемой жилой кухни. На западе это название выдерживает критику, у нас — в редких случаях культурного пользования этим совмещением функции кухни и жилья в одном помещении. Поэтому и до сих пор противоборство этому—казалось бы, безобидному—облегчение тягот квартирной оплаты зиждется на том, что жилая кухня перестает быть жилой по кричащие грязи и чада и испорченного варкой и стиркой воздуха, а сама кухня—из соседства чистого жилого угла очень унижена в смысле возможности демонстрировать, приписанные ей от века грязь и смрад.

Не верно ни первое, ни второе. Грязь и чад на кухне—это ей навязанное некультурным обращением, а не ее существом, свойство. По существу процессов, в кухне совершающихся, это наиболее чистое и здоровое помещение в квартире, обслуживающее человека. При высоком культурном уровне — а мы обязаны равняться на эту ступень, а не на низшую, хотя бы и существующую сейчас—будет стыдно говорить о грязи в кухне.

Но, если кухня перестает быть грязным помещением, если ее рационально оборудовать, то вполне возможно под кухню отвести часть действительно жилой комнаты.

Так возникли кухни-ниши на Западе. Эта ниша обычно задернута портьерой, и буржуазная совесть приличной гостиной спокойна, и „красивая" обстановка жилой комнаты не шокирована оборудованием кухни.

Но мы идем дальше. Опыт устройства в химических лабораториях вытяжных шкапов, в которых производятся сложнейшие химические процессы, часто с отравляющими химикалиями, убеждает нас в следующем: Устройство вытяжных шкапов абсолютно гарантирует от отравления, т.-е. газы и процессы, которые происходят внутри шкапов, не проникают в помещение где находятся шкап и окружающие люди.

Устройство вытяжных шкапов аналогично оборудованию кухни—в них сконцентрированы: мойка (водопровод и слив), газ (очаг), рабочий стол. Это три элемента оборудования кухни, без которых она не мыслима. Остальное лишь большее или меньшее рафинирование оборудования.

Устройство таких шкапов, несущих определенную функцию, является собственно частью омеблирования.

Если переход от кухни изолированной к кухне-нише делать только механическим устранением изолирующих перегородок, без какой-то последующей затраты умственной энергии архитектора, то и ребенку ясно, что решение

жилой кухни терпит фиаско, ибо то, что хорошо решено при одних условиях, не годно при условиях, ставших иными. А у нас жилая кухня так именно решалась. А если вспомнить химич. лабораторию и баньку с черным этакетом и перекрещенными костями, то опять-

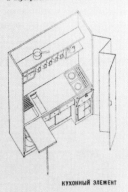

КУХОННЫЙ ЭЛЕМЕНТ

**24**

50

4 *Contemporary Architecture,* a journal published
by the Organization of Soviet Architects.
(Photo by Victor Perunkov)

3-Х КОМНАТНАЯ СЕКЦИЯ МОССОВЕТА 1929

ЗАМЕНА ИЗОЛИРОВАННОЙ КУХНИ КУХОННЫМ ЭЛЕМЕНТОМ

ГРАФИК ДВИЖЕНИЯ

СХЕМА ПРОПОРЦИЙ

8

РАЦИОНАЛИЗИРОВАННАЯ 3-КОМНАТНАЯ СЕКЦИЯ

# СТРОЙКОМ РСФСР

**РАБОТЫ СЕКЦИИ ТИПИЗАЦИИ В СОСТАВЕ: РУКОВОДИТЕЛЯ М. Я. ГИНЗБУРГА И СОТРУДНИКОВ: М. О. БАРЩ, В. ВЛАДИМИРОВА, А. Л. ПАСТЕРНАКА, Г. Р. СУМ-ШИК.**

BAIKOMITÉE DES OEKONOMISCHEN PATES RSFSR. ARBEITEN DER ABTEILUNG FÜR TYPISIERUNG: DER LEITERPROF. M. GINSBURG; MITLEIDER—ARCHITEKTEN M. BARTSCH, ALEX. RASTERNAK, G. SUM-SCHIK UND W. WLADIMIROFF.

## А-3

План обычной трехкомнатной квартиры с отдельной кухней, ванной и уборной. Рационализованная по графику процессов производства, кухня значительно сокращена против обычно преувеличенных площадей. За счет снижения этой площади увеличена жилая площадь соседней комнаты. При ненадобности изолированного помещения кухни, перегородки устраняются, ремонта капитального не требуется, т. к. самый кухонный элемент уже заранее установлен для возможного устройства кухни указанной на перспективном рисунке жилой комнаты. Спальные комнаты ориентированы все на одну сторону. Жилая общая комната со спальной кабиной связана окном - передачей с кухней. Наиболее благоприятная ширина корпуса для общей планировки квартиры — 9.00 м в чистоте. При 10 м в чистоте получаются (при равноценной жилой площади квартиры) более глубокие помещения, увеличиваются без использования (при каркасной системе конструкции дома) вспомогательные площади, и помимо худшей планировки получаются и худшие измеритель. Так сравнивая три случая планировки, равноценной площади квартиры в 9,00, 9,50, и 10 м ширины корпуса, мы имеем отношение жилой площади к полезной (в порядке указанных глубин) 0,79, 0,78 и 0,77. Отношение кубатуры (считая высоту помещения с перекрытием

=3,35 м) последовательно — 5,70, 5,62 и 5,65; последняя цифра указывает на то, что в смысле распределения жилой и вспомогательной площади наилучшее решение дает корпус наименьшей глубины, в кубатуре оно дает более благоприятное отношение, чем корпус средней глубины. На чертеже А3 показана возможность замены отдельного помещения кухни кухонным элементом, находящимся в жилой комнате. Сравнивая подсчеты как в первом, так и во втором случае, мы получаем следующую таблицу.

| | при отдельн. кухне | при кухонном элементе |
|---|---|---|
| Жил-площадь | 54.19 | 60.94 |
| полезная пл. | 69.50 | 69.50 |
| кубатура | 307.26 | 307.26 |
| отнош. $\frac{\text{жил. пл.}}{\text{полезн. пл.}}$ | = 0,78 | 0.88 |
| отнош. $\frac{\text{кубатура}}{\text{жил. пл.}}$ | = 5.67 | 5.05 |

Следовательно переход к общественному питанию, т. е. к жилью с коммунальным центром, радикально меняет рентабельность жилища, одновременно приближая его к типу жилищ, отвечающих запросам нового быта.

Схемы квартир показывают график движений и функциональную связь помещений между собой, а также проверку планового решения квартиры в целом и в частях (отдельные помещения) в смысле их пропорциональной внутренней координации. Система этих взаимоотношений в данном случае взята как отношение квадрата и его диагонали, за сторону квадрата принята длина кровати как наиболее постоянный стандартный размер мебели.

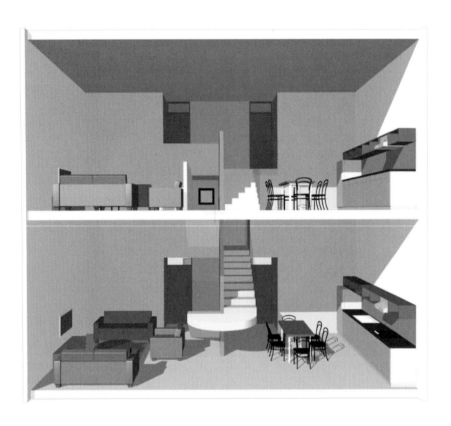

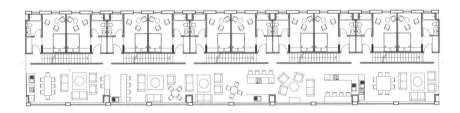

5 'Critical Spatiality', a misfits' study for improved Type F apartments.

6 'Lobby Living', A misfits' study for improved Type E apartments.

spaces with a similar generic functionality. I thought such an arrangement might be more suited to co-housing. The proposal consisted of equivalent bedrooms and two living spaces with no defined use. It was an arrangement that did not force people together if they were not related. The post received positive responses from architects, many of them sole practitioners in the United States. **(fig. 7)**

The blog is now beginning to engage with people who, like me, believe there is still a place for the application of architectural intelligence in the form of plans and sections. It connects people who are interested in collecting knowledge, applying it to real topics, and returning those solutions back into the world. That it is all happening online is not really important.

I believe in mining history for useful ideas that may have been ahead of their time or for some reason never followed up. Perhaps it was the combination of considering those square Yemeni plans together with the idea of co-living that made me think of Kazuo Shinohara's Repeating Crevice (1973) house for three generations. This house made it possible for occupants to have varying levels of awareness of each other while moving around the house. It offered more than the binary states of together or alone. I produced a proposal reimagining Repeating Crevice to illustrate how this would be useful for co-living. Two architects, one in Germany and one in the UK, wrote back to say it was a good idea. **(fig. 8)**

Around the same time, I became aware of increased crossover with my university lectures and studio work. Earlier this year, when I was preparing a lecture on one-bedroom apartments, I remembered a Japanese house I thought was called House with a Sloping Wall. The memory of it had been haunting me for decades so in early February I used that memory to design my own version.

7 The village of Hajarah in the Haraz Mountains, Yemen.
(Photo by yeowatzup from Katlenburg-Lindau, Germany)

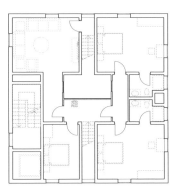

The proposal returned 50 per cent of the bedroom volume to the living room where it could be better appreciated or, as a variation showed, partially used. The main point of the post however, was to critique how buildings are often presented with misleading narratives about aesthetic considerations while their real and useful benefits are rarely mentioned. Daniel Munteanu in Romania – a follower, architect and a blogger himself – informed me that my mystery house was Hiroyuki Asai's Mochizuki House (1973). It turned out Asai had left Kazuo Shinohara's Tokyo Institute of Technology Laboratory three years before I was to arrive. Over the past two years I have seen a shift from 'finding something new to write about' to 'finding something new to investigate and then write about'. New architectural proposals don't happen every week. I am currently revisiting Repeating Crevice in an attempt to extend the idea of layers of awareness to outside the apartment, and I hope to be able to post some thoughts soon.

I have worked my way up to the present and my most recent post, which is based on a patent for a way of configuring apartments to provide the illusion of a detached house within a limited floor area. This seemed like a good idea, and so at the end of the post I suggested ways the problem could be better defined and other ways by which success could be measured. I then invited others to come up with solutions. But in publishing the post I realised I was attempting to simulate a research laboratory by combining comment and criticism with a problem that needs to be solved. I was trying to make it something it was not.

Originally, I imagined the blog platform as a thing that could frame a problem as a specific set of requirements and then crowdsource solutions in a

8  A misfits' study for apartments better suited to sharing.

process not unlike parallel computing. I imagined the result would yield an entire universe of possibilities superior to that claimed by parametricism because each of those solutions would have embedded within it all of those cultural and psychological subjectivities that resist being converted into parameters and manipulated.

The problem with this idea is that such systems already exist as international design competitions with calls for proposals and, to a lesser extent, studio design problems set at universities. Outside of these focused contexts there is no real incentive for people to contribute their time and skills to solving new problems, even if they are real ones requiring real solutions. It is instead more productive for people to share their own problems and solutions in the hope that others might find in them something of use in solving their own. This is why I see the blog platform as the natural successor to the journal of the 1920s.

And yet that system died out in the 1930s as commercial magazines took over the role of disseminating what passed for architectural knowledge. As the decline of the magazine has shown us, they were not driven by the desire to share knowledge but by a business model that used news as a hook on which to hang advertising. Magazines promoted projects that displayed the products of their advertisers. They could inflate advertising rates by publishing projects by well-known architects but were generally careful to publish an eclectic mix of projects in order to maintain wide readership.

Our architectural internet has replicated and magnified all these faults to the point that today there is a problem of insufficient architectural content on which to hang the amount of advertising that suddenly needs to be advertised. The solution seems to be that 'everything is architecture' – thus artificially inflating the amount of architectural news. In such a system, there is no difference between content and content of value. Content of value is no longer necessary. In the journal system it was essential. I am therefore happy to let the blog continue to do what it does and be what it is rather than distort it with advertising or pursue growth for the sake of growth.

Through loose collaborations with people who don't seem to fit in anywhere, the blog will continue to look for and publish worthwhile topics and, along with anyone else interested, attempt to devise solutions. This is the role of an architectural research laboratory.

As a blog, Misfits' Architecture has communicated ideas and bits of history and knowledge that are either underrated or under-represented in the history of architecture, or in danger of slipping away from it, such as a post titled 'The Analog Student', which examined the role of digital tools in architectural education and the profession. I used Victor's sketchbooks to illustrate the type of analysis we could be about to lose. **(fig. 9)**

My own various proposals are intellectual products designed to solve a prob-

9  A post titled 'The Analog Student'
published on the Misfits' Architecture blog.

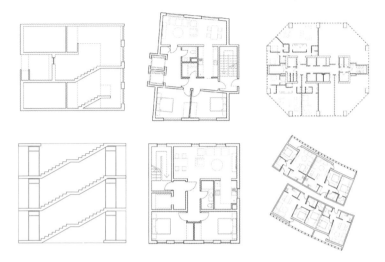

lem – as any building is until it is built. **(fig. 10)** I cannot think of them as architectural production until they either are built or have influenced something that is. Until
that happens, the blog and the contributing research laboratory can't be regarded as
having fulfilled its role. [40] But this is about to change. In 2015 I was contacted by
a student named Joshua, who was about to graduate from the University of Western
Australia, where I had also studied a few decades earlier. We also share an admira-
tion for the work of Lacaton & Vassal, and he introduced me to the work of
H Arquitectes in Barcelona. He admits the blog has helped shape his outlook.

Josh is currently managing the construction of a 140m² house in the southwest of western Australia. He designed it to have quantifiable building performance; flexibility of programme and of occupation; climatic responsiveness
through integrated passive heating and cooling techniques; appeal to its occupants rather than to external parties via media; a built expression that is the
consequence of the processes that led to its construction; and resourceful construction to deliver the building at a cost of approximately AUS$1,500 per square
metre – the midpoint between a house-builder's rate and anything upwards of
AUS$2,500 per square metre for an architect-designed home. This building will be
the first misfits' architecture that will communicate back to the world, along with
Josh's full description of his design intentions and the problems he encountered
realising them. When that information can be evaluated by others and either
applied as it is, improved upon or adapted as necessary, the cycle of architectural
research and architectural production will once again be linked.

All a blog needs to do is let that happen.

10  A misfits' layout study.

# Debate
# Criticism Today

Eunice Seng (Moderator),
Françoise Fromonot, Kamran Afshar Naderi, Graham Brenton McKay

**Eunice Seng:** Whether it's within the blog or a journal, I noticed that often the *question* is similar. It is the title for many issues and also the title of many essays. In Graham's case, 'dilemma' replaces crisis. I was wondering if you can start by talking about the motivation for initiating the journal or the blog as a space to begin to trigger questions or of posting questions.

**Graham Brenton McKay:** My blog began as a place to think through and to articulate ideas. The blog is self-aware as a critical entity and is not shy about commenting on anything. One of my persistent concerns is the dysfunction between the respective roles of the media, theory and production in architecture. It is not unique to architecture, but a couple of posts attempt to identify and describe its consequences for architecture. I notice that my observation is directly connected to what Françoise covered in her talk this morning. We actually have something in common that I didn't realise before this symposium.

**ES:** The latest 2017 issue of *Memar* was called 'Who's Afraid of Theory?' Kamran, why *that* question at *that* time?

**Kamran Afshar Naderi:** Over the past few years,

the magazine has invited guest editors to participate because we need the editorial voices of others. The guest editor of this particular issue was Nashid Nabian. As a magazine *Memar* needs to be critical about itself – in a similar way to how we critique other architecture projects and writings. This particular issue was actually a critique of our magazine. *Memar* has been called a yellow – or liberal – magazine. That is why this issue of 'Who's Afraid of Theory?' has a yellow cover.

My presentation was also trying to address that discussion and debate are the most important parts of nurturing critical thinking. In Iran, we always and still have the problem of free discussion and the difficulty of doubting what we are doing. We need to think deeper and more critically about what we are doing, including *Memar* magazine and how it has been run over the past 20 years. We need to think again about what we used to believe or still believe. We should not be afraid of opening discussions about things that we have long taken for granted.

**Françoise Fromonot**: All three presentations this morning have something in common: this lingering or explicit idea that we are lacking discussions – that we are in need of debating, connecting and exchanging all activities which are central to architecture criticism. This allows us to find a common ground in this network or platform of criticality. In fact, the lack of critical discussions is a question that is reluctantly addressed in academia. However, it is no less important that we talk about the role of questioning and debating projects, rather than 'just' about practising and building. For example, questions such as 'in what condition is this project *situated*?' and 'what does it do, in terms of its relationship to society at large?' are paramount issues for criticism. Each of us sitting on this panel somehow practises criticism differently but also recognises a similar set of questions.

**GBM**: I am still thinking about this question, 'who's afraid of theory?' Maybe people are afraid of theory because they think it is too difficult. I think there is a detachment of theory or the perception of theory from issues we are all related to. This is the gap I am trying to bridge with the blog. I am trying to translate complex forms of neoliberalism and architecture into simpler languages, and at the same time have a better understanding myself. These topics are important, and yet they seem to exist only in academic journals and have not flowed down to where a greater variety of opinions could be expressed. To be frank, I was afraid of theory myself, but am less afraid of it now.

**FF**: Defining theory is probably even more complicated than defining criticism, isn't it? If theory is a definition of architecture, then how is it present in the debate today? Should architects be asked to phrase explicitly what architecture is for them and present their work as an illustration of their claims? Or should they just build, and critics will formulate their 'theory'? Should critics base their criticism on a stated idea of what architecture is and gauge the value of any building on this given ideology? Perhaps we have misused these two words, theoretical and critical, to the point they are often mistaken for one another. In fact, theory and criticism are opposites: theory is meant to establish, and criticism is meant to destabilise.

**ES**: On that note, let's talk more about crisis. For many of us − whether architecture students or practitioners or educators − crisis belongs to another kind of historical force. For example, architecture

was extremely productive due to the crises of the 1960s. Through your experience in the production of journals or the blog, how do you locate or identify this crisis in order to be generative? How to break things down? As Françoise said, it is a task that is as daunting as establishing a theory.

**GBM**: What I have been trying to do with the blog is to simplify and make sense of things. Recently, it came together in a post titled 'Misleading Narratives', in which I mentioned a house with a sloping wall. The actual architectural proposal of the house was one thing, but the main point of the post was to criticise how buildings are often presented with misleading narratives about aesthetic considerations while their real and useful benefits are never mentioned. As architects, we are responsible for designing a building as criticism. This would be a way to generate valid proposals to illustrate a critical point, rather than serve as criticism in themselves.

**KAN**: At *Memar*, we are trying to promote critical thinking, but I don't think we are very good at it. The lack of critical thinking might have a lot to do with the education we received. Students in an Iranian university are used to following the rules, the paths and the frameworks set by the professors without questioning or challenging them. Architecture students are trained as scientists who use rational thinking rather than critical thinking. As you can probably imagine, it was extremely difficult when we first started *Memar* magazine. We couldn't get contributors to write for a magazine that aims to be critical about the architecture profession. For the first couple of years, I used to write all the pages dedicated to architectural criticism. Aside from *Memar*, I think being critical is a matter of life, a way of being. The first step is to observe daily life and our surroundings. Then, we can start to have a critical opinion on what we have observed and to imagine something different.

**FF**: I would like to continue the argument just put forward by Kamran. I think it's important to relate the issue of critical thinking to education, to the way in which architecture is taught. Today a 'cool' architecture school is more or less like an open bar, where students can taste a little bit of everything throughout their programme of studies. They go from one design studio to another, often taught by practitioners who are tailoring the studio subjects to their own concerns and who evaluate the students' work based on what they think architecture should be, based on their own practice. Architecture education has become the reproduction of established knowledge and thinking. This condition can be seen not only in France, but also in other parts of the world.

Going back to the differences between theory and criticism. For me, criticism is about constantly questioning the validity of established knowledge – its origins, its motives, its sense (of course, you have to have some basis to be able to do so), putting it into a state of crisis in order to reach another state, where things are re-stabilised before being questioned again. It is very hard to engage this dynamic process in the academic world as everything conspires to maintain things the way they are, as testified by the ubiquity in the pedagogical discourse of the word 'transmission', because graduates should be able to fit in the professional world. And the profession, because of its dependency on commissions, has very little 'critical' leeway. It is not only students that are copying images from journals or the internet; mainstream architectural practices have more or less always worked like that. In this context, initiating a *real* critical discussion on architecture in academia, in professional journals and in society is both needed and extremely hard.

**KAN**: I want to add a few words. When I started *Memar*, very few architecture magazines existed in the 1990s. Within that context, the purpose of starting a magazine was not only about writing what I was thinking, but also debating what mattered the most at that time. It was a process of trial and error. One of our many efforts to establish a better architecture discipline in Iran was to promote the younger generation of Iranian architects. Later, when this young generation of architects established their practices, they also started to create their own architecture magazines. I would say, the goal of *Memar* – the critical project that was first established almost 20 years ago – is always changing, evolving, and adapting to the needs of the society.

**FF**: Indeed, being critical is more than simply saying, 'this is bad' or 'that doesn't work'. You can be critical by promoting work you truly believe in because you find it establishes new ground through the questions it contains. Positively putting forward people, practices and ideas that are challenging the status quo can be a critical act.

**ES**: There is a kind of self-criticism of your own evolution of the space within which you operate. This leads me to my next question: what does it mean when an architect engages in criticism? How do you actually formulate your thoughts? Maybe all of you have already partially answered this question. Pardon me if my reading of what you have said is incorrect. I think Françoise was looking very specifically at certain architects' repertoire as a kind of criticism in itself. This is distinguished from what we have heard from Graham, who as an architect is writing the blog to figure out your own position. This is opposed to the larger identity project that Kamran has taken on, which is very country specific. What does it mean to have a magazine that presents, reveals and also facilitates national discourse? What does it mean when architects perform architectural criticism within a different space, like text and blogs? What kinds of struggles do you encounter? How do you actually make it as discursive as you want it to be? I guess the context of my question is this really grand view of architecture criticism. For example, there was a split in the academic and technical or trade journals after the 1930s, which was the space where Le Corbusier could write criticism, theory and practice simultaneously.

**FF**: The 1920s was a period of certainties for architects. *Architecture d'Aujourd'hui*, *Domus*, *Casabella* were founded on the crusade for modern architecture in the 1930s. It was a moment to promote ideologies and accomplish their promises for architecture. Just like those wonderful little pamphlets Graham showed from the Soviet Union that promoted new architecture for a new society.

Today, we are going through the reverse. We are in absolute uncertainty. You can choose among all kinds of trends in constant flux and witness the works of many architects, who are more often than not opportunistic in terms of the forms they choose because commissions are also very whimsical –

and there is no architecture without commissions. Of course, architecture can exist in the utopia of pure representation, but our times do not seem so conducive to utopia.

As far as I am concerned, I left practice to become a critic, not so much to judge the work of others but to try to elucidate where I stand, where I could stand. Being a critic is not to assert your certainties, but to investigate your doubts through the works you are looking at – by visiting them, by reading on them, by elucidating where they are standing in the history of ideas, of forms, etc – and formulate these findings in a constructed form to share them with others. For me writing criticism is like designing a series of written projects. All these things are a way of mapping a desire for architecture, and of defining a position.

**ES**: This is a very good moment to open to questions from the floor.

**Audience**: Who has the authority to criticise architecture?

**GBM**: As a self-appointed critic, I think anybody has the authority to criticise architecture. Everybody who uses architecture is entitled to his or her opinion. If images are going to be proposed and accepted as architecture, then the intended consumers of those images also have the right to a critical opinion on how or why those images were chosen, and what they were intended to convey. Aside from liking or disliking an image on social media, anybody should be able to add a few words explaining why. That is a form of criticism.

**FF**: This question about legitimacy of the critic is always around. I totally agree with Graham: anybody should have the right because everyone lives in architecture. Everyone goes to public spaces, everyone has lived in badly designed apartments or lectured in schools with over-air-conditioned lecture halls! So, on the one hand, yes, everybody is entitled to have an opinion. On the other hand, there are many levels of opinion, with very diverse origins: a carefully expressed view by a layperson or by a user of a building on the basis of experience, an analysis by someone who has professional knowledge – let's say an expert, etc. While I am saying this, I am think-

ing that one of roles of critics could be to hear them all, identify them and weave them into a coherent, meaningful narrative that could bring together all these critical voices.

Therefore, the question is not only if anybody has the right, but what does the expression of that right do, and what do we do with it? Going back to social media. My problem with social media or the internet is that I find the origin of what I read hard to figure out. Who and what is behind the opinion expressed? When you used to buy your newspaper in the morning, you knew what you wanted from it, because you knew, and generally shared, this newspaper's persuasion. If you wanted different points of view you could buy several newspapers, knowing for each of them where they stood. The success of social media is largely based on the fact that they value opinion *per se*, in the name of everyone having the right to have one. For me this is *not* criticism. When I turn to social media, I feel lost, not only because of the massive volume of text and the streams of images that they provide, but because of the difficulty of understanding who and what stands behind a piece of information I read. I miss the 'wings', the background, the context of opinion.

**GBM**: I think things on the Internet are increasingly confusing as well. A while ago, I was befriended on Facebook by Zaha Hadid. I found the whole thing quite bizarre. This person on Facebook created a post with a screenshot of an article from Misfits' Architecture, which was actually quite critical of Patrik Schumacher. The post was circulated around for a while.

**Nasrin Seraji**: I would like to join this discussion in a *misfitting* way. I am trying to stitch all of these earlier comments together by going back to the role of *Memar* magazine that Kamran talked about earlier. After being an exile for 22 years, I went back to Iran for the first time when I was invited to be on a jury panel. I remember Soheila Beski's work very well. Soheila basically started the precursor of *Memar* magazine. Since she was not an architect herself, Soheila invited people like Kamran to become editors of this magazine (Soheila Beski, Seyed Reza Hashemi and Kamran Afshar Naderi are the founding partners of *Memar*). I think Soheila not only created a way of protecting works of architecture and inducing another type of architecture, but also started an architectural magazine that functions as a place where people can actually express themselves. Expression in Iran was a very different question.

However, how do you express yourself freely in an environment that doesn't really allow you to do so? For example, we knew the party secretary was there when we went to a lecture in Shanghai five years ago. It is similar in the public places in Iran. This surveillance atmosphere did exist. Although it is less so now, there are still eyes watching when you go to a public lecture with an audience of 1,000 people. When architecture becomes the forum that allows us to talk about these issues with a different 'veil' – for the better of use of the word – and allows architecture to become that thing that unveils, we can start to see the capacity of architecture criticism to feed into other types of democracy. Maybe Kamran can talk about this a little bit more. After not being in my own country for 22 years, I am not even able to speak my own language fluently. That is why I felt strongly about the importance of what *Memar* was doing. It created a forum where people could speak, read and write in a critical manner – into an atmosphere that did not exist in Iran at that time.

**KAN**: Sohelia was a very tough lady. I remember one day she came to the office, laughed and said, 'Democracy is there to allow me to exercise dictatorship in my magazine.' Since its establishment, *Memar* has been accessible to anyone who is willing to purchase it. Many years ago, I would receive emails from people who criticised my writing in *Memar*. I replied to their emails and invited these people to send their comments so that we could publish them in the correspondence column. Inviting people who completely disagreed with us to participate in a discussion was our way of exercising democracy at *Memar*. However, for some reason, most people that I reached out to would not allow their letters to be published.

Perhaps blogs and other types of social media allow people to be less hesitant about sharing their thoughts. With new media, people can participate in public discussions no matter where they are phys-

ically located. The point of creating a platform for discussion is not to say that 'we are right'. It is about allowing everyone to express his or her opinion. That is the strong point that *Memar* has always tried to make. For sure, we have a lot of difficulties. I have to admit that often we are not completely happy with what we have published. Sometimes, issues managed by guest editors were of relatively low quality. Again, this is a trial-and-error process. This is how *Memar* magazine continually grows and evolves. We see the value of having more people, especially young people, participate in the editorial work. It was also great to see that many young people who used to work for *Memar* have started their own architecture magazines in Iran.

**FF**: Criticism can be subversive of many things. The constraints of political regimes in Iran or in China cannot obviously be compared to what we have in Europe. Europeans should feel very privileged to be able to say something like, 'Why are we not able to say what we want?' But even in a so-called democracy there are things that seem to be forbidden to say or show in architecture publications. As mentioned in my presentation about the Centre Pompidou-Metz, the side of the building opposite to its entrance is never presented in journals. However, it is the view that you experience when you arrive in the city of Metz. And it is a total mess – Metz, mess! Publishing a picture of it in *Criticat* was a simple, basic act of criticism. Of course, I am aware that this minute example cannot compare with the kind of fight for free speech that Nasrin and Kamran are talking about.

**GBM**: But let's not overestimate democracy.

**FF**: Of course, but let's not underestimate dictatorships.

**Audience**: I am a design assistant at HKU. I totally agree that there is a need for a broader debate in the field of architecture and am curious about your experience with the blog, particularly the language on a blog. For example, are you able to tell the intellectual positions of your blog readers based on their comments? Have you ever deleted a comment because it was too radical?

**GBM**: I approve everything that arrives. I might not

always reply to it because there are some discussions that I don't want to get into.

**Audience**: There is no editing of readers' comments?

**GBM**: Right. Going back to your question about the language of the blog. Because readers are from a variety of countries, I try to keep the language simple. Sometimes, I link my articles to other websites or to an online urban dictionary.

**FF**: This question of language is extremely important. Graham is perhaps one of the few people in this lecture hall for whom English is his native language. I suppose that for many of us whose mother tongue is not English, we speak English simply to communicate with each other. Since almost all of us have this shared experience, I am sure you have noticed that you don't think or articulate ideas in the same way when using different languages.

This internationalisation of criticism is the problem we are having now at *Criticat*. The official language of *Criticat* is French because it is the language of our culture as writers and editors. In order to make the journal accessible and readable to anyone interested in architecture, we try our best to write in a clear and un-academic style. However, translating some of those texts from French into English for a book, was extremely difficult for our translator. It was not only a process of translating the words. The essential concepts as well as the types of reasoning had to be recast in another version altogether.

I am sure anybody who has done some translations knows this. You need to project yourself into the mind-set of not only the author, but also his or her linguistic culture, with its structure. You don't want the quality of your translation to be like those done by the Google translator. However, we do read more often than not texts that are close to a generic Google translation, even in so-called good journals. While English has become a global language that makes information more accessible to diverse groups of people, it is not well used compared to what English as a language could really offer. I don't have a solution to this dilemma, but I think it is an important question to raise.

This challenge is also related to the question of the place from which you stand or speak. We need to keep this in mind when we read criticism from other places. I am actually curious about the Persian language. I don't know much about it, but it seems an incredibly sophisticated and literary language. I wonder what happens when you translate articles from Persian to English?

**KAN**: I have done a lot of translation from my mother tongue Persian, to my second language Italian, and to English, which is actually my third language. I come across similar difficulties when I translate Persian into Italian or English. There is always something that makes perfect sense in Persian, but doesn't make any sense when translated directly into Italian or English because the ways in which these languages express ideas are very different. We don't assume that readers of the texts we translate think in the same way as Persians. Oftentimes, you need to add more information when you translate. I am not sure if I am a good translator, but at least people understand what I translate.

**FF**: I am sure that those of you who are also editors have been confronted with this situation where through the process of translation, you can actually improve an article.

**Angelika Schnell**: What has not been mentioned here is the golden age of criticism, which was actually the 1970s. It was a time when critical theory – the combination of 'criticism' and 'theory' – was a very important issue. Language of critical theory was never simple. In contrast, from what I have seen and heard this morning, each of you has a different way of practising criticism. I was wondering whether this critical theory – by Theodor Adorno, Max Horkheimer, Herbert Marcuse, or even Manfredo Tafuri, which of course is not easy to include, to understand or to practise – still plays a role for you or if it is completely over. What is your position towards it?

**GBM**: I think I operate and write outside those hidden ideological structures not to live up to the name of the blog but because the type of criticism lacking today needs to bump up against other more immediate positions. The battles criticism faces are not going to be won or lost on the grounds of intellectual rigour, so I am content to comment on the mainstream of theory or criticism in whichever direction they lead. I don't see myself as a devil's advocate. I am just putting forward my thoughts. I hope to provide a useful position and not merely a false certainty, but we will see.

**KAN:** When I started my first year of college in Italy, I studied a few books by Manfredo Tafuri. However, I soon realised that Tafuri's writing could be understood by very few people. His writings are very difficult. If I write like Tafuri in *Memar* magazine, we could probably only be able to sell the magazine to three people in Iran. I thought that maybe it would be better to use a different kind of language, and maybe not link a specific theory to my criticism. Criticism for me is just a way of discovering things, not knowing things *a priori*.

**FF:** There is the Italian branch of critical theory represented by theorists such as Manfredo Tafuri, and there is the American version of it. As far as the Italian branch goes, its Marxist ideological cast seems difficult to sustain – at least in a similar form – in the 'liberal' condition of today. For me criticism is the opposite of the use of an all-encompassing, *a priori*, ideology; one needs to 'travel lighter' in order to be more agile. As far as the American so-called critical theory is concerned, I have always been perplexed by the alliance of these two terms. As mentioned earlier, criticism and theory in a way are opposites. Are there really that many dialectics at play in most of this so-called critical theory? Furthermore, it is mostly issued from the exclusive limits of American architecture schools. It may be interesting to study it as a phenomenon, though, particularly as a social phenomenon within academia of that particular period of time. But for me, its heavily interpretative aspect is built up at the expense of first-hand knowledge and true investigation: it is not what criticism should be today, not at all.

**Cole Roskam:** In each of your talks, I heard a lot about the specific platforms for criticism, but not a lot of specific methods of criticism that those platforms might enable or allow. I was curious to hear a bit more about the interplay between form and method, platform and method with respect to criticism.

**GBM:** My examples are from my blog. There is an extended series on Misfits' Architecture, in which I was reading Patrick Schumacher's *The Autopoiesis of Architecture* chapter by chapter. It has been extended for about four years and I still haven't finished it. This series is meant to break the book into simpler sections in order to explain concepts and critique those concepts to a wider audience. That is an on-going project, and I still have one more chapter left to go. I think all of these allow me to create a style of writing that is easy to understand by readers of my blog.

**FF:** When it comes to method I could stress one main principle, which is to *visit* what I write about: never write about a building that you have not seen in the flesh. Critical practice in our field includes visiting and revisiting the built matter in its environment, physical and social. Sometimes you only get the chance to visit the project once, if it is far away. Sometimes you visit it five times if necessary, you see its uses change, its materials age, etc. I don't mean that a kind of phenomenology of space could be enough as a basis for criticism. The informed experience of a building, preferably with people in it – users that you can talk to – as well as meeting clients, is very important. And before writing on something I also like to read everything that has been written about it, to visit the texts it has generated. Because the discourses that construct architecture are as relevant as the architects that construct the buildings.

**Audience:** Have you had the equivalent experience of translating between languages of different professional cultures? Some of the issues you face when translating to different languages and to different cultures may also be found in 'translating' architecture into other areas of practice.

**KAN:** I think translation is a way of rebuilding the text. And related to Cole's question of method, it is important to reveal the thinking behind a project. My first published article was written by talking to the architects, going through all their sketches and excavating their hidden processes. Architecture criticism is about discovering and re-discovering the work.

# History's Role in Contemporary Criticism

# History and Criticism
Cole Roskam

In introducing an academic panel devoted to the relationship between history and criticism in architectural discourse, it feels both cliché yet necessary to make obligatory reference to Italian architectural historian Manfredo Tafuri, who famously began his 1985 interview with another architectural historian, Richard Ingersoll, by stating 'There is no such thing as criticism, there is only history. What usually is passed off as criticism, the things you find in architecture magazines, is produced by architects, who frankly are bad historians.'[1]

My intent is not to further mythologise a seminal figure or the complexities that surround his work. Nevertheless, revisiting Tafuri's pronouncement feels instructive at a time of uncertainty about the state of architectural criticism and history today, particularly in parts of the world where notions of criticism and history in architecture may depart from what they were in Europe and the US in the early 1980s.

Was writing history in the age of collage and pastiche such a different project than the task of producing history in today's frenetic globalised world of fake news and the insatiable online consumption of Instagrammable images? Now, as then, we exist in what Tafuri identified as 'a state of constant anxiety'.[2] Tafuri's exhortation to architects that they should 'just *do* architecture' echoes in David Huber's critique of the 2017 Chicago Biennial as 'an adventure in disengagement' in which 'architecture felt small, isolated, gutless, and inconsequential'.[3] The biennial itself, titled History Again, invoked a very particular version of the past in ways that reminded a number of observers of postmodernism's own superficial efforts to recover history.[4]

Nevertheless, distinctions do exist that demand architecture's attention and present opportunities for further reflection. For one, we use technologies on a daily basis that, in theory, allow for a much broader architectural engagement with people and context than what was available in the 1980s. Architectural history and criticism, too, consist of much broader

1 'Manfredo Tafuri interviewed by Richard Ingersoll', *Design Book Review* 9 (Spring 1986) pp8–11.
2 Ibid.
3 Ibid; David Huber, 'History Again', *Artforum International*, 25 September 2017. https://www.artforum.com/diary/david-huber-at-the-2nd-chicago-architecture-biennial-71309.
4 Matthew Messner and Matt Shaw, 'What's up with the Chicago Architecture Biennial?', *The Architect's Newspaper*, 5 September 2017.

engagements with building practices and discourses than each did 40 years ago. Both the critic, generally understood as a judge of value or merit in contemporary works of cultural production, and the historian, who seeks to understand and organise past events into a coherent framework of analysis in an effort to illuminate process, now have access to objects, sites, and forms of knowledge that expand what was considered to be acceptable fields of inquiry in the past.

The essays that follow illuminate these exciting new realms. Seng Kuan's work argues for the agency of buildings, essays and exhibitions in redefining notions of tradition in postwar Japanese architectural discourse. Kenzo Tange is highlighted as a key figure in the deployment of display, presentation, and viewing – all vital exercises in historical Japanese visual culture – to connect postwar Japanese architecture to global debates then taking place over architectural modernism and the role of history in architectural making.

Anthony Acciavatti's work as an architect, historian and founding editor of *Manifest: A Journal of American Architecture and Urbanism*, positions him squarely within questions of the role of criticism and history in contemporary architectural discourse and production. In its focus on American architecture, cities and territory, *Manifest* seeks to interrogate notions of America itself – an important and timely exercise amid ongoing debate as to where American boundaries begin and end, and how to protect them. His essay tackles the question of discernment – the ability to judge – in determining value in relation to architectural inquiry and scholarship.

Here, then, we return again to Tafuri, and to the process of selection that determines which architectural objects and sites are deemed worthy of criticism and history. We live in a world of unprecedented access to things and ideas. Given such overwhelming scope, how and why do particular works and figures enter into the architectural canon, and are there ways in which an effort like *Manifest* can contribute to the construction of a defined yet expanded architectural field through critical and historical inquiry? In particular, can discernment and its assorted curatorial and editorial frameworks be used to push the parameters of architectural discourse outward and upward rather than reinforcing the authority of those few institutions that continue to dominate the rules of the discipline? The potential for new theories, practices and histories awaits.

1  Tange Kenzō, Hiroshima Peace Center, Exhibition Hall (1951–55).
(Photo by Ishimoto Yasuhiro, courtesy Tange Associates)

# Architecture Criticism in Postwar Japan

Seng Kuan

Few ideas loom larger in the critical literature of Japan's modern architecture than that of tradition.  Since the term was formally invoked in 1955 by Kawazoe Noboru in the essay 'Kenzō Tange's Japanese Character',[1] published in the journal *Shinkenchiku* where he was also serving as an editor, the suggestion of an innate continuity between the splendours of ancient Japan with modernism has continued to entice and vex us.[2]  Within Japan's architectural community the Tradition Debate, or *dentō ronsō*, refers to a specific moment of coalescence in the 1950s, lasting no more than three or four years, of specific ideological trends in artistic and literary communities. Willingly or not, architect Tange Kenzō was cast as the poster child of this discursive moment, and his long and complicated career became inextricably tied to this set of causes especially in later critical reassessments.[3] Through polemical writings and design projects from this period, Tange's enthusiasm for tradition needs to be carefully qualified, despite his apparently robust participation in the debates of the 1950s. In fact, a careful parsing of Tange's commentary on Japan's architectural heritage, as well as his own design work, shows how thoroughly he internalised the conditions of his own time and especially the potential of technology. Tange is seen by many as the first non-western architect to have produced works inducted into the canon of modern architecture that were not merely of regional interest but had universal

1 Iwata Kazuo (Kawazoe Noboru writing as), 'Tange Kenzō no Nihon-teki seikaku: tokuni raamen kōzō no hatten wo tōshite', *Shinkenchiku* (Jan 1955) pp62–69.
2 The exhibition 'Japan in Architecture: Genealogies of Its Transformation', on view at the Mori Art Museum as this draft is finalised, is organised entirely on this premise of a continuity that stretches from prehistoric Japan to the present.  Fujimori
3 See Tange Kenzō and Fujimori Terunobu, *Tange Kenzō* (Tokyo: Shinkenchiku-sha, 2002). Fujimori's position on Tange's early work, tracing backwards from projects from the 1950s to his competition schemes produced during the Second World War, owes in part to the dissertation of Jacqueline Eve Kestenbaum, 'Modernism and Tradition in Japanese Architectural Ideology, 1931–1955', (Columbia University, 1996).

value. Against the backdrop of Japan's geopolitical situation of the early postwar period as the country emerged from the devastation of the Second World War and six years of American occupation, tradition also emblemises the culmination of a cultural and aesthetic discourse that was based largely on a facile and often unhelpful attitude toward historical and cultural continuity. **(fig. 2)**

Publishing in the January 1955 issue of *Shinkenchiku* under the nom de plume of Iwata Kazuo, Kawazoe situates Tange's early rationalist designs – such as the *Rahmen* rigid-frame reinforced concrete structures – in Japan's historical space-making and construction techniques, while referencing ancient sites such as the seventh-century grand Ise Grand Shrine, Shōsō-in treasure house and the Zen garden of Ryōan-ji. The publication of this essay is conventionally seen as the official starting point of the Tradition Debate, at least as it pertains to architecture. Kawazoe, who joined *Shinkenchiku* in 1953 after graduating from Waseda University, was highly effective in turning his editorial position into a powerful platform of ideological instigation.[4] Founded in 1925 and in essentially uninterrupted monthly print since, *Shinkenchiku* is Japan's premier trade journal for architecture. Just a few years later, in 1960, Kawazoe would reemerge as a founding member of the Metabolist movement that debuted at the World Design Conference in Tokyo.

4 See an oral history account with Kawazoe: 'Nihon bijutsu ooraru hisutorii aakaive, Kawazoe Noboru intavuu', by Nakatani Norihiko and Washida Meruro (March 24, 2009).

2 'Tange Kenzō's Japanese Character' by Kazuo Iwata, from *Shinkenchiku* 1955:01.

As art historian and critic Noriaki Kitazawa has reminded us, the Tradition Debate in fact derived from historicist currents of the avant-garde that first emerged in the 1930s and resurfaced in the early postwar period, developing largely independent of architects.[5] In the early 1950s, several events in the Japanese art world signalled an attempt to revisit Japan's cultural patrimony, manifesting most notably in the exhibitions on Tawaraya Sōtatsu and Ogata Kōrin's *rinpa* school and Japan's ancient culture, both held in 1951 at the newly reorganised National Museum of Tokyo.[6] The first exhibition, on *rinpa*, was devoted to the work of two seventeenth-century painters later heralded as the progenitors of a uniquely Japanese pictorial style. The exhibition on Japan's ancient culture, prominently featuring recent archaeological finds, rekindled interest in the origins of Japan's sui generis plastic arts culture, particularly resuscitating the two prehistoric eras of Jōmon and Yayoi with modern aesthetic significance.[7] The political message of these two shows, to mark the end of the six-year-long occupation of Japan by the United States, was unequivocal, embracing two major historical episodes of Japanese art and culture seen as unencumbered by foreign influences.

Within the international community of architectural modernism, there was a parallel and complementary sentiment toward Japan's architectural heritage, embraced from overseas by powerful figures such as Arthur Drexler, curator of architecture and design at the Museum of Modern Art in New York, the powerful philanthropist John D Rockefeller III, and Walter Gropius who was then teaching at the Harvard Graduate School of Design, that largely inherited a reductive view of historical Japanese architecture and design as proto-modern first proposed in the prewar period by the likes of Bruno Taut. In this sense the Tradition Debate as a critical movement grew out of not one existential crisis but two: first, in the ruinous destruction of Japan in the final months of the Pacific War in which we saw the obliteration of scores of Japanese cities, including Tokyo; and the second, in the Treaty of San Francisco between the US and Japan, signed in 1951, which included a treaty of mutual defence through which Japan came within the American sphere of influence. A few months before the publication of Kawazoe's essay, a Japanese *shoin* building, Shōfu-sō, designed in the style of a seventeenth-century aristocratic residence by the great modern architect Yoshimura Junzō, was constructed at the Museum of Modern Art in New York,

5 Kitazawa Noriaki, 'dentō ronsō : 60 nendai avangyarudo he no airo', in Bijutsu hihyō ka renmei ed, *Bijutsu hihyō to sengo bijutsu* (Tokyo: Buryukke, 2007) pp103–22.
6 The two exhibitions were 'Sōtatsu Kōrin-ha ten' (4 April–6 May 1951) and 'Nihon kodai bunka ten' (10 Oct–25 Nov 1951).
7 The central role of Okamoto Tarō in the promotion of the Jōmon/Yayoi framework is discussed extensively om Jonathan M Reynolds, *Allegories of Time and Space: Japanese Identity in Photography and Architecture* (Honolulu, HI: University of Hawaii Press, 2013). Okamoto and Tange collaborated closely on a number of projects between 1955 and 1957 at the height of the Tradition Debate. This work is showcased in the exhibition catalog *Okamoto Tarō x Kenchiku: Shōtotsu to kyōdō no dainamizumu*, eds Suzuki Reikō and Kinoshita Saeko (Kawasaki: Okamoto Tarō Bijutsu-kan, 2017).

adjacent to the recently redesigned sculptural garden.[8] In the spring of 1954, just as the Japanese house was being assembled in the MoMA courtyard, Gropius and his wife Ise embarked on a historic journey to Japan, ostensibly to attend the opening of the Bauhaus exhibition in Tokyo led by his former Japanese students from the days of Dessau. Gropius was lavishly feted by Japan's architectural elite and treated to an extensive tour of Japan's ancient buildings and gardens, particularly in the Kyoto and Nara region.[9] His impressions from this experience are documented in the essay 'The Architecture of Japan', the first version of which appeared in the journal *Perspecta* the following year:

> You cannot imagine what it meant to me to come suddenly face to face with these houses, with a culture still alive, which in the past had already found the answer to many of our modern requirements of simplicity, of outdoor-indoor relations, of modular coordination, and at the same time, variety of expression, resulting in a common form language uniting all individual efforts.[10]

Gropius's favourable impression of what he saw – both ancient and contemporary – were reiterated a few years later in Tange's photo album on Katsura Villa, first published in English in 1960 by Yale University Press.[11] Built in the early seventeenth century as an aristocratic villa complex, Katsura itself has been appropriated in the modern era to establish an intrinsic affinity between Japan's architectural patrimony and modern architecture.[12] Tange's own essay in the Katsura volume, titled 'Tradition and Creation in Japanese Architecture', is usually cited as the smoking gun of tradition's paramount role in his architectural design. This perception, situated in the context of Tange's substantial portfolio of large institutional buildings with representational and ceremonial qualities, tempts one to conclude axiomatically that Tange embraced of a prewar notion of monumentality, with the implication that this architecture is inherently conservative and possibly undemocratic.[13] This was the stance of many scholars and critics until only very recently.

---

8  Arthur Drexler, *The Architecture of Japan* (New York, NY: The Museum of Modern Art, 1954).
9  The visit in 1954 by Walter and Ise Gropius is documented in *Guropiusu to Nihon bunka* (Tokyo: Shōkoku-sha, 1956).
10  Walter Gropius, 'The Architecture of Japan' *Perspecta*, no 3 (1955) pp8–21.
11  The collaboration between Tange and photographer Ishimoto Yasuhiro that resulted in the book *Katsura: Tradition and Creation in Modernism Architecture* (1960) is discussed in Yasufumi Nakamori, *Katsura: Picturing Modernism in Japanese Architecture: Photographs by Yasuhiro Ishimoto* (Houston: Museum of Fine Arts, 2013).
12  For an excellent overview on Katsura's role in the discourse of Japanese modernism, see Benoît Jacquet, 'La Villa Katsura et ses jardins: l'invention d'une modernité Japonaise dan les années 1930', in Nicolas Fiévé and Benoît Jacquet eds, *Vers unes modernité architecturale et paysagère: modèles et saviors partagés entre le Japon et le monde occidental* (Paris: Collège de France, Institute des Hautes Études Japonaises, 2013) pp99–139.
13  In 1942 and 1943 respectively, Tange won two national competitions for the designs of the Monument to the Greater East Asia Co-Prosperity Sphere and the Japan Cultural Center in Bangkok. His postwar success at the Hiroshima Peace Memorial is often considered together with these two wartime projects as a triad of Tange's monumental architecture. This position was first proposed in a series of essays by Naka Masami (nom de plume of Sasaki Hiroshi) in the journal Kenchiku in 1963–64. The collected volume was published as *Kindai kenchiku-ka no shisō: Tange Kenzō no joron* (Tokyo: Kindai kenchiku-sha, 1970).

As I try to argue, in the context of these cultural anxieties and political realities both inside and outside Japan, Tange adopted a nuanced and opportunistic attitude to the issue of tradition in the middle of the 1950s, the height of the Tradition Debate. He looked for ways to incorporate aspects of historical Japanese architecture most sympathetic to modernism, sometimes rhetorically and often in collaboration with artists. At the same time, he maintained his research on the scale of the modern city, extricating himself from regionalist marginalia in order to be recast by the end of the decade as an architect with global aspirations and relevance.

Tange's deep engagement in local networks and domestic debates was conditioned from the outside by his position as a world architect. He came of age at a time when world architecture began to be ensconced in the university curriculum and became a precondition for the imagining of modern architecture. Precluded from an education abroad by the war, his mentors – Kishida Hideto, Maekawa Kunio, Sakakura Junzō, and Takayama Eika – placed a resolutely cosmopolitan outlook on design during Tange's formative years. He debuted on the world stage at the 1951 CIAM meeting in Hoddesdon, on the Heart of the City, with a presentation of his Peace Memorial and reconstruction scheme for Hiroshima. Throughout his career Tange's reference points would remain Rome, Michelangelo and Le Corbusier, while his discursive formation was owed in equal measure to his participation in CIAM, teaching at MIT, and long-standing correspondence with overseas interlocutors as it was to Japanese networks of architects, artists and critics. **(fig. 3)**

Operating one of world's first true global architectural practices, Tange captured his image of the world in the age of jet travel and advanced telecommunications in the diagram 'The Shrinking Pacific'.[14] Here the distance between Tokyo and San Francisco, a route he knew well, is mapped in terms of time, which is shrinking, and volume, which is expanding, enabled by advances in airplane travel. Although it reflects a chronotope firmly situated in its time, this worldview also suggests the inadequacy of defining Tange and his work even loosely in national or regional terms. It is important to recognise Tange's profile as, and aspiration to be, a world architect, primarily because of the potential it holds to further conceptualise the multi-nodal origins and expressions of architectural modernism.

Before we return to Tange and the architectural culture of the 1950s, it is useful to examine first the writings by Itagaki Takaho.[15] The ideas of this most important of architecture critics of the 1930s is useful to untangle of the complex intellectual threads that preconditioned the theoretical anxieties of the postwar

---

14  Tange Kenzō, et al., eds, *21 seiki no Nihon: sono kokudō to kokumin seikatsu no miraizō* (Tokyo: Shinkenchiku-sha, 1971).
15  Itagaki's position on classicism is discussed in Yasumatsu Miyuki, 'Itagaki Takaho to 'koten': kenchiku hyōron to bannen no sakuhin 'kasai Junhachi ō kinen monyumento' o musurnde', in Omuka Toshiharu ed, *Kurashikku modan: 1930 nendai Nihon no geijutsu* (Tokyo: Serika shobō, 2004).

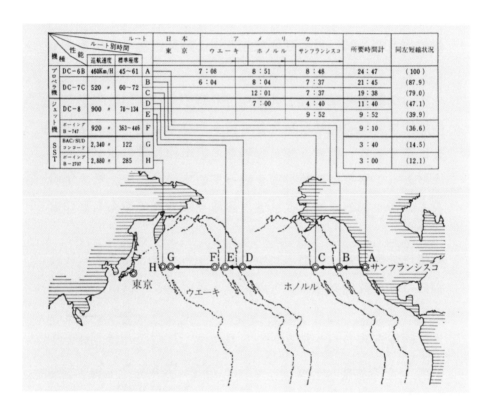

3 'The Shrinking Pacific', from *21 seiki no Nihon kenkyūkai* (Tange Kenzō et al.), *Japan in the 21st Century: A Vision of Its Land and Its People [21 seiki no Nihon: sono kokudo to kokumin seikatsu no miraizō]* (Tokyo: Shinkenchiku-sha, 1971).

period, when a similar set of issues was reintroduced in a different guise. The revisionist stance we find in the postwar era, under the mantle of tradition or even more frustratingly as *nihonteki na mono* – or 'the pure Japanese thing' – has largely blurred our understanding of a crucial period of ideological development in Tange and his cohort.[16] With the escalation of the war effort in the early 1940s, the word 'tradition' began to supplant the role that 'classicism' had fulfilled in Japan's elite academic art and architectural study in the 1930s. Itagaki was one of Japan's leading scholars on renaissance art and architecture and can be considered among Japan's first architectural critics, although mainstream historiography has largely brushed over Itagaki's immense influence in the 1930s. He was personally close to two of Tange's mentors: Kishida Hideto, the powerful professor at Tokyo Imperial University and Tange's first major patron, and Sakakura Junzō, with whom Itagaki organised the 1942 Leonardo da Vinci exhibition held in Tokyo. In revisiting the work of Itagaki we are able to reframe the historicist yearning of Tange and others of the postwar period in terms of a more robust and universal idea of classicism.

Itagaki's writings reveal a subtle and nuanced view of classicism, particularly in its application to the modern context. In Japanese the word 'classical' is typically rendered in two ways: either as a translation into *kotenteki* or transliterated phonetically as *kurashikku*. The former is a compound *kanji* word meaning, literally, 'that of ancient texts'. This is consistent with its etymology in the west, where its earliest modern uses were to describe the revived interest in Greek and Roman texts by Petrarch and other late-medieval humanists. The abundant usage of the term 'classicism' in all its forms – classical, classic, classicising – in western art and architecture history has been subject of continued scrutiny and retuning, oscillating between classicism as style and as ideology as David Freedberg has highlighted.[17] Albeit trained as a scholar of renaissance art and architecture, Itagaki's prolific writings as an architecture critic convey an enthusiastic and persistent endorsement of modernism. His first essay on architecture was published in 1929 and titled 'Manifestations of Modernity in Architecture'.[18] He was particularly sympathetic to the works of the Ministry of Communications produced under Yoshida Tetsurō and Yamada Mamoru, two of Japan's earliest and most progressive architects of the modern movement. In his 1933 publication *Modern Architecture*, Itagaki traces the ideals of the rationalist strain of modern architecture to that of Greek temples. Itagaki was far more profligate in using 'classical' to describe modern works of architecture than Japan's premodern buildings. He

16 Isozaki Arata has translated *nihonteki-na-mono* as 'Japan-ness'. Cherie Wendelken calls it 'the pure Japanese thing', which I prefer both for its proximity to the Japanese original and a hint of ridicule. The additional appeal of 'the pure Japanese thing' is that it somehow extricates this core set of ideas from the burdens of history and historicism and allows it to evolve into the *je ne sais quoi* of all this wonderful architecture produced in contemporary Japan.
17 David Freedberg, 'Editor's Statement: the Problem of Classicism: Ideology and Power', *Art Journal* vol 47, no 1 (Spring 1988) pp1–6.
18 Itagaki Takaho, 'kenchiku ni okeru gendai no hyōgen', *Bijutsu Shinchō* (April 1929).

praised the Bauhaus as 'it would not be inappropriate to recognise as a classic of modern civilisation'.

Although working frequently with Horiguchi Sutemi (the architect most closely associated with *nihonteki na mono*), Itagaki was wary of his collaborator's approach to historicism, or what has recently been called the *sukiya*-fication (*sukiya-ka*) of Japanese architecture after the highly refined style developed in the sixteenth century in association with tea connoisseurship. In 1934, the architectural journal *Kokusai Kenchiku* devoted an entire issue to the culture of tea and *sukiya* architecture. In contrast to the general sanguineness expressed by most of the writers, Itagaki was uniquely reserved in his review essay, titled 'A Warning'.[19] Praises lavished on Japan's historical architecture – as voiced by the likes of Bruno Taut – risked Japan's own modern architects rushing to embrace historicism without careful reflection. In the case of the architecture related to the culture of tea, Itagaki implored for in-depth study of not just the physical forms, but also its social background as well as the practice and spirit of tea ceremony. This warning against what he refers to as 'elite dilettantism', or a one-dimensional infatuation with a historical phenomenon, was reiterated in the 1940 essay 'Relics and Modernity'.[20] The essay was written partly in response the special number of *Gendai Kenchiku* that was entirely devoted to Sen no Rikyu and the culture of tea connoisseurship. Beyond the cultivation of taste and sensibility, Itagaki doubts anything substantive can be gleaned from *sukiya* architecture without extraordinary intellectual cultivation and self-reflection. Most importantly, the elite origins of *sukiya* architecture represented a fundamental departure from the needs of contemporary society.

Against this historicist debate between more universalist implications of classicism and the particularities of *sukiya* style and *nihonteki na mono*, as an architect emerging out of the 1930s Tange clearly leaned toward the former in the essay 'Ode to Michelangelo: As a Prologue to a Theory on Le Corbusier', published in *Gendai Kenchiku*.[21] For the rest his life Tange never veered from his devotion to the renaissance master. Tange attributed his own classicist stance on modern architecture to his mentor Sakakura, who returned to Japan in 1939 after six years in Le Corbusier's atelier. Sakakura's formal education at Tokyo Imperial University was in art history, where he purportedly took an interesting in Paul Frankl's writings on medieval architecture. In fact, the illustrations used by Tange in 'Ode to Michelangelo', including those of the Medici Chapel and Pasteum, were mostly lent to him by Sakakura. Writing in 1938, Tange was keenly aware of the potential irony in situating his reading of Le Corbusier in the tradition of western classicism. The esoteric and cryptic essay, Tange would later explain,

19  Itagaki Takaho, 'hitotsu no keikoku', *Kokusai Kenchiku* vol 10, no 1 (January 1934) pp29–30.
20  Itagaki Takaho, 'ikō to gendai', *Kokusai Kenchiku* vol 16, no 9 (September 1940) pp268–70. Tange
21  Tange Kenzō, 'Michelangelo no shō: Le Corbusier ron he no josetsu toshite', *Gendai Kenchiku*, no 7 (December 1939): pp36–47.

was intended to be a critique of doctrinaire functionalism narrowly abided by Japanese avant-garde architects at the time. Le Corbusier's contribution, which Tange intended to follow, was to resuscitate architecture from this dogmatism of rigid geometry, or in his words, the 'palace of ice (*koori no dendō*)'.

The early postwar period saw a major turn in the west's pursuit of academic architectural history. Among the new generation of studies, probably the most influential to architectural practice, certainly in the English-speaking world, were: Colin Rowe's 'The Mathematics of the Ideal Villa' (1947); Rudolf Wittkower's *Architectural Principles in the Age of Humanism* (1949); and Emil Kaufmann's *Architecture in the Age of Reason* (1955).[22] In situating Japanese architectural ideology of the 1950s, particularly the discourse of tradition in the second half of the decade, it is crucial to consider this international context. Wittkower distilled the relationship between history and practice with the following: 'As I see it, renaissance architects saw this problem in terms of employing ancient theory and practice in support of contemporary requirements.'[23] This book led a generation of architects to look to the past to reenergise modern architecture in the postwar period. Rather than acting as a definitive guide on classicism's harmonic proportions – which the book in its whole is not – the central thesis of the book is to present renaissance architecture as manifestation of a universal and absolute hierarchy of values and knowledge.

Unlike the previous generation of Japan's modernist architects who came of age before the Second World War, Tange and his cohort largely shied away from direct reference to the culture of tea and its corollary visual and design culture, as epitomised by the later works Sutemi Horiguchi. Tange preferred working with other self-proclaimed avant-garde interpreters of the traditional arts and pursued new directions of artistic creation and collaboration that were inherently modern and un-nostalgic. In 1949, he was among the first architects to be inducted into the Shinseisaku Art Society, an association of Japan's leading modern painters and sculptors. That same year he designed the exhibition space for the group's prestigious annual show and described his design in a catalogue essay titled 'On the Unity of Architecture, Sculpture, and Painting'.[24] Taking a cue from Le Corbusier's call for *vers l'unité*, first sounded in 1944, and the theme on aesthetics discussed at the seventh

---

22    Kaufmann began publishing on Ledoux and the neoclassical architects of pre-revolutionary France in the 1920s. *Von Ledoux bis Le Corbusier* was published in 1933 in German and was broadly received. It was formally presented to American audience at Philip Johnson's house in Cambridge for the Society of Architectural Historians in 1943. His first English-language work, titled 'Three Revolutionary Architects: Boullée, Ledoux, and Lequeu', appeared in the *Transactions of The American Philosophical Society* in 1952.

23    Rudolf Wittkower, *Architectural Principles in the Age of Humanism* (New York, NY: Norton, 1949).

24    Tange Kenzō, 'kenchiku, chōkoku, eiga no tōitsu nit suite: shinseisaku ha kyōkai ten ni kanren shite', *Shinkenchiku* vol 24, no. 11 (November 1949): pp372–73, 380.

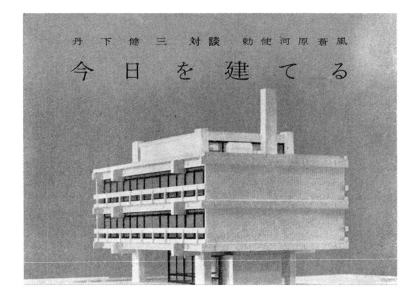

meeting of (CIAM), Tange initiated a series of fruitful collaborations with Japan's cultural arts, most notably with calligraphy, mural art, *ikebana* flower arrangement and gardens. A significant number of his exhibition designs also reveal a critical engagement with the allied arts. **(fig. 4)**

Tange designed a series of buildings for Teshigahara Sōfū and the Sōgetsu school of *ikebana*. The first Sōgetsu Kaikan opened its doors in 1958 and was a monument to the collaboration between Tange and Teshigahara, where spaces of display and its architectural vessel became fully integrated into *Gesamtkunstwerk* of visual unity and sculptural tableau. One of Tange's most enigmatic and least understood buildings, the first Sōgetsu Kaikan encapsulates the key aesthetic problems of Japan's postwar architectural culture, including the display of works, the evolving media of fine art, approaches to presentation, the spatial arrangement of viewing space, and the consideration of gardens and buildings in and of landscape.

Teshigahara came from a long line of prominent *ikebana* flower arrangement artists. He started teaching on his own at the age of 13 and rebelled against his father at 25, forming his own school, *sōgetsu-ryū*, a year later in 1927.[25] Deeply influenced by avant-garde currents in the plastic arts – cubism, Russian constructivism and, above all, surrealism – Teshigahara steadily moved away from

25    See Thomas R H Havens, *Radicals and Realists in the Japanese Nonverbal Arts: the Avant-garde Rejection of Modernism* (Honolulu, HI: University of Hawaii Press, 2006).

4 Tange Kenzō, early study model of Sōgetsu Kaikan, ca. 1957, courtesy Sōgetsu Foundation.

the mere arrangement of flowers towards the production of three-dimensional objects composed of steel, glass, wire and wood – a transition that gradually evolved between the 1930s and 1950s. In 1933 he founded the New Ikebana Society (*shinkō ikebana kai*), along with Shigemori Mirei and several others who were part of this rebellion. The central tenets of their 'New Ikebana Declaration' were: the rejection of nostalgia (*kaikoteki kanjō*); the rejection of fixed forms (*keishikiteki kotei*); the rejection of botanical constraints; and the free manipulation of flower vessels.

The agglomeration of reformist *ikebana* artists in the 1930s was coupled with the importation of the surrealist *objet* into Japan to describe works of art that cannot easily be categorised as sculpture. The art critic Takiguchi Shūzō, who would wield almost peerless influence among the artistic and architectural avant-garde in the postwar period, translated André Breton's *Le Surréalisme et la peinture* (1928) into Japanese in 1930. The reforming efforts of Shigemori and Teshigahara were part of a crucial move to establish *ikebana*, or *kadō*, as a discipline of fine art in the 1930s as the boundaries between fine art and craft were being drawn in Japan's cultural reconstruction.[26] As early as 1934, Teshigahara had already started to embrace the surrealist potential in modern *ikebana* through his friendship with Fukuzawa Ichirō, who along with Takiguchi championed the surrealist cause in Japan. Takiguchi first articulated the potential for objet-discourse in *ikebana* in the in 1938 essay 'Freak Flowers and Objet,' and in 1940 Teshigahara started submitting to the annual autumn show of the Bijutsu Bunka Art Society, organised by Fukuzawa. In the postwar period, Takiguchi revisited the genre of *ikebana* with a review of Teshigahara's 1952 solo show. According to Takiguchi, one of the foremost themes in modern Japanese aesthetics was the tension between the rationalism of modern plastic arts and the irrationality of flowers:

> People in the West call *ikebana* "flower arrangement", which means the ordering of natural flowers in an artistic way. This is no longer adequate for today's designs. Flowers of course have their naturalistic appeal, but this is left out of the rationalist approach to the plastic arts. In other words flower arrangement is surely placed outside the boundaries of fine art.[27]

Modern *ikebana* was to elevate the sensual beauty of flowers by rejecting its looming tradition. Many of the pieces created by Teshigahara in the early 1950s incorporated the surrealist idea of *objets trouvés*, and vases are often dispensed with. Favouring material such as steel, stone and dead root, Teshigahara enthusi-

26    Omuka Toriharu, 'Kadō to obuje: Teshigahara Sōfū to Fukuzawa Ichriō no taidan (1938) wo megutte', in Omuka Toriharu and Kawada Akihisa eds, *Kurashikku modan: 1930 nendai Nihon no geijutsu* (Tokyo: Serika shobō, 2004), pp 225–29.
27    Takiguchi Shūzō, 'Obuje no hakken', reprinted in Endō Nozomi and Sugiyama Nobuko, *Sengo Nihon no kakenuketa ishiki no zeni* (Tokyo: Setagaya bijutsukan, 2001), pp204–05. Originally published in *Sōgetsu Bessatsu* (February 1953).

5  Teshigahara Sōfū, 'Locomotive', 1951, courtesy Sōgetsu Foundation.

astically pursued what he called *musui ikebana* (waterless *ikebana*), which is actually an oxymoron that specifically denies its *ikeru* (living) aspect. (fig. 5)

Notwithstanding the publication of Katsura, Tange did not relish in gardens or nature. In the late 1950s, Tange nonetheless assumed a particularly intense interest in garden-making and took direct charge of these garden designs. In examining this series of gardens Tange designed in the late 1950s, it emerges that Tange was less interested in the formal aspects of modern garden making – a task the architect can always subcontract – than in the mediation of architecture with the surrounding environment; the spatial composition of objects in architectural scenography; and the formal design of plazas as social space.

Teshigahara's *ikebana* and sculptural work necessitated a new display approach. At his 1953 solo show at the Takashimaya Department Store, he had begun to decouple *ikebana* from its traditional setting in the *tokonoma* (alcove). As architectural critic Kōjiro Yūichirō writes:

> In the modern age as the *tokonoma* has been exiled from our homes, Teshigahara has liberated *ikebana* from the *tokonoma*. Whereas previously *ikebana* could only be seen in one direction in the *tokonoma*, it has now been transformed into a "floral object" (*hana no obuje*) that can be seen from any angle. This is not the obstruction of space, rather the colour scheme of space through which our fields of vision traverse ... "Floral objects" do not require frames or walls, stands, nor *tokonoma* or vases. It is ideally suited for modern architecture, which need only consist of ceiling, floor, and windows.[28]

As this essay endeavours to make clear, the Tradition Debate in postwar Japanese architectural development was a historical episode specifically ensconced in the cultural and political anxieties of the 1950s, as Japan sought to redefine its place in the postwar world order. If we look beyond images of Katsura and Ise, we find Japan's most talented architects marching to the same beat as their peers everywhere else, exploring new technologies and creating new spaces in the global context of the postwar city. After a handful of projects produced at the height of the Tradition Debate, most notably the Kagawa Prefectural Government Building (1955–58), Tange returned to his focus on the city with ever-expanding scales of imagination, culminating in the incomparable revisioning of the modern metropolis in his 1960 plan for Tokyo.

28    Kōjiro Yūichirō, 'Kindai kenchiku, obuje, ningen: Teshigahara Sōfū ten, hyō', *Kokusai Kenchiku* (January 1954), pp70–71.

# On the Decay of the Art of Discrimination and Description in Architectural Writing

Anthony Acciavatti

My role as an editor is markedly different from my role as a writer or a historian. In my estimation a good editor listens carefully, scans the lay of the land, locates overlooked holes in the topography and attends to the slightest tremors. A good editor sharpens and cultivates another's work. These practices that I value and aspire to as an editor are not at odds with my work as a historian, but they certainly operate on a different bandwidth. As *both* a historian and an editor, I will inevitably oscillate between speaking as an editor and speaking as a historian at a symposium dedicated to architectural writing.

With that out of the way, I would like to talk about an intrinsic virtue – an art of the highest order – that is, in my own estimation, on the decline. I am here to talk about the decay of discrimination in architectural writing. I do not want to suggest that the practice of discrimination has suffered any falloff or underutilisation. My complaint is in the decaying state of its art. And by art of discrimination, I mean the ability to discern and describe differences between things.

What does it mean to have a discriminating eye and what the deuce can we do with such a thing? While today discrimination is often used as a weapon to explain unfair biases against individuals and communities as well as against entire races and nations, I will briefly sketch out its virtues in a world where our abilities to describe are encumbered by our inability to discriminate.

Discrimination is a prevailing and acknowledged characteristic of humans: a powerful practice that makes it possible for all of us to pass judgment. Discrimination is something we all do. And while it is everywhere, and potentially profitable to advertisers and marketers, it is increasingly relegated to our collective unconscious, so much so, that it is almost unconscionable to speak of its

[The text is an edited transcript of Anthony Acciavatti's symposium presentation.]

benefits in public company. And while everyone from art connoisseurs to orators to psychologists and defence engineers study and engage in it, we seem to have forgotten its forbidden pleasures and indeed its community-building potential.

Injurious discrimination is an unworthy thing, but so too is injurious indifference. As William James observes in his 1892 *Text-book of Psychology*, 'The noticing of any part whatever our object is an active discrimination'. People, he continues, 'spontaneously lapse into an undiscriminating state, even with regard to objects which we have already learned to distinguish.' What we must bemoan is the ubiquity of such indifference. I would argue that we should also eradicate neutrality and perhaps even broadmindedness.

That discrimination – in the way I use it today – has a history goes without saying. Indeed, discrimination can be an empowering and imaginative faculty, particularly for the hungry historian interested in traversing the great outdoors and blowing off the dust of old drawings and letters of the now deceased. Discernment is the first step in imaginatively interpreting and narrating a set of events or artefacts. At least on par with critical thinking is the ability to discern the significance of things in the world. To this end, discrimination is a performative act, a mixture of ideology and aesthetic proclamation that situates things in particular ways in specific places and times; but it is also an expression that considers its enunciation to be its own evidence.

No human act is more determinately imprinted in our consciousness than our capacity and need to make choices. It is a *matter-of-factly* manifest virtue. Yet, no virtue reaches its zenith – its greatest virtuosity – without sensible and attentive cultivation. 'The discriminating eye and judgments of the connoisseur are formed perhaps more by practice, than by any general rules,' noted Johann Eschenburg in his 1836 *Manual of Classical Literature*. It is the idea of practice, as opposed to rules or methods, which animates my pursuit of discrimination and description in architectural writing. It is impossible to appreciate let alone describe architecture without engaging in discrimination. Today there is a poverty of description when, perhaps more than ever, we need to persuade non-architects of the role architecture plays in shaping our environment. Discrimination must clearly be taught and disseminated. But how?

I leave the discussion of defining how best to teach discrimination for another day. Instead I will speak about how we exercise discrimination in our writing about architecture and cities and how we might disseminate it, using experiments at *Manifest*, a journal of American architecture and urbanism, to make my argument.

*Manifest* is an independent print journal that I co-founded and co-edited with Justin Fowler and Dan Handel in 2011. It is the first journal dedicated to the architecture and urbanism of the Americas. When we invoke Americas, we intentionally speak about it in the plural: a constellation of sites and myriad states of mind. The journal began in 2009, when the three of us came together to write a follow-up to *The American City: From the Civil War to the New Deal* (1979). Written by four Italian urbanists, namely Manfredo Tafuri and Francesco Dal Co along with Mario Manien-Elia and Giorgio Ciucci, this critical tome focused on the entangled histories of capitalism and urban form in the shaping of the United States. At a certain point during our discussions, it became clear that rather than attempting to conjure the polemical tone of our Italian forbears, we were interested in exploring the Americas in a different way: through description, rather than circumscription. We took the often-cited advice from publishers to authors (write the book that you can't find but want to read) and with a gimlet eye to the topic, embarked on an exploration of the Americas.

With *Manifest* we wanted to offer a format where those who like to read and those who like to look at images could converge. We soon found ourselves gravitating less to a series of arguments and more towards a range of narratives, from the panoramic to the miniature, that recast our understanding of how the Americas are artificial, peculiar and intriguing. A print journal seemed an excellent way undertake this adventure: a journal that was in a sense a field guide, a record unto itself as well as an object that directs a person – through a building, under a city, or across a landscape – while simultaneously working to teach readers how to discriminate specific objects, routes and ideas.

For the inaugural issue, we chose the theme of looking inward. Looking inward was broadly construed as an interrogation of a new world taken for granted. Assuming the Americas deserved scrutiny, we asked what parts had been overlooked and were deserving of attention. After receiving more than 150 submissions from across the globe, we had far more provocative and insightful proposals than we could publish. These submissions ran the gamut of Gunnar Birkerts' design for the headquarters of Domino's Pizza (a one-kilometre-long Prairie-style structure based on Frank Lloyd Wright's work), to exploring the industrialisation of the Atacama Desert in Chile. We were amazed by the overwhelming interest in narrative and the diminished claims for specific positions. Indeed, there was a paucity of texts that examined the Americas in the critical vein that we had read throughout our years in school. It felt less like critique had run out of steam than that critique itself had switched axes beneath our feet.

Thinking little of this at first, we went about editing and enjoying the pieces, which looked at the relationship between 'Bob Dylan's 115th Street Dream' and Thomas Pynchon's *Mason & Dixon*; the making of the chicken 'broiler belt'; and the architect–president of Peru, Fernando Belaúnde's forest and highway project of the late 1950s and early 1960s. What we came to realise post-facto was that all these pieces were crafted with an intriguing set of discriminating eyes. And while genres varied – from reportage to cunning historical fiction – the desire to write imaginatively and persuasively permeated the texts and visual contributions.

Perhaps this is why *Manifest* has been described as the "first literary journal of architecture." From that first issue, we have been invested in writing imagined histories and new stories about architecture, cities and landscapes.

I would like now to think through a range of ways that the experimentation and practice of writing and editing has developed within the pages of *Manifest*. In particular, I will speak about three literary forms that we either intentionally engaged or that we noticed in the new architectural and urban histories proposed by our writers: ekphrasis, fiction and what we called para-tours. All of these are attempts at enlightening how history can be imaginatively presented and experienced.

*Ekphrasis*

With its roots in ancient Greek poetry and philosophy, and later in art history, ekphrasis is at its most basic, an imaginative description of a non-verbal work or works of art. And like any description, the author of an ekphrastic poem or piece of prose trains the discriminating eye on an object of regard. However, when something is truly ekphrastic, description goes above and beyond the object and transforms our perception of the nonverbal work of art. Perhaps the most well known examples of this 'beyond the object' are Homer's description of Achilles' shield and Virgil's description of the shield of Aeneas, which together began a lineage of incredible poets who undertook such descriptions, including, in the last century, WH Auden's poem 'The Shield of Achilles'.

In 'Wuthering Immensity', an essay from the first issue of *Manifest*, landscape historian John Stilgoe partakes in an ekphrasis to examine the American continent. He begins by stating:

> 'Five hundred years into the settlement of North America by Europeans and Africans, intellectuals, and designers especially, lack words for bigger-than-big. An unwholesome, stubborn refusal to confront the immensities of the continent, indeed the immensity of the continent itself, now hobbles conception and design in the global era. *Scale*, as designers glibly use the world, demands redefinition. But the wuthering giant frightens them back to urban and other small scales.'

Stilgoe looks at how the poverty of our abilities to discern and describe the Americas beyond words like 'immensity' and 'bigger-than-big', is attached to an early didacticism. He turns his attention to Anglo-American children's books, such as Frances Hodgson Burnett's *The Secret Garden* (1911) and Barbara Cooney's *Miss Rumphius* (1982). In these texts, 'bigger-than-big' spaces are to be eschewed at all cost for they are often described as monotonous, boring or without scenery. Both Hodgson Burnett and Cooney encourage children to retreat to scales that are far more controllable and circumscribed, like that of the garden itself. A lifelong historian of where landscape and city meet, Stilgoe witnesses a similar poverty of expression and indeed an inability to confront immensity in writing on the city.

Another example of the power of ekphrasis, at a far more intimate scale, is an essay by art historian and critic Caroline Jones titled 'Talking Pictures: Clement Greenberg's Pollock', published in Lorraine Daston's edited volume *Things That Talk: Object Lessons from Art and Science* (2004). Jones argues in her essay for the important role that description played in defining the relationship between the work of the painter Jackson Pollock and the writings of the art critic Clement Greenberg. For Jones, the relationship between the writing and the object was the 'thing.' A book and its reader resemble this kind of 'thing' as does the image in the mind's eye. Jones describes the relationship in order to address a pressing question about art, objects and things, asking 'If it is said, then is that what is historically available to be seen? If it is not said, then is it not seen at all?' This strikes me as a particularly important point: besides indirectly lauding the ekphrastic capacity of Clement Greenberg, the essay encourages us to see writing about works of art as translations – which ekphrasis certainly is not – but instead, to quote Valentine Cunningham, *as* 'ek-phrasis, literally a speaking-out, an audible speaking out now in the present text, a speaking made out of the silence of the past, and of the past and very silent aesthetic object, the painting, the sculpture, whatever'.

We the humans – not objects and not things – do the talking. We do the interpreting. We do the making. Perhaps objects have a social life as anthropologist Arjun Appadurai theorised in *The Social Life of Things* (1988). But should we believe they speak? Is it not their silence that provokes within us and in our experiences, the motivation to speak, to interpret, and not just translate or transcribe that which is seen?

*Fiction*

Building on the imaginative prospects of ekphrasis, I would like to turn to the historical possibilities of fiction. When it comes to the writing of history, I would argue that professional historians juxtapose fact and fiction. And it is with good reason, is it not? For fiction is tantamount to a lie. However, fiction, deep in its etymology, has a set of practices that are shared between the fiction writer and the historian; the word comes from the Latin *fingere* for 'form-giving, shaping'. Besides implicitly engaging in a process of discrimination, this practice of form-giving and shaping shares similarities with the process by which historians take historical evidence and shape a narrative that can be shared and experienced as a story. Our collective interest in fiction is not to produce new untruths or resuscitate dead lies; we are invested in artfully experimenting with how we might reconstruct and interpret objects and events from the past.

A number of our writers experiment with the art of writing history, playing with these common traits of fiction and history. Colleen Tuite and Ian Quate, who make up the duo known as GRNASFCK, have experimented with mixing and matching historical artefacts with fictional characters and landscapes in a gonzo journalism style. In 'Field Transmissions West Texas', they recount a ten-day expedition in one of the harshest landscapes of the US. Due to its deep geological history, this site, once covered in limestone, eroded over millions of years to reveal an undulating landscape of volcanic rock. Within this terrain, the authors travelled to 777 Ranch for their story. The 777 Ranch raises over 60 breeds of African mammals as prey for big-game hunters from all over the world. Colleen and Ian explain how this ecology of imported African mammals is less a geographical perversion than a temporal reversion to pre-ice age Texas, which was not unlike the African savannah of today. At a ranch gate marked 'Botswana', the big-gamers are in fact going back in time to hunt animals that may very well have once roamed the Texas landscape.

The kind of gonzo reporting and archaeological work done by GRNASFCK is akin to what Carrie Lambert-Beatty christened parafiction – a form of art practice that exists at the intersection of fact and fiction and appeared in the late 2000s all over the world. She argues that 'Fiction or fictiveness has emerged as an important category in recent art. But, like a paramedic as opposed to a medical doctor, a parafiction is related to but not quite a member of the category of fiction established in literary and dramatic arts. It remains a bit outside. It does not perform its procedures in the hygienic clinics of literature, but has one foot in the field of the real.' Unlike historical fiction's fact-based but imagined worlds, in parafiction real and/or imaginary personages and stories intersect with the world as it is being lived. Colleen and Ian's work, much like that of artist Walid Raad's Atlas Group and works on display at the Museum of Jurassic Technology in Los Angeles, recovers and reanimates the past with an imaginative eye on the present.

*Para-tours*

In our public programming for *Manifest*, we have developed what we call *Manifest* Para-tours. These tours are something akin to a ghost tour for architects. For us, spaces and architecture develop through the stories we tell about them. As a layer of programming that could complement the more traditional installations and events at the first Chicago Architecture Biennial, *Manifest* was invited to make a set of para-tours that were led by some of our most prominent contributors. The hour-long tours took participants to various locations around the city determined by real or para-fictional narratives. Our contributors/tour guides were also asked to produce a printed field guide for their para-tour. One, led by architect Andrew Kovacs, was structured around a full-scale replica of the Leaning Tower of Pisa in the suburbs of Chicago. Another para-tour, led by GRNAS-FCK, descended into the basement of the Chicago Board of Trade to explore the 'meteorological capitalism' of this once frenetic futures market. These para-tours, along with Enrique Ramirez's exploration of the site of the Eames Office's film *Powers of Ten* (1977) and the blockbuster *Top Gun* (1986), assembled an eclectic and imaginative set of objects and events to sharpen how we experience parts of the city's history.

Our contributors and guides not only exposed unexpected spots around the city, but also reimagined parts of Chicago through reflections on a by-gone past and persistent projections into an unforeseeable future. Where many urban walking tours emphasise lost and forgotten aspects of the built environment with an aim towards preservation or the recovery of minor city narratives, the *Manifest* para-tours worked to intensify the imaginative stakes of such an engagement.

Here, too, narrative worked toward a hybrid genre that wove together an obsession for the period detail often found in historical re-enactment with the speculative attitude of contemporary fantasy societies, all conjured through the critical voices of our guides.

More recently, both the School of Architecture at Princeton University and the Princeton Mellon Initiative in Architecture, Urbanism & the Humanities sponsored a series of travelling para-tours across the New Jersey/New York metro area. After spelunking through the teak caverns of the Armoury on Park Avenue in Manhattan and catching glimpses of architectural ghosts strewn about northern New Jersey strip malls, we convened all the guides for a dinner where we shared and discussed experiences. Combining field excursions with critical and creative reflections from across a range of disciplines, the para-tours are indicative of the overarching spirit of our practice and our pedagogical mission to explore the architecture, cities and landscapes of the Americas.

I would argue that all of the aforementioned modes of narrating architecture are predicated on the ability to artfully discriminate. Now is this all low-hanging fruit and just a throwback to late-nineteenth-century connoisseurship? I hope not. I hope that I have been able to share why and how we at *Manifest* not only cultivate discriminating sets of eyes in our writers and fellow explorers, but also how we go about combining word, image and form to undertake experiments in writing and rewriting history. Such practices in writing are an effort to encourage others to pursue the guilty pleasure of making the most of their own discriminating eyes.

# Debate
# History's Role in Contemporary Criticism

Cole Roskam (Moderator),
Seng Kuan, Anthony Acciavatti

**Cole Roskam**: Perhaps we can start with the question I led with in the introduction on the relationship between criticism and history. Both projects presented – in the case of Anthony Acciavatti, the *Manifest Journal*, and Seng Kuan's historical project on postwar Japan – seem to engage and interrogate the intersections, the overlaps and the frictions between criticism in architecture and architectural history. Can we speak a bit more about mapping and interrogating those points of contact?

**Seng Kuan**: I will start by talking more specifically about the case in Japan, which is unusual in the robustness of its architectural publication industries, whether those are books being produced and being read or the sheer number of architectural journals and other venues for publications. Similar to *L'Architecture d'Aujourd'hui*, in Japan *Shinkenchiku* has been in continuous publication since the 1920s. In the 1950s, the English edition, *JA* or *Japan Architect*, launched. In the early 1970s, a third imprint of the same publication appeared, which became *a+u* or *Architecture+Urbanism*, with which I maintain a casual relationship. In the 1950s, there were also *Kindai kenchiku* (*Modern Architecture*), *Kokusai kenchiku* (*International Architecture*) and *Kenchiku bunka* (*Architectural Culture*). At least two or three major publications emerged each decade between the 1920s and 1950s. This prolificacy makes architectural research extremely productive in the case of modern Japan. To some extent, it is still the case, where we have a lively cohesive community of like-minded individuals who come together.

The central role of Tokyo Imperial University (currently Tokyo University) as an institution should also be emphasised. This has been the mothership of architectural education in Japan since its establishment in the 1870s. The traditional debate that we are talking about here is a really an elite subset of architectural discourse. All those people mentioned in my presentation essentially went to the same school and received a rigorous education. For instance, all had strong foreign language skills – until recently English and German were required foreign languages at Tokyo University. People like Sakakura Junzo, Maekawa Kunio and Itagaki Takaho travelled outside of Japan and were able to sustain elite educations and grand tours because of their privileged backgrounds. They all knew each other and belonged to the same social circles.

**CR**: How about your roles as a historian, a designer and an editor? Do you find mining the potential overlaps and confluences between criticism and history to be productive, or is it something you don't necessarily see as part of your work?

**Anthony Acciavatti**: For me, history is about writing a coherent narrative. Similar to Françoise Fromonot's point about how architectural criticism can enter into the field of cultural criticism, we are interested in the ways in which you can use narrative to draw people in. Through that, you can form critiques. In many ways, foregrounding the critique or the critical analysis is quite important for a lot of the work we do.

Because we are all PhDs we see our journal, *Manifest*, as a way to explore, imagine and experiment with modes of writing history. A lot of people who submit to *Manifest* think that it is going to be a peer-reviewed journal. We have had academic publishers such as University of Minnesota Press approach us, talking about taking us on, but for us, it is important to remain independent. Because *Manifest* is only exists in print we work slowly, producing maximum one issue per year, in order to hold our ideas closely and work with our authors. This is all a very roundabout way of saying that the work we are trying to do is less about 'history versus criticism' and more about making a coherent narrative, as opposed to a coherent analysis.

**CR**: That's a good segue to my second question, which is about building or constructing narratives. I heard two modes of narrative-building in your presentations. In Seng Kuan's case, it is perhaps the exhibition. While in case of *Manifest*, it is not merely the journal, but also these para-tours that are a fascinating engagement in exercising discernment. Could each of you address the exercise of narrative-building as it is captured in these modes of criticism?

**AA**: In respect to the para-tours, if I have to describe it, it is like a pre-modern version of using your averted vision to see stars. Averted vision is the technique of using the periphery of your eye to actually draw dimmer objects into focus. If you want to see a set of stars but do not have a telescope, you can actually use your averted vision to observe some faint objects in the sky. In a similar way, para-tours are kind of like meditations on spaces. They draw in many other aspects of the built environment that

people may take for granted or that go unnoticed.

For example, during one such para-tour led by New York-based GRNASFCK, we obtained access to the Chicago Mercantile Exchange floors and vaults. GRNASFCK has been looking at natural gas resource extraction in North Dakota and Saskatchewan adjacent to the Canadian–US border. The Chicago Board of Trade used to be where those kinds of futures would be traded. GRNASFCK took a series of recordings from the natural gas extraction sites and played those clips on different sites within the Chicago Board of Trade. Although the trading floors no longer operate, by getting the sound of resource extraction resonating in an old trading space, GRNASFCK allowed people on this para-tour to experience two different places at the same time.

Another para-tour was led by Pedro Ignacio Alonso, a Chilean architect who looked at a series of sites in New Jersey with prefabricated housing and building structures made by NASA. In the 1960s, NASA was testing out a set of these structures in the space-race with the Soviets. What Pedro did was compare and contrast those structures in New Jersey with Soviet models. By doing this sort of architecture ghost tour and visiting former NASA pre-fab buildings, people had the chance to look for traces of those landscapes as archaeologists or ghost hunters.

I think these experiences train people to be a little bit more discriminating when it comes to the larger environment.

**Audience**: I wanted to pick up on two points from the earlier discussion: Cole Roskam brought up the idea of 'narrative versus analysis', which seems to parallel the idea of 'history versus criticism'. And the other thing is about this kind of 'constituency' that Seng addressed in his comment. I think economists may call it demand, and for us, let's just say it is about audience.

I am wondering if you can talk about history versus criticism – whether there is a 'versus' between the two words – in relation to the audience and constituency. Also, since we are now in Hong Kong in the year 2017, I am wondering whether there are cultural specificities – or lets say cultural gene co-efficiencies – that make differences in this set of relationships.

**SK**: I'll answer the second half of the question first. I was thinking about the relationship between narrative and cultural specificity while preparing for this symposium. At the University of Tokyo, I was presenting a talk to an audience that was completely conversant with the present as well as the historical names and events in Japan that I covered. But talking outside of Japan about its architectural tradition is completely different things. I recently did an exhibition at the ETH in Zurich on Kazuo Shinohara and had to add significantly more background information than what would be required for a Japanese audience. Also, the questions and the reactions I get from each audience are completely different.

**AA**: I don't quite like the demarcation between criticism and analysis, but I will go with it. I recently had to give a job talk for the department of anthropology, and I mentioned something about creating instruments for my work in India that not only measure soil but also measure cultural aspects of the soil. A student asked, 'What's culture for you?' I said something like 'culture is a very large umbrella that I like to put all these different things under'. The answer was quite vague, but the anthropologists from the faculty came up to me afterward and said, 'You were so good at answering that question. We would have said that culture doesn't exist.'

I kind of like that culture maybe doesn't exist. This is what anthropology has showed us for the last 20 years. Culture is just like a lot of those instruments, which became dull once we have used them too much. Whether culture exists, I think we can try to sharpen it. At *Manifest*, we certainly experience differences, although maybe not necessarily cultural differences. Let's say, when working in Mexico or Brazil, versus the US or Canada or parts of the Caribbean, we have encountered differences in terms of ethics or aesthetics. We are definitely attuned to those differences.

They just don't always need to be cultural.

**Angelika Schnell**: I also want to focus on this relationship between analysis and narrative. This linguistic turn over the last decade has changed the role of history. Every history book is now also called a narrative – something that is constructed. The point that history has become a constructed narrative has been well addressed in both of your lectures and comments. However, what you did not talk about is that history is also a science. There is a need to at least attempt to do serious research on architecture. What is your personal or general relationship to this scientific side of architecture research.

**SK**: Architectural history is very much a science, and there are rigid protocols that you have to follow. You can't make things up. However, in addition to this scientific aspect is the imaginative or even creative aspect that runs parallel to the same method. You can think of a million things to investigate from the archives. You can go through every drawing. You can go through every book.

Let me sidetrack for a moment. When I first decided to take on Japanese architectural history for my PhD studies, I was amazed by the sheer amount of available resources related to this topic. I am not just talking about architectural history, but rather Japanese history in general. The incredibly rich information in Japanese and foreign languages allowed me to have a fairly good grasp on what was going on in almost every discipline in Japan: histories of architecture, anthropology, art, economics, social studies politics and so on. This very neat database of historical events allowed me to package and reconstruct certain narratives scientifically. My research has to be accurate and systematic. However, I was also free to make my own associations, speculations and imaginings. I personally found this to be the most satisfying and compelling aspect of working.

Architectural historians must be able to handle an incredible amount of data and material. At the same time, we also need to speculate on what these people from the past were thinking. Of course, you don't make these speculations out of thin air. We need to make specific and surgical decisions in order to draw out specific relevance. This brings us back to the critical aspect of architectural history. As historians, you try to tease out something from this rich historical data. Architectural historians should be able to draw out ideas of interest for people, let's say, in the field of architectural practice.

**AA**: Because I am a historian of science, I would want to historicise what you mean by science. I think philosopher Willard Van Orman Quine writes a kind of empiricism of history through a set of evidentiary processes. He has this unique way of adding footnotes to master evidences. I don't have any problems or issues with that. In *Manifest*, we also look at how you master and assemble evidence. However, much like an archaeologist, when you are working with broken bits, you put things together and they don't always align perfectly. I think there is a lot of room for interpretation with respect to evidence. In a similar way, it is a productive and interesting to have these differences in *Manifest*. Part of what we try to do is to bring clarity to that narrative. I think that is where the kind of critique and critical analysis comes in, with respect to constructing these coherent and hopefully persuasive narratives.

Also as an historian of science, I know that the scientific method enters the field of humanities – at least in the English language lexicon, especially the US – in the period between the First and Second World Wars. It was a time when the social sciences were being side-lined by all of the physical sciences. Still, there is a growing idea that what humanities can offer is a set of practices or methods that are similar to the physical sciences. This methodological turn, or the interdisciplinary turn within the field of social sciences is tied to a certain kind of withdrawal or fear about not being recognised and appreciated, or giving more authority to the physical sciences, especially physics. I worry that if we do that with research – with architecture or the humanities in general – we risk losing a great deal of what humanities have to offer. I don't think social sciences can be placed on the same value scale as the physical sciences. I don't know if we can apply the same kind of quantitative or Euclidean way of

using data. I think there is a lot more that we have to offer even we have to fight for its relevance.

I am also a bit intimidated by the idea of equating history or rendering history as science completely. I just tend to think that rather than demarcating what is and isn't science, I would just say that science is what scientists do, and architecture is what architects do. I always find it a bit tough to start to demarcate where something ends and begins, because it becomes very difficult to define what's in and what's out when you do that. I know people who do it and seem to get very far by themselves. I am not very good at it, and I rather prefer not being good at that I myself.

**Audience**: You mentioned that *Manifest* is a literary journal of architecture. What is the literary dimension in history or criticism?

**AA**: Great question. We didn't call ourselves a literary journal, but someone said to us 'You guys are *The New Yorker* of architecture.' We didn't really quite aspire to something like that at all. In fact, my co-editor said: 'We would rather be *Cosmopolitan* magazine than *The New Yorker*.' When we look at the journals around us, there is a real need and thirst for narrative in architecture. Whether it is *October*, an academic journal published by MIT Press that nobody really reads, or trade journals such as *Architectural Record,* periodicals seem to be completely fading away. We felt that in the context of the US, there was a lot of room to play with and to tease out narratives about American architecture to engage larger audience than just architects themselves. We also saw a pedagogical opportunity to teach people about architecture through narrative, which is something we find more appealing than doing a formal analysis of a building. There are ways that I think you can nest that within the narrative, and that is what we are trying to do.

**Nasrin Seraji**: I think *Manifest* is probably doing something for architecture similar to what *Cabinet* did for art. After displacing a series of issues that are within the realm of architecture, *Manifest* does not bring those different points of view back into architecture itself, but rather allows them to become a necessity of thinking about other broader issues. Maybe Anthony can talk a little bit more about that.

**AA**: I would love it if people said we were the equivalent of *Cabinet*. I do think that what is interesting about *Cabinet* is that it is about aesthetics, but it is definitely not about what you find quickly at the Museum of Modern Art. That is also important for us. In the same vein, we are interested in playing high and low. We certainly have significant figures that people write about, but we are interested in a broadening process, as you are saying. As *Cabinet* opens up aesthetics, we are trying to do the same with the architecture of the Americas. One of the faculty members at Harvard told us that no one seriously works on the Americas. We didn't take that personally, but we just thought that was a little bit strange, given this person was from the American south. We really felt that there was a lot to explore, a lot to open up, as you say.

**Chris Brisbin**: Building on Nasrin's observation regarding the things that *Cabinet* does very well, I am reminded of the term *fictocriticism*, coined by Australian cultural anthropologist Michael Taussig, which emphasises the idea of mixing different kinds of voices and different kinds of forms of communication, representation or projection. It seems to me that this is similar to what you are doing with *Manifest*. Then, within this strange context where we are struggling to deal with architectural polemics, exhibition curatorial practices or objects of exhibition seem to have their own meta-narrative.

Perhaps the metanarrative is actually *Manifest*, rather than the singular conversations that can sometimes be, as you said, parochial about the Americas. The idea of metanarrative gives you and gives us an opportunity to stand back from the body of work.

**AA**: I don't know what metanarrative means. I feel like I am so embedded in the journal itself, so I don't know if I can pull back enough. Just as it is hard for people to lie to their children and say that they are the best child in the world, it is hard for me to do the same especially

since we are just working on the third issue.

**SK**: I am trying to remember this comment made by someone when I was an undergraduate. Essentially, his professor put three disciplines – namely literature, philosophy and history – into a hierarchy. I am trying to remember how this hierarchy ought to be organised. But I am pretty sure, history was at the very top.

**CB**: As a historian you will say that.

**SK**: Yes, as a historian I would certainly say that. I think the implication of his comment is that all literature boils down to philosophy, and all philosophy boils down to history. I think this is what you mean by the metanarrative. It is about levitating it onto a more abstract level. Is that what you mean?

**CB**: No. I think it is about understanding and cutting down the bias that exists in any form of history. I think writing history is actually about juxtaposing different kinds of narratives, or about telling a metanarrative, rather than telling a singular truth. It is about opening up an opportunity to interpret multiple aspects or multiple readings of the same work. This relates back to an earlier question about the audience. Oftentimes, we are talking about the writer, and we don't tend to talk much about the reader. However, the audience also brings with them a particular set of culturally constructed baggage that predicates how they understand the work. So that is what I mean by metanarrative.

**Eunice Seng**: I have two different types of questions. One is concerning aesthetics. Could you please talk a little bit about your approach to image? In the case of *Manifest*, how do you approach the image? Quite literally, how do you frame it or how do you even select it? Also, how does that go back into the positioning of your magazine? In Seng Kuan's case, how do you select images in your curatorial practice?

The other question is slightly different and probably directed more at what Anthony has said. When you opened your talk by positioning the

Americas in relation to the Orient, I was a little puzzled. The Orient has been very problematic as a term: where it is and what it is. In fact, we try *not* to talk about the Orient. For example, Japan was in the Orient but it is no longer presented in such way. As you said, *Manifest* focuses on architecture of the Americas, I wonder what is the problematic of the Americas? Is there one?

**AA**: I might have been speaking quite quickly. I talked about the historical category of the Orient, and that where the Orient began and ended has flummoxed people for a long time. In the same way, when we say the Americas, we mean it both as a geographic thing but also a state of mind. After we did our first launch of *Manifest* at the Philip Johnson Glass House, we did another talk at Princeton University. There was a historian who said, 'This is the problem. You really need to just do the continental United States.' But that is not what we are after. What interests us is the fact that, when you talk about the Americas, you could be talking about Iraq, you could be talking about the fact that the Philippines used to be part of the US, or the fact that, even with the Jeffersonian grid tattooed across it, Arizona didn't actually become a state until 1912. So, we are interested in the elasticity about what constitutes the Americas. We don't have a definite answer, but we are interested in how strange, bizarre, peculiar and sometimes sharp that term is. When I talked about the Orient, it was a critique of the idea of the Orient as much as a critique of what constitutes the Americas. And in fact, when we say America, we mean the Americas.

With respect to your question about aesthetics and images, we work very closely with our graphic designer, Neil Donnelly. He and his team are kind of like our fourth editor. It is important for us that images don't just become illustrations but are embedded within the text. Since we exist only in print, we are very concerned about material quality and tactility. We are concerned about the physical object itself, in terms of its representation and reception. I don't know if they read it or not. People from different parts of the world – Australia, Croatia, North Africa, Egypt and Morocco

– actually photographed the magazine when they received it and sent us the photos. In that way, we got a sense of how people appreciate it. That is important to us because we are so committed to it being a physical thing rather than a digital thing.

**SK**: To answer Eunice's question, let me talk about two book projects that I have been working on. The first one is about Kenzo Tange, which I started a couple of years ago. I am currently working on a similar analogous project on Kazuo Shinohara. Tange and Shinohara are opposite poles of postwar Japanese architects, in terms of personality, style and types of projects they worked on. With three or four exceptions, all of Tange's projects were public institutional buildings. In other words, they remain in the public realm. For example, on either Pinterest or Google Image, you can find millions of photos of Tange's Yoyogi National Gymnasium, including both interior and exterior views. Also, it is not that difficult to visit the building and take similar pictures as those you find online.

Shinohara is a completely different story. All of his projects, barring a few exceptions, are private houses. They are difficult to visit either because some properties have changed hands, or the owners are rather advanced in age so that it is no longer feasible to intrude. Furthermore, Shinohara took a restrictive attitude towards the presentation of his buildings. Until he passed away, he took extreme care of how his projects were featured in magazines, in terms of not only the text, but also the selection and the layout of drawings and images. In fact, very few people who study Shinohara's architecture have been into a building designed by him. Therefore, when working on this book about Shinohara's architecture, we actually had a limited repertoire of images to use.

**Audience**: Do you think a good historian could also be a good architect? I think the crisis is that architects do not normally know how to contextualise things properly. What I found interesting in your talk is that, you try to contextualise the present for the future. How do you see your role as a historian, a scholar and an architect?

**SK**: I think what I am going to say is more like a confession. I actually dropped out of the MArch programme at Harvard Graduate School of Design and switched into the PhD programme in architectural history. I had a great time and a great run in the design studio but ultimately realised that it was not for me. I know lots of people around me who are far more talented in design than I ever would be. I would never pretend to be an architect or even a good architect, because this is simply not what I do.

**Audience**: I am really curious about Itagaki Takaho's role in relating traditional Japanese architecture to modernity. It seems that Japanese architecture has a kind of superiority complex because of the persistent myth of being proto-modern. Historians within the field of architecture may not agree, but I think generally people do feel that way.

**SK**: I don't think it is necessarily an issue of Japanese architects having a superiority complex. That being said, Japanese architecture somehow has enough of an appeal and enough of a mystery. The aspect of mystery– which applies to both cultural aspects and anthropological aspects of this community – is very important. And because of this somehow impenetrable quality of Japanese architecture, you need specific interlocutors, such as myself, either as a historian or as a curator, to repackage the material for consumption. I think that's the service I provide to the field.

**CR**: Seng is a historian and a diplomat.

**AA**: To answer the audience member's question, I couldn't quite tell if you are saying I can be a good architect because I am a bad historian. What I would say is that I do conventional history writing, which relies on a set of guidelines that are commonly used among historians of science. But I do think for us, *Manifest* is a place that hallucinates upon alternative practices and methods. It is a testing ground to try out things that we don't usually get to do in our daily routine.

Aside from doing conventional or unconventional writing, I also go out to map and explore things.

When working on projects in South Asia, especially on the history of the Ganges river basin, I had to go out and be what John R Stilgoe would call 'a barefoot historian'. In that case, I borrowed techniques from architecture. Even though I am not really practising as an architect, I have the ability to read and maps. I am able to form arguments using visual materials. I think it is something that makes those of us who have a training in architecture different than other historians.

Architectural history is actually similar to the history of science because a lot of what we do in the history of science is look at the tools, the lab spaces and the way that space actually shapes the practices of others. For me, there are a lot of parallels between the two. At *Manifest*, we really try to cultivate and tease that out of our authors, whether or not they have the background in architecture. Treating built artefacts as things to be studied, almost like an archaeologist, is a useful way of working.

# Criticism in China

# 'From Defeat to Defeat', 'From Victory to Victory'
Tao Zhu

The symposium's title, 'From Crisis to Crisis', cuts particularly powerfully through two master narratives that describe writing about modern history in China. The first is 'From Defeat to Defeat'; the second, 'From Victory to Victory'. The first describes history writing about China from the middle of the nineteenth century to the early twentieth century: a semi-colonial society that suffered endless defeat at the hands of western powers. According to this narrative, China had nothing for which to be proud. Its entire cultural heritage was a burden that prevented its people from moving forward with modernization. This narrative generated an extreme psychology toward China's tradition and history, which one could describe as an 'inferiority complex'.

Contrary to this first mode of self-doubt and sincere self-deprecation, the narrative used to describe China's history from the 1920s to the present offers an entirely different trajectory: the newly born Communist Party leading China to shake off its dark past and conquer the future, marching from one victory to another toward the present.

These polarized modes of story-telling pose problems for the articulation of China's past experience and its current condition. As historical accounts oscillate between permanent defeat and permanent victory, the country's cultural psychology swings from an extreme inferiority complex to extreme pride. This polarization is also present in China's assessment of its own architectural development. One can see this symptom in architectural writing and in general discourse: either a total lack of confidence or an extraordinary self-satisfaction, with little careful critical articulation in-between.

This morning's panel focuses on writing about Chinese architecture that explores gradients between the two extremes of China's master narratives. In '(The Crisis of) Chinese Whispers', Chris Brisbin blurs the boundary between 'defeat' and 'victory' by expanding the definition of crisis from both western and eastern perspectives: crisis is not only a state of being or an idea but also a performative action that acknowledges equal measures of 'danger' and 'opportunity'.

By evoking the active, or performative aspect of 'crisis', Brisbin argues that Chinese 'knock-off' culture, viewed with a certain intentionality, can be reconsidered as a critical project. By recognizing the duality of 'crisis' – as offering both danger and opportunity – the copy can be reconsidered within a cultural confluence where the superiority of western values and the inferiority of eastern values are challenged, making it possible to reveal discourses on broader social and cultural concerns as they relate to Chinese society's ongoing identity formation.

In 'Cultivating a Critical Culture', Wenjun Zhi outlines over three decades' efforts – beginning with China's economic reform in the late 1970s – to shape a critical voice on architecture in China with the journal *Time + Architecture.* In his survey of the major thematic debates curated by the journal, Zhi's text highlights two elements that play an essential role in nurturing a critical position towards both the practice and theory of Chinese architecture. First, the editors of the journal have scrutinized the singular narratives that accompany most architectural projects. *Time + Architecture,* along with other venues for architectural debate emerging in China, have become testing grounds for independent critics whose writings unfold multiple narratives on a single project while also articulating larger positions about architecture's relationship to society and cultural identity. Second, contemporary critics in China have begun to challenge the uncritical use of western theoretical discourses to interpret architectural practice. This new consciousness is markedly different from the cultural anxiety that resulted from the influx of western books and architectural thinking that began in the early 1980s and reflects the emergence of an informed awareness.

By re-examining the definition of crisis, this panel repositions the practice and theory of Chinese architecture within a more inclusive and nuanced articulation of the relationship between 'defeat' and 'victory'. 'From Crisis to Crisis' contributes to this nuancing by asking some basic questions: when architectural culture is indulged in its complacency and euphoria, can critical writing open cracks, single out problems and send out alarms? When this culture crashes into complete hopelessness and desperation, can writing help to identify opportunities? I see this kind of critical questioning as the goal of the conference.

# (The Crisis of) Chinese Whispers: Consumption, Assemblage Aesthetics, and the Globalisation of Meaning in China

Chris Brisbin

What constitutes a crisis? At what point do we acknowledge the profundity of a crisis in transforming who we are and how we behave? Crises come in many forms, ranging from crises of confidence, of faith, of identity, to crises such as environmental degradation and climate change. Crisis is, often understood in the west as the perception of emergency or disaster, which refers not only to the traumatic event itself, but also to our reaction and response to that event. Crisis thus conceived is not only a thing and idea, but also a performative action. Some crises are so profound and complex so as to resist effective response, such as Horst Rittel's and C West Churchman's 'wicked problems'.[1] The ingrained systemic complexity of these problems is such that they challenge our existence and are potentially irreconcilable with our current lifestyle and value system. While crisis is perceived in the west pejoratively as a harbinger of pain and suffering, the Chinese word for crisis, *wéijī*, consists of conjoined semantic segments that acknowledge equal measures of 'danger' and 'opportunity'. This duality offers initial insight into the aim of my research: what is at stake for status consumption and cultural identity within the slippage in meaning that often occurs as ideas move between geographies and cultures, such as that between the US and China? For example, how might we understand Chinese 'knock-off' couture as a critique of capitalism and western aesthetics, and what insights might we garner into the cultural functioning of architecture in China? In particular, when these ideas are consumed by China, how does this semantic slippage productively manifest in a range of creative and cultural pursuits across art, design and architecture? What examples can be used in both western and Chinese cultural practices to

1  Richard Buchanan, 'Wicked Problems in Design Thinking', *Design Issues 8*, no 2 (1992) pp15–16.

understand this paradigm, and how do appropriation and cultural assemblage practices act as unwitting cultural identity signifiers in China today?

Works created by through the disciplines of art, design and architecture can be understood to bear witness to the cultural contexts in which they operate. They express the cultural beliefs of their designers, the values and aspirations, or equally the successes and failures of the broader society in which the works are conceived.[2] Scrutinising these works can therefore provide potential insights into the impacts of the broader social and cultural concerns of society's ongoing identity formation. This is particularly relevant in societies whose overt forms of critical discourse (both written and verbal) have been repressed. My career up to this point has pondered one not-so-simple question: what can, and does, architecture say about us? Furthermore, how does globalism and commodified forms of cultural signification disrupt the specificity of cultural identity? In the east, there is no author – just content.

The chapter will draw upon a brief history of shifting ideas about western architecture that relate to how meaning was conventionally carried and understood, and how the 'social contract'[3] shared between the signification system and its reader was subsequently undermined by neo-classicism, and later the pluralism of postmodernism and poststructuralism. It will discuss the relation shared between the perceived original and conceptual approaches to copying, including semantic deviations in imitation, replication, 'knock-off,' homage and so on. It thus attempts to move beyond simplistic binary differentiations between 'original' and 'copy,' and the related western moral and legal frameworks that respectively associate 'right' (legal) and 'wrong' (illegal) to this relationship. This discussion will then attempt to understand a parallel history in Chinese contemporary culture, one specifically focusing on the slippage in meaning that occurs as concepts, ideas and designs (and their associated, embedded meanings), move from the west into China.

The enlightenment of the eighteenth century challenged truth claims and assumptions about the legitimacy of meaning as bound to religious 'revelation'. Instead, intellectuals proffered the birth of the age of reason based on scientific rationalism.[4] The power structures of church and state, as Max Horkheimer and Theodor Adorno observed, were thus replaced in the late nineteenth century

2 Umberto Eco, 'Function and Sign: The Semiotics of Architecture', in *Signs, Symbols, and Architecture*, eds Geoffrey Broadbent, Richard Bunt and Charles Jencks (New York, NY: John Wiley & Sons, 1980) pp11–14.
3 I am specifically referring to the philosophical structures through which different forms of agreement that are made in society and the rights that are relinquished by all to a collective authority in the best interests of the collective. John M Parrish, 'Collective Responsibility and the State', *International Theory: A Journal of International Politics, Law and Philosophy* 1, no 1 (2009). I am inferring that we share a 'social contract' as designers with the people who occupy our buildings, in the most literal sense, obliged to ensure that they do not harm those who occupy them. Equally, I am using the concept of a social contract here to support the assertion that a broad social contract was in place between designers and the occupants of their buildings about how signification systems were applied in/on buildings to communicate meaning up to the neo-classical period. In order for these sign systems to operate, there must be broad agreement by the collective as to what meaning they convey.
4 Thomas Paine, *The Age of Reason* (London: Broadview Editions, 2011).

by new political and ideological systems including national socialism, Stalinism and capitalism.[5] Tropes of classicism were initially redeployed to speak to the inherent values in systems of architectural signification that no longer responded to or embodied the defining spirit of the eighteenth and nineteenth centuries.[6] Systems used to project meaning through architecture gradually became less legible and more concerned with stylistic aesthetics than semiotics. Simply put, what became legible was no longer symbolic narrative or semantic content, but rather the signification of recognisable forms of architectural language reduced to an aesthetic or imagistic 'likeness'.

As western Europe was undergoing its enlightenment, the Chinese Qing Dynasty continued in relative indifference, if not outright hostility, towards the western 'barbarians'. The direct cultural engagement between China and the west was generally catalysed by the expansive Dutch and English sea-trade in the eighteenth century. China's philosophical practices and cultural traditions continued relatively uninhibited by the lure of trade with the west or Christian religious incursions that followed. The scientific, intellectual and philosophical revolution fostered by the western Enlightenment did not affect China until the late nineteenth century, when increasing numbers of students who travelled to Japan and the US to study came into direct contact with the philosophical traditions and content of the enlightenment. Such examples include Jean-Jacques Rousseau and Voltaire's influence on Japanese writers' thinking about the concept of suffrage and civil rights.

Cultural exchange was much more effective between China and the west through architecture and art. While there were western-style buildings in nineteenth-century China, they 'were neither widespread nor created an extensive influence on Chinese architecture'. Free trade ports such as Shanghai, in particular the Bund district, encapsulated the widest variety of architectural stylistic tropes and were directly influenced by China's extensive global trading partners. Its vernacular and civic architecture therefore remained unaffected by western influence. Foreign architectural styles applied as follies and aesthetic curios, rather than serious agents of formal stylistic change. (fig. 1)

5  Max Horkheimer and Theodor W Adorno, *Dialectic of Enlightenment*, ed Gunzelin Schmid Noerr, trans Edmund Jephcott (Palo Alto, CA: Stanford University Press, 2002).
6  Here I am referring to advancements in construction technology that allowed for dramatically reduced structural member sizes, due to iron reinforcement and concrete construction, for example as applied to Claude Perrault's design for the east facade of the Louvre (1663). While these new construction technologies could have transformed, and refined the formal composition of the facade, Perrault designed it in the neo-classical style. It would not be until the nineteenth century that designs would adopt the essence of the classical style while adopting the opportunities offered by new construction systems, exemplified by projects such as Joseph Paxton's Crystal Palace (1850) and Thomas Newenham Deane's and Benjamin Woodward's Oxford Natural History Museum (1855–60).

China's relative stability during this period can be contrasted with the dramatic social, ideological, political and economic change the country underwent throughout the twentieth century. Even through this period of relative instability, China maintained a proud national identity that was often in direct ideological opposition to the west. Specifically, such attitudes were exemplified throughout the chaotic period of social and political upheaval created by Mao's cultural revolution of the 1960s and 1970s. As Karl Gerth notes, through Mao, 'nation-making included learning, or being coerced, to shape preferences around something called the Chinese nation and away from items deemed foreign'.[7] (fig. 2)

Mao's China fuelled national sentiment through the segregation of consumptive goods into categories of Chinese-made and foreign. Foreign goods were demonised as 'treasonous'. They embodied a deliberate mechanism of the state through which to instil a sense of nationalist pride and preference for the consumption of Chinese-produced goods.[8] But since the 1980s this attitude has dramatically changed, and for today's Chinese middle-class, the state-sanctioned demonisation of foreign-made goods is no longer prevalent. The projection of modernity and social status is no longer directly associated with Chinese-made or foreign, nor with authentic originals or copies. China is happy to embrace a mish-mash of pluralist, postmodern assemblages in which an original has no cultural hegemony over a copy. Rather, the aesthetic 'likeness' of the 'proximate' copy maintains the allure of the original without the ideological hang-ups of its western-based production: 'nationalists today allow for a Sino-western space

7    Karl Gerth, 'China Made: Consumer Culture and the Creation of the Nation', *Journal of Consumer Research* (Cambridge, MA: Harvard University Press, 2003).
8    Ibid, p3.

1  Giuseppe Castiglione, Yuanming Yuan (Gardens of Perfect Brightness), Haiyantang, Xiyang Lou (Western mansions) Beijing, People's Republic of China, 1786.

where Chinese can love China without hating the West.'[9] It is no surprise that, when left to freely appropriate preferred architectural styles from the west, the Chinese have embraced a pluralist postmodern assemblage of Western aesthetics to distance themselves from the overtly nationalist and austere Beaux-Arts-inspired communist architecture curated by Mao from 1949 to 1976. But this open embrace of all things western arguably comes with a cultural cost.

The appropriation and re-translation of canonical architectural styles from abroad has continued into the twenty-first century in China, evident in re-productions of Le Corbusier's Ronchamp (1954) in Zhengzhou in 2004; in the reproduction of the architecture and engineering of Haussmann's nineteenth-century Paris in Tianducheng's 2007 Eiffel Tower (built at one-third the original size) and its surrounding baroque cityscape; the eight themed towns surrounding Shanghai under the 'One City, Nine Towns' 2001 urban development, including Gaoqiao (Holland), Pujiang (Italy), Fengcheng (Spain), Anting (Germany), Luodian (North European), Fengjing (North America), Songjiang (England), and Zhoujiajiao (based on a traditional Chinese town). Derided in the western press as being Disney-esque assemblages of western cultural symbols and failed 'ghost towns', the reproduction of the aesthetic likeness of contemporary architectural styles has continued China's traditional approach to the consumption of cultural others' creative capital. This cultural appropriation and reproduction is also demonstrated in the widely published Meiquan 22nd Century building in Chongqing (2012–14), an imitation of Zaha Hadid Architects' Wangjing SOHO complex (2011–14) in Beijing. The social signification of power and success is conveyed through the iconography of modernity draped, as Jeffrey Kipnis has

9    Lily Dong and Kelly Tian, 'The Use of Western Brands in Asserting Chinese National Identity,' *Journal of Consumer Research* 36, no 3 (2009).

2 The Great Hall of the People, Beijing, People's Republic of China,
courtesy Thomas Fanghaenel (2007).

3  Le Corbusier's Notre Dame du Haut in Ronchamp,
France and its copy in Zhengzhou, China.

4  One-third scale Eiffel Tower copy in Tianducheng, Hangzhou,
People's Republic of China, courtesy Chris Brisbin (2016).

5  Anting, German-themed satellite town outside Shanghai,
People's Republic of China, courtesy Chris Brisbin (2016).

6  Zaha Hadid's Galaxy SOHO in Beijing,
China and its copy in Chongqing, China.

argued, as a form of 'cosmetic skin'.[10] **(figs. 3-6)**

Whether framed as a cosmetic veneer or as a cultural or formal assemblage, China continues to fashion itself as simulacra of other cultures' creative production, but often absent of any culturally specific adaptation to the idiosyncrasies of its Chinese context. However, Chinese attitudes toward this trend appear to be shifting. In 2014, at a literary symposium, President of the People's Republic of China Xi Jinping cited the need to move away from the 'strange-looking buildings' being built across China.[11] President Xi's observations were no doubt a response to a number of contentious projects designed by foreign international architectural practices across China, including OMA's CCTV building (2002–08, facetiously nicknamed Big Pants for its silhouette's striking similarity to a pair of trousers), Zaha Hadid's Galaxy SOHO (2011–14) and Wangjing SOHO (2009–14), Herzog & de Meuron's Beijing National Stadium (2003–08, nicknamed the Bird's Nest), and PTW Architect's Beijing National Aquatics Centre (2003–08, nicknamed the Water Cube), to name a few. Arguably, Xi's goal is to see a more Chinese-based spirituality embedded within contemporary architecture (whether designed by foreigners or locals), though whether this results in expressions of authentic Chinese culture and a return to a legible 'social contract', both between the Chinese and the semiotic system applied in the semiotic construction of their cultural goods, is yet to be determined. ( figs. 7, 8 )

There are enough examples of the Chinese copying the Chinese in clichéd assemblages of traditional or heritage-mimicking stylistic tropes to suggest that Xi's aspirations are far from easy to achieve. What does it mean to look Chinese today without an over-reliance on historical references to what it meant to be Chinese in the past? This construction of cultural identity is formed by many developing nations whose vernacular traditions are subsumed by colonising impacts of a global capitalist economy, which raises questions about what it means to be original in this capitalist framework. Indeed, if such an end is even possible.

Where does originality dwell in today's world of digital reproduction? For Walter Benjamin, who asked this question in his 1936 'The Work of Art in the Age of Mechanical Reproduction',[12] the coming age of mass, systematised reproduction technologies provoked serious questions about the role of mechanical reproduction's impact on affecting aesthetic experience. The ability to

10    Jeffrey Kipnis, 'The Cunning of Cosmetics: [Herzog & De Meuron]', *Du* (May 2000) pp25–27. While Kipnis is specifically using 'cosmetics' to discuss the minimalist oeuvre of Herzog & De Meuron's work, in the context of this chapter I am using it to suggest that what is being often copied in China is simply the outer skin of the symbol, redeployed as a form of aesthetic plastic surgery applied on a Chinese doppelganger.
11    Alyssa Abkowitz and Ma Si, 'Xi Jinping Isn't a Fan of Weird Architecture in China', *The Wall Street Journal* (2014). This has been followed up by an offical change in policy on 21 February, 2016 by the People's Republic of China which aims to 'ban odd looking buildings'. However, the criteria by which to differntiate what an 'odd' building looks like has not be disclosed. Zheng Jinran, 'China Looks to Regulate City Growth', *China Daily* (2016). http://english.gov.cn/news/top_news/2016/02/22/content_281475294306681.htm.
12    Walter Benjamin, 'The Work of Art in the Age of Mechanical Reproduction', in *Illuminations* (New York, NY: Schocken Books, 1968).

7  Rem Koolhaas's CCTV building in Beijing,
courtesy Chris Brisbin (2016).

8  Herzog & de Meuron's Beijing National Stadium,
courtesy Chris Brisbin (2016).

mass-produce millions of copies of an artwork directly challenged the prevailing belief in the existence of 'originality' as somehow dwelling in the authentic artefact. Benjamin introduced the concept of 'aura' to account for the existence of a metaphysical cultic condition that must operate in the artwork's cultural function, which ultimately gives it its originality. For example, in the facture – the legible trace of artisanal manufacturing in the surface and medium of the artwork's production – we can identify, according to Benjamin, the authenticity of its production by the artist's hands and tools. Mass reproduction risks flattening this facture and stripping the artwork's cultural allure as an original. What we are left with are copies of artworks that lack an authentic aura, and also contain an imagistic flattening that redefines how we collectively understand the aesthetic value of art. Stripped of art's aura, we are transformed from active participants of aesthetic production into passive onlookers of aesthetic consumption.

Further complicated by the legal frameworks through which these creative production strategies are applied today is the semantic slippage in meaning associated with terms such as copy, replica, duplicate, reproduction, facsimile, simulation, likeness, index, forgery, imitation, counterfeit, knock-off or fake. Language complicates the relationship shared between the original and the copy in describing how objects, ideas and meaning relate to one another. Meaning is further complicated when bridging between cultures with very different language systems; in some cases, no exact words exist with similar meaning, and there are very different cultural attitudes towards the terms themselves.

In China, what is often being consumed and copied is not the original's form, but rather the original's aesthetics and iconic signification of modernity and cultural status that is reproduced and consumed in the copy. As Winnie Yin Wong notes in her research into the artwork-copying mecca Dafen Village in Shenzhen, the production of the majority of copied European artworks were sold through multinational western retail chains, such as K-Mart and Wal-Mart, to an American audience unaware of the specific compositional structures of the original beyond its broad aesthetic and social appeal.[13] Furthermore, the Dafen painters responsible for the reproductions had never seen the original artworks they were copying. In fact, the Dafen reproductions were more often dramatic deviations from the original artworks: Mona Lisas painted in Dafen are almost always larger, and the strokes of *The Starry Night* always thicker. Jacques-Louis David's *Napoleon Crossing the Alps* smiles more, and Yue Minjun's pink faces smile less cynically.[14] Their copying thus concerned the attainment of an aesthetic likeness and not the realisation of indexical replication. As Wong outlines, both painter and consumer operated from a limited disciplinary knowledge of the meticulous

13    Winnie Yin Wong, *Van Gogh on Demand: China and the Readymade* (Chicago, IL: University of Chicago Press, 2013), p5. For a discussion of distribution of copied works through K-Mart, see p52; and for discussion of distribution of copied works through Wal-Mart, see pp58–59.
14    Ibid, 20.

ideological and technical characteristics of the original artwork. Benjamin's aura and warnings about the destructive power of mechanical production are equally contested here, as the works themselves potentially become a different kind of copy. **(fig, 9)**

Wong further illustrates the conceptual irreconcilability between originals and copies in Chinese linguistics to demonstrate how Chinese society understands, for example, the philosophical relationship between each painting in Monet's early twentieth-century *Waterlilies* series, and copies of them in Dafen. Each of the *Waterlilies* paintings is understood as iterative copies of an overarching series of impressionistic representations of waterlilies. This relationship is conceived as a *gǎo*, which encompasses relations that exist between versions of artworks that can be understood as a series. For example, an analogue photograph, a scanned digital image or a digital photograph of Monet's *Waterlilies*, or indeed any other iteration in the study of waterlilies by Monet – in each case, the *gǎo* is simply one iteration of a potentially infinite series of representations of the waterlilies, inclusive of all of Monet's *Waterlilies* as a 'singular work' or *huà*. As Wong concludes, the 'original … is conferred no absolute hierarchical status, and is merely a *yuán gǎo*, or if you will, an "original copy".[15] There are certainly semantic, legal and moral principles associated with copying nomenclature in the west. Yet as I have outlined the complexity of meaning between original and copy in Mandarin has exasperated intercultural resolution of copyright infringement, or our nuanced understanding of the linguistic and semantic slippage that occurs as concepts move between cultures. **(fig. 10)**

There are numerous examples of the hazards that arise from not fully appreci-

15    Ibid, 18.

9 Dafen Village painting reproduction, courtesy Stephen R Woolverton (2006).

ating these nuances, as demonstrated by marketing mistakes when western companies have attempted to directly translate their brands and jingles to a Chinese audience without understanding how meaning shifts from language to language, or from culture to culture. In the 1920s – so the story goes – as Coca-Cola entered the Chinese market, the company chose Chinese characters to mimic the phonetics of the word Coca-Cola without adequately understanding its actual semantic translation into Mandarin. Coca-Cola thus was translated as 'bite the wax tadpole' or 'wax-flattened mare'. Pepsi spooked Chinese consumers when it failed to realise its 'Come Alive with Pepsi' slogan translated to 'Pepsi brings your ancestors back from the dead'.[16] KFC mistakenly translated its 'finger-lickin' good' tagline to 'eat your fingers off'.[17] Nike made similar missteps when it released a pair of special-edition sports shoes: sewn into the left shoe was the character *Fa*, which translates as 'getting rich'. On the right shoe, was the emblazed character *Fu*, meaning 'fortune arrives'. 'Unfortunately for Nike, when combined, *Fa* and *Fu* translate as "getting fat"'.[18] In 2015, in celebration of Chinese New Year, Burberry released a special edition of its classic tartan scarf, adding in bold red the

---

16    Larry Roellig, 'Designing Global Brands: Critical Lessons', *Design Management Journal* 12, no 4 (2001), p41.
17    Leo Paul Dana, 'Kentucky Fried Chicken', *British Food Journal* 101, no 5/6 (1999) p495.
18    Will Heilpern, 'The Biggest Lost-in-Translation Mistakes Made by Western Brands in China', *Business Insider Australia* (2016). While popular culture sources are widespread outlining these supposed 'brand disasters' in China, they are unverified in academic literature.

character *fu* for 'fortune'. Context is critical.

In returning to the architecture example cited earlier the Meiquan 22nd Century building in Chongqing bears striking aesthetic similarities to the Wangjing SOHO shopping complex it copies. While the Wangjing SOHO consists of three buildings, and the Meiquan 22nd Century building only consists of two, the overall aesthetic form and compositional inter-relationship between each building to the whole remains consistent. Similarly, the silhouette and compositional approach to the façades of each building are very similar. However, the built expression, performatively realised in the Meiquan 22nd Century building, and supposedly drawing upon an illegally procured set of Wangjing SOHO construction drawings, is very different.[19] The copying of Wangjing SOHO raises interesting and provocative questions about the validity of copyright law that privileges 'construction work' over other physical and digital forms of expression. What is being copied here? This includes virtual models of a design's proposed form, or its embedded informational systems, such as BIM (Building Information Modelling), or the variety of physical drawings used to understand, represent and communicate the embedded intellectual property of the work. While there are subtle variations between Wangjing and Chongqing, the overarching relational outcome seems suggest they are estranged siblings, rather than fundamentally different. Or in drawing upon Wong's linguistic categories, perhaps their conceptual relationship should be understood as a series of works in a new form of copy, a *yuán gǎo* (original copy).

In returning to the chapter's initial search to determine how the embedded meaning within a building or artwork can expand our understanding of its cultural value, I argue that the assemblage practices inherent in post-critical theory and creative practices prevalent in China today may provide insights through which to critique the economic and political power structures that influence a work's creative production. As such, critical and post-critical theory provide a theoretical scaffold upon which to demonstrate how copied works in China can be interpreted as critiques of contemporary Chinese identity and capitalism, and the role of the architectural discipline in redefining and reframing how this identity can be read.

The critical project of the 1970s and 1980s applied a deliberate position that questioned the prevailing market system of capitalism and its disaffecting power structures. It instrumentalised the deliberate disturbance of common structures of linguistic meaning to undermine the structuralist's idealisation of binary relationships in semiotic theory. This binary relationship bound meaning in language to a universalising system that supported the belief in a singular 'ultimate

---

19   Zaha Hadid Architects' Project Director Satoshi Ohashi believed that 'the Chongqing pirates got hold of some digital files or renderings of the project' upon which their copy of the Wangjing SOHO was based. Jessie Chen, 'Twin Buildings Appeared in Beijing and Chongqing', *China Intellectual Property* no 50 (2012).

truth', which structuralists believed underpinned how meaning was derived and understood by the beholder. Critical theory and architecture happily co-existed with the shared goal of transcending the repetitive traditions of language, culture and built form to conceive a new autonomous architecture through the 'immaculate conception' of authorless anti- and post-human environments.[20] This was achieved initially through the application of theory drawn from Claude Levi-Strauss, then Michel Foucault and Jacques Derrida, and finally the architectural theory and practice of Peter Eisenman's 'decomposition and deconstruction', among others.[21]

While Eisenman sought a theoretical basis for his architectural practice, the underlying neoliberal structures of the global capitalist economy marched on, unhindered by Eisenman's claims for the reinvention of architectural discipline. Conversely to Eisenman, as Jean-François Lyotard identified in his critique of the postmodern condition, it is not theory that binds the apparent randomness of postmodern plurality and the market, it is money.[22] The cultural value associated with the artistic practice of appropriation and assemblage has been challenged by an ontologically flat conception of the world, no greater than its commoditised financial value. All aspects of life and creative production are thus reduced to quantifiable financial investments, such as those driving reproduction practices in China. According to Hal Foster, in the last 20 years American society has demanded a familiar and affirmational quality in its art and architecture,[23] one uncritical of its mode of production and commoditised into familiar aesthetic styles and franchised brands. Originality, or claims for originality, are increasingly commodifiable concepts in the face of the affirmational allure of the unconfrontational and familiar.

Thus, the growing disenfranchisement with the critical project's failure to realise social liberation or critical resistance against the alienating structures of the market gave way to the 'projective' project of the post-critical.[24] The post-critical was therefore proposed by Rem Koolhaas, Michael Speaks, George Baird, Robert Somol and Sarah Whiting, as a juxtaposition to the perceived ideological traditions of criticality and a reestablishment of disciplinary knowledge and expertise specific to the discipline of architecture.[25] According to the tenets of post-criticality, architecture had lost its way in the milieu of complexifying theory of the

20  Peter Eisenman, 'The End of the Classical: The End of the Beginning, the End of the End', in *Theorizing a New Agenda for Architecture: An Anthology of Architectural Theory 1965–1995*, ed Kate Nesbitt (New York, NY: Princeton Architectural Press, 1996).

21  Diane Ghirardo, *Architecture after Modernism* (New York, NY: Thames & Hudson, 1996) pp32–5.

22  Jean-Francois Lyotard, *The Postmodern Condition: A Report on Knowledge*, trans Geoff Bennington (Minneapolis, MN: University of Minnesota Press, 2010) p76.

23  Hal Foster, 'Post-Critical', *October* 139, Winter (2012), pp3–8.

24  Op cit, Zhu, 'Criticality in between China and the West'

25  Robert Somol and Sarah Whiting, 'Notes around the Doppler Effect and Other Moods of Modernism', *Perspecta* 33 (2002) pp72–7. George Baird, 'Criticality and Its Discontents', *Harvard Design Magazine* 21 (Fall 2004/Winter 2005). Michael Speaks, 'After Theory', *Architectural Record* 193, no 6 (2005) pp72–75.

1980s and 1990s. They sought the diagrammatic forces of the market through which to autonomously generate architectural and experiential possibilities in the affirming and familiar content of material culture. Sylvia Lavin's call for a '"cool" architecture that is unashamedly fashionable, desirable and ephemeral' demands a direct engagement with, and celebration of, the very market mechanisms that the tenets of criticality so vehemently opposed.[26] Consumptive practices thus became the primary content of architecture, and capitalism its ultimate author.

I have argued that the post-critical turn in architecture provides a lens through which to critique projects that claim for themselves no deliberate critical action.[27] In following Lyotard, as Jean Baudrillard has observed, it is important to remember that aesthetics and economics are ontologically reified as a 'single cultural form that becomes the essence of the consumer society'.[28] Works of art, architecture and design that critically respond to market forces exerted upon them within the dominant capitalist economic system are subsequently consumed by the very system that they seek to disrupt. For Firat and Venkatesh, there are only two possible outcomes: re-appropriation or marginalisation.[29] It is either subsumed into the market, or it is marginalised by it, to the point that it is no longer relevant. Faced with the undeniable agency of post-critical architecture's causal effects, the post-critical can be argued to be far more inherently critical than traditional criteria for determining criticality might infer. As Hal Foster has observed, 'the post-critical turn is not the rise of uncritical approaches to art [or architecture], but a reconsideration of what it means to be critical.'[30] As such, architecture – when conceived of as an edifice of cultural values affected by contemporary business practices and the market system – cannot easily be differentiated from its economic and political symbolism, even when its voice is left relatively mute by repressive institutional forces.[31] For example, the application of the post-critical offers a framework through which to understand cross-cultural transmissions of meaning.

Capitalist-based consumption is driving these various forms of reproduction, first driven by an emerging middle-class in Europe in the eighteenth and nineteenth centuries, then by the nineteenth and twentieth centuries in the United

26   Michael Speaks, 'After Theory', *Architectural Record* 193, no 6 (2005) p74.
27   Chris Brisbin, 'The Post-Critical U-Turn: A Return to Criticality through the Consumptive Affirmation of Glamour and Affect in Michael Zavros and Rem Koolhaas', in *Critique 2013: An International Conference Reflecting on Creative Practice in Art, Architecture, and Design*, eds Chris Brisbin and Myra Thiessen (Adelaide: University of South Australia, 2013) pp25–39.
28   A Fuat Firat and Alladi Venkatesh, 'Liberatory Postmodernism and the Reenchantment of Consumption', *Journal of Consumer Research* 22, no 3 (1995) pp239–67. Jean Baudrillard, *The Mirror of Production*, trans Mark Poster (St Louis, MO: Telos, 1975).
29   Firat and Venkatesh, 'Liberatory Postmodernism and the Reenchantment of Consumption', op cit, pp239–67.
30   Wes Hill, 'On Post-Critical Art', *Contemporary Visual Art+Culture Broadsheet* 41, no 1 (2012) pp65–67. Hill is paraphrasing Hal Foster's argument from Hal Foster, 'An Interview with Hal Foster: Is the Funeral for the Wrong Corpse?', *Platypus Review* 22 (2010) p12.
31   Mary McLeod, 'Architecture and Politics in the Reagan Era: From Postmodernism to Deconstructivism', *Assemblage* 8, no February (1989) pp23–59.

States, and now in China, India, Indonesia and other developing nations in the twenty-first century.[32] These nations are undergoing a middle-class explosion, but at a far greater rate than experienced in the west. Copying and knock-off culture is simply an outcome of these broader cultural and economic phenomena. To understand this relatively newly found consumptive thirst in China, it is important to also understand the influence of the Chinese concept of 'face' in super-charging, status-based consumption over the last 20 years.

Face is intrinsic to all collectivist cultures, which make up one-third of the world's population, but is especially important in understanding the consumption habits of China's middle-class.[33] The social practice of giving and maintaining 'face' encourages consumptive practices that allow for the consumer to aspirationally project one's self as part of a desired social group, to reinforce culturally accepted norms of behavior within that group and to differentiate one's self from others external to it.[34] Chinese collectivist culture, which is Confucian at its ideological core, is 'interdependent' in its social structuring: 'to the interdependent Chinese, class reflects not only one's achievement, but also one's social group: usually one's family, relatives and kinship clan.'[35] While the Chinese have been engaged in the process of abrupt migration and socio-economic transformation from subsistent agrarian lifestyles across rural China into its rapidly swelling urban metropolises,[36] social structures still focus strongly upon the family node and extended family networks. It is therefore due to this very need to 'enhance, maintain or save face' that Chinese consumers today still find themselves more likely to purchase luxury goods to advance their social standing than perhaps in other cultures.[37]

Even in the west, 'keeping' and 'giving' face are necessary components of everyday social practices in what Erving Goffman calls 'face-work' – a form of identity management that involves verbal and non-verbal social contracts that are conducted through either face-to-face or mediated social encounters.[38] For both Chinese and Americans, face-work is a vital social tool through which to determine and maintain social impressions of one's self, and the social grouping in which they wish to be identified by others. Face in China thus presents a complex social account of identity construction that directly conflicts with the social

32   Matthew Burrows, 'The Emerging Global Middle Class – So What?', *The Washington Quarterly* 38, no 1 (2015) pp7–22.
33   S Ting-Toomey, 'Intercultural Conflict Styles: A Face Negotiation Theory', in *Communication, Culture, and Organizational Process*, eds Stewart Gudykunst and S Ting-Toomey (Newbury Park, CA: Sage, 1988).
34   Ang et al., 'Spot the Difference: Consumer Responses Towards Counterfeits', pp219–35.
35   Nancy Y Wong and Aaron C Ahuvia, 'Personal Taste and Family Face: Luxury Consumption in Confucian and Western Societies', *Psychology and Marketing* 15 (1998) pp423–41.
36   Dieter Hassenpflug, *The Urban Code of China* (Basel: Birkhäuser, 2010); Xuefei Ren, *Urban China*, China Today (Cambridge, UK: Polity Press, 2013); Zai Liang et al, eds, *The Emergence of a New Urban China: Insider's Perspectives* (Lanham, MD : Lexington Books, 2012).
37   Julie Juan Li and Chenting Su, 'How Face Influences Consumption: A Comparative Study of American and Chinese Consumers', *International Journal of Market Research* 49, no 2 (2007) pp237–56.
38   Erving Goffman, *Interaction Ritual: Essays in Face to Face Behavior* (New Brunswick: Transaction Publishers, 2005), p5.

standards expected of western copyright law when copied goods are consumed in preference to an original.

'Face' also drives the advancement of the 'Diderot effect' and continuously fuels the consumption of goods based on the comparative perceived value of the desired artefact. For example, it is evident in comparing an iPhone 8 Plus to the fever-pitched anticipation and speculation about the panacea-like qualities supposedly possessed by the X series. The perceived 'newness' and thirst for an original artefact entices and exposes the supposed flaws of the superseded object. As Robert Crocker observes: 'We start to perceive that what we have is not "good enough" in comparison with the brand new', thus perpetuating a grand deception that the consumption of the newest and most desirable goods will continue to 'keep face' and keep us happy.[39] Face thus potentially generates a new form of post-criticality in which the act of affirmational status-consumption can be used to unpack and critique the inner machinations of consumption, as well as capitalism's impact on cultural identity and meaning in China today.

To conclude, I will provide one last example of what is at stake when meaning is lost in translation across cultures. Copyright should not, and cannot, be the only lens through which we understand and evaluate cultural appropriation and reproduction. It is a blunt instrument of subjugation and socio-economic stratification, and a direct instrument of capitalist colonialisation. The games Telephone, Gossip – or the somewhat racist variations, Russian Scandal and Chinese Whispers – can be used here as a metaphor to explain, in part, the shift in meaning that occurs when one culture appropriates through assemblage the visual elements of another. These are subsequently divorced from their linguistic and semiotic structures, or the social contract upon which their understanding fundamentally relies. All we are left with are the visual aspects of the assemblage, aesthetically read from within one culture for whom the assemblage is only as valuable as the visual pleasure and social status that it provides. Here the aesthetics of the assemblage become commodified and consumed wholly in relative indifference to the cultural specificity of its signification. Here we get to the crux of the problem. The complexity and multi-layered nature of aesthetics, and the capacity for multiple levels of sensory engagement, are lost through this capitalist flattening of the world's value to that of the ocular-centric and its ultimate commodification and amplification of status-based consumption.

The resulting 'Sino-Frankenstein' assemblages resemble the compositional structures applied by André Breton and the tenets of surrealism in their *Exquisite corpse*. The architectural and urban forms that result are an outcome of multiple cultural authors, collectively composting meaning in significantly new ways: Western on the outside, but Chinese on the inside. The traditional modes of

---

39  Robert Crocker, *Somebody Else's Problem: Consumerism, Sustainability & Design* (Salts Mill: Greenleaf Publishing, 2016), p51.

semiotic signification and meaning-making are thus radically altered as these works shift from formal and cultural to aesthetic and imagistic. This may be a transition in China's architectural, urban and cultural development as the signification of cultural identity gradually subsumes and redeploys western typologies to its specific ends. Only time will tell.

Nonetheless, the perceived crisis created by China's booming economic growth and its legacy of knock-off production and consumption yield equal measures of 'danger' and 'opportunity', mirroring the duality inherent in the Chinese conception of 'crisis' that introduced the chapter. The fusion of Chinese and western aesthetic tropes is fostering purportedly dangerous compositional outcomes and mediocre aesthetic forms that are neither Chinese nor western. Aesthetics alone cannot define a culture or its identity. However, an opportunity exists in this perceived crisis to reconceive a 'social contract' between Chinese-designed objects and their signified meanings. In this way, there is an opportunity to consider how the Chinese who use them to foster a reciprocal investment in the objects, as well as the resources we consume without creating, are no longer mediocre aesthetic assemblages of compromised, kitsch cultural fragments. This also reconceives the value of the copy: moving from copying as an inherent consumptive practice, to assemblage as a critical practice through which to proactively and productively provoke critical engagement as to what Chinese-ness means today. Perhaps Chinese knock-off culture is simply a post-critical redefinition of architectural disciplinarity, whose fundamental conceptual difference to its western counterpart is only brought to light through cultural and linguistic mistranslation. Aesthetic tropes of assemblage and reproduction in China are thus a harbinger of architecture's broader globalised meaning and commodification, reduced to the atmospheric, the affirmational, and the familiar.

# Cultivating a Critical Culture: The Interplay of *Time* + *Architecture* and Contemporary Chinese Architecture

Wenjun Zhi and Guanghui Ding

Since their first appearance in Europe about 200 years ago, architectural periodicals have played a significant role in disseminating architectural knowledge and scholarship.[1] Compared with published books, periodicals usually feature the latest architectural projects and establish the domain of criticism.[2] Given their focus and readership, architectural periodicals in the west can be classified into two categories: scholarly journals for academics and researchers, and professional trade magazines for practising architects. However, such differentiation appears to be blurred among architectural periodicals currently published in China, which tend to combine both scholarly and professional materials. Why do Chinese architectural periodicals maintain mixed features? What are the conditions and challenges of architectural magazine culture in China? How do architectural periodicals intervene in theoretical debates and material practices?

As one of the newly established journals in post-Mao China, *Time + Architecture* (*Shidai jianzhu*) has constructed a significant forum for critical practice through the presentation of critical architecture and architectural criticism.[3] Over the past few decades, the journal has published a number of special issues on the work of emerging independent architects such as Yung Ho Chang, Wang Shu, Liu Jiakun and others. The theoretical topics, projects and criticism that appear in its pages exemplify an editorial agenda that presents innovative and ex-

1    Frank Jenkins, 'Nineteenth-Century Architectural Periodicals', in *Concerning Architecture: Essays on Architectural Writers and Writing Presented to Nikolaus Pevsner*, John Summerson, ed (London: Allen Lane, 1968) pp153-60.
2    Mitchell Schwarzer, 'History and Theory in Architectural Periodicals: *Assembling Oppositions*', *Journal of the Society of Architectural Historians* vol 58, no 3 (September 1999) p342.
3    For a detailed study on the journal, see Guanghui Ding, *Constructing a Place of Critical Architecture in China: Intermediate Criticality in the Journal* Time + Architecture (London: Routledge, 2016).

ploratory work. Perhaps more than any other periodical, the journal's presentation of both disciplinary and socio-political issues illustrates the role of academic publications in shaping a critical culture for architecture in China.

The dual nature of the discipline of architecture (both scholarly and professional) profoundly influenced the character of the journal, which sought to expand its impact in both academic and design fields. At the turn of the millennium, the journal's substantial reform of editorial policy focused on thematic editions, within which editors selected essays and projects to respond to a particular theme. This essay uses *Time + Architecture* as a medium to inquire into the role of the periodical in forging a critical culture of architecture. It offers a brief examination of the journal's history as well as its character and programme. It argues that the journal's engagement with the work of emerging independent architects and critics has demonstrated the editors' and contributors' collective endeavour to develop a critical position for confronting the dominant ideology of architecture.

*History*

The origins of *Time + Architecture* date back to 1984, during an extraordinary era when China was experiencing profound social, political, economic, cultural and ideological transformations after the end of the Cultural Revolution (1966–76). The journal was based in the Department of Architecture at Tongji University in Shanghai, then on the frontlines of China's Economic Reform and Opening programme. On its initiation, the publication attracted the attention of both the leaders of the university and the department that supported its launch. **(fig.1)**

The appearance of the journal is associated with a number of internal and external factors. First, before its establishment, in the early 1980s two volumes of a small publication titled *Architectural Culture* (*Jianzhu wenhua*) appeared. These issues are, to some extent, considered an experiment in anticipation of *Time + Architecture*, both in terms of their editorial operations and ideological underpinnings.

Due to the relatively loose political climate of this time, the early 1980s witnessed a wave of publications in the field of architecture and beyond that actively responded to the official call for a liberation of thought (*jiefang sixiang*) – an intellectual call to arms after the fall in this new post-Mao context. Aside from the journal *Time + Architecture*, architectural periodicals in this period included *Architect* (*Jianzhushi*, 1979) in Beijing, *World Architecture* (*Shijie jianzhu*, 1980) at Tsinghua University, *Southern Architecture* (*Nanfang jianzhu*, 1981) in Guangzhou, *New Architecture* (*Xinjianzhu*, 1983) at Huazhong Institute of Technology, *Huazhong Architecture* (*Huazhong jianzhu*, 1983) in Wuhan, *Traditional Chinese*

*Architecture and Gardens* (*Gujian yuanlin jishu*, 1983) in Beijing, and *World Architecture Review* (*Shijie jianzhu daobao*, 1985) at Shenzhen University.

In the Mao era (1949–76), the state-run *Architectural Journal* (*Jianzhu xuebao*, founded by the Architectural Society of China in 1954) was the only important platform for scholarly communication related to architecture – individual publications or the promotion of architectural ideas not officially recognised by the state were severely constrained and even repressed. In the 1980s these new periodicals, sponsored by public institutions or professional bodies, jointly provided scholars and practitioners with crucial venues for academic debate, documenting the flourishing of architectural writing and building in the reform era.

The second issue of *Time + Architecture* was published in 1985, and the editorial board – comprising academics, local architects, government officials and others – was established the next year. Luo Xiaowei, a professor of architectural history in the department, became the editor-in-chief, and a founding editor, Wang Shaozhou, became the deputy editor-in-chief.[4] Despite publishing in the

---

4    In the early 1980s, Luo Xiaowei travelled to the US as a visiting scholar, where she lectured at Harvard University and MIT. She also visited a number of architects, including Robert Venturi, Michael Graves and Peter Eisenman, as well as historians such as Stanford Anderson, Kenneth Frampton, Joseph Rykwert and others. See Lu Yongyi, 'On Teaching History of World Architecture in Tongji: An Interview with Professor Luo Xiaowei', *Time + Architecture*, no 6 (2004) pp27–29.

1 The inaugural issue of *Time + Architecture* (1984).

heyday of postmodernism in China, the editors were more inclined to present experimental work and maintain a clear pro-modernist position. The first editorial claimed that:

> In China, in order to change the stereotyped state of architecture, it is important to treasure the exploratory spirit in the process of design. It is more than ever necessary to concern and support people who are devoting great effort to innovation and overcoming adversity. Therefore, we are not only willing to introduce mature works, but also happy to present immature but innovative works. We certainly do not advocate a censorious attitude to successful work, and conversely we do not assume an apathetic face to exploratory work. Supporting creation and encouraging innovation are not only common hopes for the field, but also the popular demand of our readers.[5]

Further, they wrote:

> Modernism in architecture is the result of large-scale industrial production and new technology; and is the reflection of advanced productive forces in the field of architecture. Its historical progress has already been affirmed in real life and still plays a role. We should no doubt take its essence to accelerate the pace of our progress during China's modernisation.[6]

The intention to create a platform for the open discussion of architectural theory and practice, which set the tone for the journal's future development, was revealed by this lucid editorial statement, best described as a critique of the previous political interference in scholarly debate. At the same time it explicitly reflects the editors' and sponsors' preoccupation with the ideologies of modern architecture, a position with deep roots in the department's origins in the 1930s at St John's University. There the founding director of the architectural programme, Huang Zuosen (Henry Jorson Huang), promoted progressive modern projects and used architecture as an instrument to deal with urban and housing problems.[7] This teaching philosophy had a strong influence on Luo Xiaowei, who studied architecture under Huang's tutelage in the late 1940s and became a lecturer at St John's and Tongji University.[8] Another influential figure at Tongji was Feng Jizhong, who promoted progressive modernism and advocated the principles of space (*kongjian yuanli*) in education during his tenure as the head of the department from the late 1950s to the early 1980s.

The interest in intellectual exploration in architecture remained a crucial

---

5    Editors, 'Editorial', *Time + Architecture*, no 1 (1984) p3.
6    Ibid.
7    Huang Zuosen was trained at the Architectural Association School of Architecture in London in the 1920s and at the Graduate School of Design at Harvard in the 1930s.
8    See Luo Xiaowei and Li Dehua, 'Department of Architectural Engineering of St John's University, 1942–1952' *Time + Architecture*, no 6 (2004) pp24–26.

characteristic of *Time + Architecture*. The 1990s saw an intensive publication of articles related to architectural production in Shanghai written by local academics and architects from state-owned design institutes. In the the past two decades, the journal has paid particular attention to the work of independent architects and critics, and was dedicated to the exchange of ideas between Chinese audiences and international architects and scholars.

Of particular significance is the fact that the journal began to publish thematic issues at the turn of the millennium. This theme-based editorial policy redefined the journal's character from a 'presenter' of received materials to a 'producer' of selected collaborative work. It also enabled *Time + Architecture* to remain editorially distinct from the Chinese architectural publishing scene. Editors were able to choose specific themes, commission potential authors to write essays and also select individual projects. This pattern led to a higher level of selection criteria. Later on, the viewpoints and selections of both the contributors and their projects would play a pivotal role in forging the character and quality of the journal.

*A Magazine of Dual Natures*

Edited by academics and sponsored initially by the university, *Time + Architecture* was once a purely academic publication and was, like other publications in the 1980s, financially dependent on the state funding. As academic faculty, the editors were also paid by the state. Their concerns were primarily focused on scholarly debates, rather than economic income or material rewards. Although two local and state-owned design institutes became co-sponsors in the late 1980s, the journal maintained its academic position. By 2000, however, the journal started to take a more market-oriented approach within the context of a socialist market economy. Its original, purely academic existence has since been transformed into a more complex juxtaposition between academic and professional features.

Initially the editors' primary responsibility was to develop an academic position for the journal, but by maintaining a close relationship with professional design firms, the journal accessed current information about built projects and some indispensable funding. This was crucial in the late 1980s and early 1990s, when individual architects and private design firms were largely absent in China. At that time, architects working for state-owned design institutes were the only practitioners in the field. Its simultaneous appeal to academics and professionals was further strengthened in 2006 with the founding of a council for professional design firms and commercial real estate, as well as material and construction companies.[9] The editorial committee, under the leadership of Luo Xiaowei, is

---

9    In commemorating its 25th anniversary, editors of *OASE* claimed that the journal's emphasis on editorial intervention

now responsible for the thematic direction and specific content published in each issue, while members of the council are obligated to offer financial support and informational resources. What makes this well organised management model unique is the way in which an 'independent' editorial position is guaranteed, while additional information can also be presented in the form of advertisements or other relevant content in the journal's pages.

*Time + Architecture*'s dual nature distinguishes it from both purely scholarly journals and professional architectural magazines in the western sense. Its preoccupation with academic topics demonstrates the editors' cultural ambition to promote theoretical debate, while its presentation of professional issues implies their intention to include a vast readership in the publishing market. The current condition of architectural magazine culture in China can help us understand this dual character:

> Compared with western architectural periodicals, most architectural magazines today in China were established by universities and, yet, the scholarly journal, in the strict sense, has not appeared. Two reasons could explain this: on the one hand, Chinese architectural journals mainly sponsored by the large-scale state-owned bodies were deliberately inclined to be all encompassing; on the other hand, the overall academic resources and architectural achievements here are not enough to support a purely scholarly theoretical journal. In this sense, the Chinese architecture magazine was either obscurely positioned or intentionally crossing the boundary. In fact, the majority of them were based in the middle ground between the academic and the professional. The obvious advantage is the more intimate link between the two fields, while the consequence is to blur their differences.[10]

*Time + Architecture*'s intermediate position was co-shaped by the dual nature of the architectural discipline, the journal's complex relationship with both academic institutions and professional design firms, and by the general condition of cultural production in contemporary China. In a precarious situation in which architectural practice, in the broadest sense, was primarily driven by immediate profit, a purely academic publication would be constrained by the inadequate production of scholarship and limited funding. It would thus be confined to a small audience of people within academia.

In order to survive in the current publishing market, selling printed copies could hardly sustain the journal's expansion and development. Rather, it functioned as an architectural media platform, using its accumulated resources (personal networks, accessible projects) to organise design competitions, exhibitions, architectural study tours aboard and to edit and publish monographs.

was different from professional magazines and academic journals and thus became a magazine of neither. See the editorial board, 'OASE: A Magazine of Neither', in *OASE*, no 75 (2008) pp2–7.

10  Wenjun Zhi and Wu Xiaokang, 'The Development Prospect of Architectural Journal in China, 2000-2010', *Urbanism and Architecture*, no 12 (2010) pp18-22.

While these commercial activities do increase the journal's professional influence and its economic income, they also present challenges for editors who need to consistently expand their academic horizons and maintain a critical position towards the status quo. To balance the contradiction between a scholarly focus and professional consideration in this regard became a dilemma.

The 'oeuvre' of *Time + Architecture* can be considered a persistent documentation of – and reflection upon – the changing conditions of architectural culture in the Chinese cultural context. The division of content for each issue, however, has remained a constant. Although some columns might occasionally be added and removed, consistent categories include thematic debates, projects and architects, criticism, history and theory, and a back section of interviews, book reviews, exhibitions, annual events, profiles on young architects, bulletins and news from online. This final section is an opportunity to present a diversity of information: from politics to culture, from the academic to the professional, from the institutional to the individual. However, the journal's dedication to covering both scholarly and professional issues helps bridge the gap between theory and practice, between academia and the architectural professions. This endeavour is exemplified in the journal's engagement with theoretical debates, critical projects and architectural criticism.

*Thematic Debates*

The first category, thematic debates, was one of the most important topics, as the journal's primary editors were not practising architects, but scholars in architectural history, theory and criticism. During its first decade many articles that appeared in this section tended to discuss architecture from an analytical rather than a descriptive point of view. Although without a specific theme in each issue, these articles, in one way or another, were edited and classified following similar concerns. More than 100 specific themes related to architecture and urbanism have been presented to date. Theoretical articles published in the journal were not peer-reviewed, although editors would give feedback to the authors who were commissioned. It is difficult to classify these themes in a comprehensive way; however, one of the most significant topics that repeatedly appears in the pages of the journal is contemporary experimental architecture in China.

Over the past two decades, the emergence of a new generation of architects educated in the post-Mao era can be seen as a transformation in Chinese architectural circles. Grouped together as experimental architecture, the works of independent practices that strove to resist the dominant commodification of architecture have been documented and discussed consistently in *Time + Architecture* through a series of themes: Experimental Architecture, Young Architects,

Tectonics, New Urban Space, Group Design, Art and Exhibitions, Education and others. Although experimental architecture became a hotly debated topic at the turn of the twenty-first century, *Time + Architecture* was probably the most important periodical dedicated to the presentation of this discourse.[11] The journal's engagement with the innovative work of a younger generation of architects dates back to its 2000 publication on the topic. **(fig. 2)** This special issue presented an intense discussion of marginal yet critical projects by emerging architects whose avant-garde spirit and creativity, for the editors, seemed to indicate a new tendency. As they wrote:

> Although Chinese experimental architecture had initially been inspired by experimental art in terms of concept, it displayed a new scene with poetic spatial expression and a rich formal language. The purpose of letting a hundred schools of thought contend is to promote the communication of thought and voice. At the same time, we attempt to introduce works objectively and truthfully and to judge them by a third party.[12]

In this special issue, several works by emerging architects such as Yung Ho

11  In 1998, the architectural critics Wang Mingxian and Shi Jian used the term 'experimental architecture' to describe the practice of a number of young and independent architects. A year later, in 1999, Wang curated the exhibition of Experimental Architecture by Young Chinese Architects during the International Union of Architects (UIA) Conference in Beijing. Shortly after that, experimental architecture was widely discussed in newspapers, architectural periodicals and fashion magazines. See Wang Mingxian and Shi Jian, 'Chinese Experimental Architecture in the 1990s', *Literature and Art Studies*, no 1 (1998) pp118–37.
12  Editors, 'Editorial Issue', *Time + Architecture*, no 2 (2000) p5.

2 **Wang Shu's interior design for the Room with a View Gallery (dingcenghualang) in Shanghai, featured on the cover of *Time + Architecture* (2000-2).**

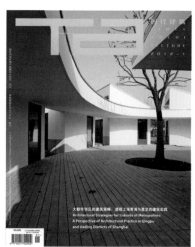

Chang, Wang Shu, Liu Jiakun and Dong Yugan were presented together. Chang used the tiny interior design for the Xishu Bookstore completed in 1996 as a point of departure to question the dominant Beaux-Arts approaches toward decoration and symbolism. He employed bicycle wheels as a characteristic construction element to sustain bookshelves and to redefine the space in a creative way. Chang's long-term interest in bicycles, which first appeared in his student work at Ball State University, is an influence on this design, as is the fact that the space previously functioned as a bicycle store. Chang's advocacy of *jiben jianzhu* (basic architecture) highlighted ontological issues of architecture, such as construction, materiality and space that are largely overlooked by Beaux-Arts principles. This special issue on experimental architecture can be read as both a continuation of the journal's tradition of publishing projects by young architects, and as an extension of the journal's engagement with alternative architectures. It was a turning point not just for the journal, but also for Chinese architecture in general.

Since then, *Time + Architecture* has paid considerable attention to the work of younger generations of architects. Its tendency to critically embrace so-called experimental architecture was revealed in its 2002 publication of these architects' theoretical, material and pedagogical practices with a 135-page special feature on emerging architects. Alongside three theoretical essays on experimental architecture were four pieces of criticism that addressed the work of Chang, Wang and Liu. (**fig. 3**) Indeed, this edition explicitly reflected both the journal's critical position *vis-a-vis* the publication of work by emerging figures and the burgeoning of experimental architecture during the process of urbanisation. (**figs. 3, 4**)

3 Left: Ming Ke's criticism on Yung Ho Chang/FCJZ Atelier's Southwest China Bio-Tech Pilot Base, published in *Time + Architecture* (2002-5).

4 Right: The topic 'Group Design Projects in the Qingpu and Jiading Districts, Shanghai' was explored in *Time + Architecture* (2012-1).

开合 聚散 驻游

新城建设背景下的上海嘉定司法中心

Opening and Enclosure, Gathering and Dispersal, Sojourn and Wandering

Jiading Centre of Justice in context of New Town Construction in Shanghai

Another thematic debate repeatedly published in the journal is group design (*jiqun sheji*), illustrating the journal's commitment to the collective practices of emerging architects. Group design projects for Songshan Lake New Town in the city of Dongguan, Guangdong Province, and for Jiading New Town in Shanghai demonstrated a joint interaction between local authorities (sponsors), architects, magazine editors and contributors. Whereas experimental architecture was a kind of spontaneous exploration by individual architects, group design practice was deliberately orchestrated, offering emerging architects an opportunity to engage in creation and coordination. As the architect Liu Yuyang stated, such practices were characterised by how embeddedness in the public realm provided an alternative mode of architectural production, one different from the dominant commercialisation of urban expansion.[13] The endeavour to compensate for the lack of public character was embodied in the Jiading Justice Centre, designed by the Original Design Studio, a project with typological exploration that transformed the predominantly bureaucratic appearance of institutional headquarters into a civic landmark. (fig. 5) In doing so, the architects incorporated different programmes (public security bureau, procuratorate and people's courts) into a complex with a unified facade. The project constructed the courtyard, plaza and landscape in dialogue with the context, rather than simply enclosing the site with walls or fences.

13   Liu Yuyang, 'A Refined Public-ness: Contemporary Architecture in Qingpu and Jiading New Towns and Their Civic Significance', *Time + Architecture*, no 1 (2012) pp34-36.

5 Original Design Studio's Jiading Justice Center in Shanghai,
featured in *Time + Architecture* (2012-1).

*Projects and Architects*

Another crucial category for the journal is its focus on projects and architects, revealing a consistent commitment to presenting critical architecture in China. One may claim that this contribution reflects the editors' initial ambitions to publish innovative and exploratory practices of architecture. This category can be defined as a window through which it is possible to demonstrate the latest developments in the Chinese architectural field. The primary editorial require-ment in this section is that published work must refer to architecture that is built in China and should show a degree of innovation and quality. Most of the time the editors visit these projects before making a final judgment about their appearance in the journal. It is this critical selection of work that plays a signifi-cant role in the promotion of contemporary Chinese architecture and enhances the journal's reputation in an a-critical publishing scene; indeed, it has proved to be quite difficult to consistently sustain close attention to the kind of work that shows a certain degree of criticality in a market-oriented climate.

Although the journal has been sponsored by a number of state-owned design institutions, its devotion to emerging design forces and independent architects has made it both stand out and elaborate on its experimental nature. Publishing the work of private studios and firms represents new tendencies in architectural practice that are characterised by energy and vigour.

What is remarkable among these practitioners is that many overseas returnees (*hai gui*) moved their primary design offices from abroad back to cities in China. As the majority of these young architects had international educational back-grounds and working experience, their dynamic design, writing and teaching activities gradually increased the intellectual depth of architecture practice. For example, in the 2003 special issue, the journal's contributing editor Bu Bing intro-duced the emerging firm, Standardarchitecture (*Biaozhun yingzao*). Established in New York in 1999, Standardarchitecture moved to China after winning the competition for the Ming Dynasty City Wall Relics Park at Dongbianmen, Beijing in 2001. One of the partners, Zhang Ke, who received a masters in architecture from Harvard University in 1998 (while already holding degrees from Tsinghua University), attempted to adopt an a-stylistic approach in their design, explaining:

> As a group, rather than only one or two people, we represent an upcoming or emerging phenomenon in China. Our work only reflects architecture itself rather than a style, a social identity or other. Standard architecture means neutral architecture.[14]

It seems that this neutral attitude does not allude to any specific form. By maintaining the original appearance of the city wall and adding a few accessible

14   Bu Bing, 'Standardarchitecture', *Time + Architecture*, no 3 (2003) pp46–51.

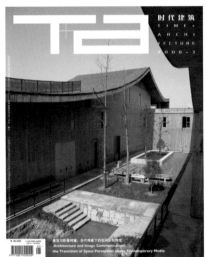

facilities, the aforementioned park design subtly transformed crowded, abandoned urban fragments into a public place. This urban intervention explicitly showed the architects' sensitivity to dealing with the contradiction between the preservation of historic relics and the creation of new objects. By far their most interesting works have been the Micro-Yuan'er in Beijing, the Yangshuo Storefronts, the Tea House in Qingcheng Mountain and a series of buildings in Tibet, all of which have been addressed in *Time + Architecture*. In all of these projects, a continued focus on the reinterpretation of traditional architecture culture in specific historical contexts is vividly demonstrated. More specifically, these buildings embodied a distinctive character – with a degree of continuity – through the synthesis of abstract formal language, local materials and mixed construction techniques and structures. **(fig. 6)**

The journal's consistent publication of Standardarchitecture's work convincingly reflects its commitment to alternative practices of architecture that emphasise subtle formal experimentation, social engagement and intellectual intervention. This publishing inclination is also demonstrated in the projects of Wang Shu and Lu Wenyu. The journal's intensive discussion of the Xiangshan Campus at the China Academy of Art in Hangzhou showcased a critical attitude toward the current condition of architectural production – the architects' preoccupation with tectonics and materiality protested against the domination of visual effect and the overlooking of traditional building intelligence. **(fig. 7)**

6 Standardarchitecture's Yangshuo Storefronts, featured in *Time + Architecture* (2005-6).

7 Wang Shu and Lu Wenyu's Xianshan Campus, the China Academy of Art in Hangzhou, featured in *Time + Architecture* (2008-3).

*Architectural Criticism*

Another feature that should be underscored is that *Time + Architecture* has sought to publish architectural criticism by architects, academics and independent writers. This section represents the journal's most consistent contribution to the development of architectural criticism in a socio-political environment that often restricted critique. The absence of professional critics in the Chinese architectural community gave rise to an extraordinary phenomenon – that is, academics and practising architects often taking responsibility for producing criticism.

The journal's commitment to architectural criticism is largely tied to the background of its editors. As a historian and critic, Luo Xiaowei had contributed to editing a national textbook on the history of western modern architecture. Similarly, her pupil and successor Wenjun Zhi has written books and articles on architectural criticism. In the late 1980s and early 1990s, the journal organised several conferences to discuss the conditions of architectural criticism. It also held competitions for critical essays and published a number of the cited articles in the journal.

Perhaps more importantly, the editors demonstrated a clear intention to seek talented writers who specialised in critical writing. For instance, in the 2002 special issue on experimental architecture, the journal reprinted a piece on the work of Yung Ho Chang and Liu Jiakun. Written by the young architect and critic Tao Zhu, it was originally published online as a blog post analysing the tectonic expression in Chang's office building in Chongqing and Liu's Luyeyuan Stone Sculpture Museum in Chengdu. The article presented a significant contribution to understanding the complexity and limitations of the discourse of tectonics in China during the early 2000s.

Throughought the pages of the journal, it is interesting to note that the work of Liu Jiakun received much more criticism than that of other architects. Although Liu was well known for writing literature, most of his published projects were covered by his peers (including Tao Zhu, Peng Nu, Li Xiangning, Deng Jing, Zhong Wenkai, Yuan Feng, Liang Jingyu, Yin Hong and Wang Wei, among others). Nevertheless, the publication of his own writing is also crucial to perceiving his design ideas. The appearance of criticism related to Liu's projects in the journal can be considered a deliberate and productive collaboration between editors, architects, critics and photographers. This interaction presents several implications that deserve critical examination.

First, the editors were interested in Liu's work and believed that it maintained a special quality for contemporary Chinese architectural practice and would attract a large readership. Second, it appeared that Liu was inclined to respect his peers' comments and maintained a willingness to have an intellectual dialogue

新集体
论刘家琨的成都西村大院

The New Collectivity
Liu Jiakun's Big Yard at Chengdu

with his critics in the public domain. Third, the journal's devotion to architectural criticism produced by critics, rather than architects themselves, implied that it tended to explore more cultural meanings beyond material production.

What made Tao Zhu's criticism remarkable is the way in which he was able to embed architectural creation into a broader historical network. In doing so, he was able to critically analyse, compare and reflect on the connections between what was currently built and what existed historically. For instance, in his writing on Liu's 2015 project Big Yard in Chengdu, published in the journal in 2016, Zhu was able to historicise the project within a sophisticated sociocultural condition. He reviewed the historical origin of the big yard prototype (or perimeter block) in the west, and argued that the project oscillated between a neutral, anonymous housing that refers back to an urban background and a singular monument that stands out to celebrate collective values and city life.[15] **(fig. 8)**

15    Tao Zhu, 'The New Collectivity: Liu Jiakun's Big Yard at Chengdu', *Time + Architecture*, no 1 (2016) pp86–97.

**8  Tao Zhu's Criticism on Liu Jiakun's Big Yard Project,
published in *Time + Architecture* (2016-1).**

*Conclusion*

*Time + Architecture* has created a public sphere by providing an opportunity for architects, academics, officials, company managers and others to discuss disciplinary, professional, social and cultural issues. As a discursive platform, the journal has helped architectural intellectuals to enter into dialogue and has even contributed to a transformation of the understanding of contemporary Chinese architecture. The journal's own development can be considered an ongoing response to a changing climate of society, politics, economy and the architectural profession. Through a close association with academic institutions and commercial companies it has established a singular standpoint between the scholar and the professional in the contemporary Chinese architectural publishing scene.

The journal is located at a critical position in the process of knowledge production, dissemination and consumption. Previously, as a commodity, it satisfied the demand for knowledge consumption by academics and professionals. Today social media, blogs and online platforms, whose immediate journalistic reports speed up knowledge circulation and consumption, challenge the journal's mission. To maintain their relevance, architectural periodicals like *Time + Architecture* need to focus on intellectual depth, particularly in curating thematic editions. It is precisely the editors' interventionist directions that have enabled contributors to reflect on the possibilities and limitations of architectural discourses, and also to transform dispersive materials into thoughtfully framed projects in which theory and practice can interact.

# Debate
# Criticism in China

Tao Zhu (Moderator),
Chris Brisbin, Wenjun Zhi

**Tao Zhu**: I'll start with Chris Brisbin and your fascinating and complex paper. To borrow Françoise Fromonot's term of the criti-cat versus the co-py-cat, in your lecture you argued that criti-cat could emerge out of the copy-cat in China, and then you elaborated on that reasoning. First, you point out that the copy phenomenon in China is cultural – that Chinese people have more relaxed attitudes towards copying. This puts the difference between 'original' and 'copy' into question. Second, you argue that western notions of authenticity and originality are complicated by commodification. China's freer use of copying can work against proprietary commodification. Finally, and perhaps most interesting, you argue that China's President Xi Jinping has been instrumental in transforming the copying movement to a criti-cat movement, with his banning of 'odd-shaped buildings' a few years ago and his advocacy for a more contemporary vernacular architecture. In other words, President Xi is like Peter Eisenman in China. He has helped to reinvent the architectural discipline in this country.

There are many questions we could ask to address these three points. Let me ask just one. Suppose there are two versions of copying mentioned in your lecture. The older version of the knock-off culture, or the copy-cat, is largely driven by the collective and unconscious action. In contrast, the newer version could possibly allow for new opportunities. It suggests that a criti-cat project requires intentionality and positioning. So aside from identifying these two versions of copying, how would you suggest a more intentional shift from the less conscious project of knock-off culture to a critical project? What are the forces or agencies that can catalyse such processes?

**Chris Brisbin**: One point that I want to make is about the empowerment of the collective. There is no individual that can alone manifest the shift from copy-cat to criti-cat. This requires a shift in how we understand our agency to inform our identity and our decisions. That is why I am interested in tracking issues about consumption and resource use. Both offer a way to discuss more grand narratives about social status and middle-class consumption, which I think drives a lot of these consumption practices. Architecture has become one of such agencies, albeit a small and elitist component.

So is shift possible? I don't know. But I think one way to enable such change is to have symposiums like this one, and to open them both to the public and to professional practice to engage architects in that discussion. We tend to keep these conversations within academia, with those who already have an interest in this change. It is necessary to empower a broader public in this conversation. Essentially, we need to start having this conversation with the public and the people we serve, and this is why my own work is less about architecture and more about trying to understand the motivations of people who use architecture. If we can understand that, I think we can make more informed decisions about what kinds of architecture are needed and what kinds are consumed.

**TZ**: That helps shift to the question of 'writers as independent critics' brought up by Professor Wenjun Zhi. You gave a few examples of the independent critic and how critical writing helps us understand an architect's design intentions. In a way, the role of a design critic is not to repeat what the architects are saying. Instead, we need to go deeper into the architects' statements to disclose what has been overlooked or made invisible to the public, or even to the architects themselves. In many cases, architects are just too busy producing new work to truly reflect on what they have created. Going back to the idea of crisis, as Françoise Fromonot brought up earlier, critics have to deal with cultural critique at large, or let's say to deal with the crisis, rather than writing an architect's monograph. Could you give an example of how *Time + Architecture* has responded to crisis, as opposed to celebrating architectural achievements?

**Wenjun Zhi**: *Time + Architecture*'s shift to a theme-based editorial policy redefined the journal's character from a 'presenter' format, which only published received material, to a 'producer' of selected collaborative work. In fact, the exploration as well as the selection of each issue's topic is a process of excavating the crisis, or the pressing issues in China's urban and architecture development. In other words, the theme of each issue emerges through a process of re-defining the ever-changing crisis. One example is a series of issues published in the past two or three years that focus on the challenge of China's urban regeneration. The scale and scope of China's urbanisation have reached new heights after three decades of development, and now the challenge is regeneration rather then continued development. Again, the themes we have selected, or the topics

we choose to focus on reflect our efforts to address the ever-changing issues affecting Chinese society.

**TZ**: I think the position of *Time + Architecture*, which aims to promote young architects' work rather than commercially driven projects by mainstream companies or design institutes, has been well received and clearly addressed. However, I think one of the biggest obstacles for nurturing critical discussion in China is that western theoretical discourses are borrowed to interpret Chinese practices. Introducing these discourses to China often seems inappropriate for the context.

For example, arguments against a 'critical architecture' and for 'post-criticality' have been going for more than a decade with authors such as Michael Speaks, Robert Somol, Sarah Whiting and George Baird. The debate between critical and post-critical was also mentioned in Chris Brisbin's talk. In 'Architecture of Modern China: A Historical Critique' Professor Zhu Jianfei writes that China is already a post-critical country because of its pragmatism. I wrote a severe response to Professor Zhu Jianfei's article. I argued, in contrast, that China is actually in a pre-critical state. Western theoretical concepts are so out of context in China, and it's frustrating to see them being uncritically applied. Lacking its own theoretical practice, China seems like a free site where everyone can project his or her future vision.

Going back to Chris Brisbin's argument for the possibility of transforming the cultural practice of copying into a critical project, how do you think a critical discourse can develop in this out-of-context situation? How important is contextualisation in critical writing?

**WZ**: Tao Zhu has raised a great question. I agree with you about the importance of contextualising the issues. For example, architectural discourses from France, Iran, Japan, the US and the United Arab Emirates that have been covered in this symposium all have regional contexts. But context is spatial *and* temporal. I think time, or the era to which these discourses belong, sometimes plays an even more significant role than their context.

Discourses of context and time are extremely important if we want to situate the Chinese architectural theoretical discourses of the late 1990s to the early twenty-first century within a global context. As scholars and editors of *Time + Architecture*, we recognise two significant aspects for introducing theoretical discourse from other parts of the world to China. On the one hand, it is important to understand these international or universal vocabularies to be active in global discussions. On the other, this awareness allows us to reflect on the unique context of China and to identify what can be adopted from other contexts. Close readings of both time and place can help illustrate what China needs in terms of combining global and vernacular vocabularies.

**CB**: Yes, absolutely, thinking about Jane Jacob's observations, she showed that a good critic is one who is grounded in the place they are critiquing and deeply understands the culture in which they are operating. I think this is perhaps one of the biggest tensions within criticism of other cultures. There is a kind of drive for an immediacy about information within global criticism. And certainly, within the Australian context, this sort of critique becomes very parochial and superficial. We end up recycling particular themes and structures. I don't necessarily have a problem drawing upon a whole range of different theoretical construction, as I am currently trying this approach in my own work and using it to tease out several different kinds of narratives. I don't think there is one answer, but I do think this requires a more serious commitment to the role of culture in design. I am trying to learn Chinese so that the language is not an abstraction but a known, lived experience. More than just visiting the buildings, critique is about actually trying to understand culture. I think that's the biggest operative connection that exists within this kind of criticism. I wouldn't say it's easy for Chinese critics to be critical of Chinese architecture, but it's far more difficult for westerners to offer meaningful critiques without reducing the architecture to cultural generalisations.

**TZ**: One of the fundamental challenges for both Chinese and western scholars working on issues in China is the extraordinarily disjunctive historical experience of China. In fact, there is no such kind of continuity of experience in Chinese history. It is full of transformative developments that come to

abrupt stops. This kind of time–space compression and fast-paced development was obvious during the 1980s with the opening up to foreign investment. During that period, the lack of a mature developmental discourse created huge difficulties.

For example, from 1981- 82, three architecture books were translated into Chinese: Le Corbusier's *Towards an Architecture*, Charles Jencks' *Post-Modern Architecture* and Bruno Zevi's *The Modern Language of Architecture*. This abrupt introduction of new architectural approaches to China created a sort of mental disorder. Beijing's architecture from the 1980s is influenced by neoclassicism and eclecticism; buildings are capped with large, traditional roofs suggesting a confusion between pre-modern, modern and postmodern design approaches.

This same confusion can be applied to China's most recent growth. Is China in a critical or pre-critical or post-critical era? Is China a copy-cat or a criti-cat? Is it even possible to nurture a sense of historical continuity within China's chronological disorder? How might we make this history more legible? What are the inherent qualities of this super modernity and how might we respond?

**WZ**: The huge transformation that happened over several hundreds of years in the other parts of the world has happened in slightly more than one generation in China. Aside from this extraordinary compression of time, China's complexity also comes from its diversity, including regional and cultural diversity. Patterns of continuation and disruption dispersed throughout China's history will make it difficult to define a single position towards Chinese architecture. I think it is more important to use critical thinking to identify the challenges and issues, and then test different ideas when responding to specific dynamics and diverse needs within an extremely complex context.

**CB**: This cultural anxiety is perhaps the root of the issue, and I feel very uncomfortable in offering a solution. Again, to return to the idea I mentioned earlier, it is about informed awareness and criticality. It is a about empowerment and knowledge in a society. Those kinds of broader narratives, and the subtle idiosyncrasies of emerging narratives, point to a culture's creative expression. This sort of self-aware-ness is happening now, but perhaps in some ways it is just a response to the level of growth.

In Australia, we are struggling with the exact set of issues – about who we are as a nation, about whether identity is a brand for attracting tourists or whether it is something more authentic and genuine. We also don't have a vernacular. We don't have a cultural history that's embedded in architecture. Almost everything in Australia is imported. So, if anyone has an anxiety about who they are and how to express that, it might be us.

For example, at the last Venice Biennale, the Austra-lian pavilion was widely derided. One of the critics said it 'put forward a superficial cliché of Euro-Dis-ney'. Because all architectural models were in some ways expressions of a kind of otherness – the pavil-ion was reflecting our mirroring of European styles and tropes, not of anything that related to us as a nation. I would say it is the same in Anting German Town, a themed satellite city on the edge of Shang-hai, where German buildings designed by Albert Speer in a modern German aesthetic are now being refurbished from within by the Chinese. So, they still look western from the outside while residents are radically transforming how the interiors and the spaces themselves are reconciled to their plan-ning. I think there was a gradual shift between the criti-cat and the copy-cat. What kind of assemblage that leads to, I don't know. But we need a critical awareness to own the crisis in the first place. We should recognise the crisis before you can address it and I think that is probably the broader issue.

**TZ**: Let us now open up the floor to any questions from the audience.

**Audience**: In this morning's panel on China – specifically post-reform China – you mentioned that *Time + Architecture* came out of the 1980s. I was very interested when you discussed how from 1979 through the first decade of reform there was this kind of emergence of multiple architecture mag-azines and discourses. Could you say something about contextualising this moment for architecture magazines, within the so-called golden decade of Chinese media, specifically from 1979 to 1989?

At that time, not only in architecture magazines, but also in the public discourse or debates, there was quite a lot of criticism related to questions like: What is China? What is the Chinese government? What is communism? What should be the role of the party? I am interested in whether there is any correlation between the emergence of critical attitudes in archi-tecture, a wave of writing about the new China and post-1949 China, and a critical attitude in society in general. What happened – specifically related to ar-chitectural criticism, and more generally to the media – after the 1989 crackdown of post-political reform?

**WZ**: In the 1980s, during the period of time that Du Juan just mentioned, the policy of 'Reform and Opening' caused huge transformations in all aspects of Chinese society. Diverse ideas from other parts of the world, particularly those in the fields of arts and culture, entered China and made a big splash in the country. Compared to the rich, avant-garde criticism that emerged in the fields of art and culture in China at that time, architecture criticism seemed quite inadequate. Therefore, criticism on the architecture of China actually came from the field of art and culture in the 1980s.

*Time + Architecture* was established within the ac-ademic context of Tongji University, as well as in the social context of Shanghai, which did not serve as the political centre of China. In many ways, I have to admit that during the first decade of the magazine's run, it did not put enough effort into promoting criti-cal thinking and experimental architectural practices. In fact, it was not until the mid- and late-1990s that the mission of nurturing critical attitudes toward architecture, as well as larger social issues, was gradually established at *T+A*. As an editor, I wit-nessed this transition from the 1980s to the 1990s.

**Angelika Schnell:** As a general question what does modernism actually mean to you, particularly within the Chinese context? Modernism itself is a question, an invention. It is also the centre of criticism, or let's say, it is where criticism comes from. It was said in the 1950s that 'modernism is over, but its consequences are continuing'. These consequenc-es are called modernisation, either technological or economic modernisation. I was wondering how you discuss modernism in China and what role it plays within this complex relationship between western thinking and Chinese thinking.

**Jonathan Massey**: I had exactly the same question about what modernism means in these contexts, because it came up in each of the presentations. But I want to overlay it with a question about a Bruno Latour-ian poster in the hallway that says: 'We Have Always Been Modern.'

**WZ**: To answer Angelika Schnell's question, I have to talk about the development of the discipline of architecture in twentieth-century China. When the first generation of Chinese architects studying abroad in the 1920s and 1930s came back to China, most brought back Beaux-Arts traditions or academic classicism. There were also a group of people who were greatly influenced by modernism in Europe and then introduced these ideas to China upon their return. Therefore, the 1930s and 1940s witnessed a process of disciplinary development with classical and modernist ideas intermingled. That was basically phase one of the development of the discipline.

The second phase was launched with the establishment of the People's Republic of China in 1949. This phase was greatly coloured by socialist ideology, where the ideas in the field of architecture were greatly influenced by Soviet neoclassicism, which effectively expressed state power. I would say that this was the period of time when Chinese architecture was least influenced by modernist thinking in the twentieth century.

The third phase, or the real discussion of modern or modernist architecture in China didn't appear until 1979, upon the launch of the 'Reform and Opening'. For example, my own graduate thesis focused on modern architecture. These are the three phases of architecture's disciplinary development in China.

**CB**: Let me also briefly respond to the question about modernism in China. I think for me – as an outsider, as someone who does not have a 'lived' cultural history in this country – I do not have an innate understanding of the narratives that Wenjun Zhi is talking about, I have read Jianfei Zhu's *Architecture of Modern China*, which is one of the few texts published in English on the subject.

It appears to me that you are facing a conflation of the enlightenment industrial revolution and modernisation all within a 40–50-year period. The kinds of distance within the western discourses that are able to use or to filter and understand, contextualise and then critique and make sense of, what it means to be modern with an upper-case 'M', is far more distinct. I don't see that necessarily in China. I don't see that from the various conversations I have had with colleagues, from the limited English texts on the subject within the west, or the translations that are actually read in Chinese texts on the subject. The original question was what is the role of modernism in China? That is a question practising Chinese architects and critics need to answer. I feel very uncomfortable with the concept of being able to answer what Chinese modernism is and how it operates.

**TZ**: I will try to give a simple answer. If we want to identify one modernist ideology that unifies Chinese intellectuals and political leaders, I would say it is an uncritical faith in science and technology, when everyone believes that technology is the ultimate truth and embraces science and technology as driving forces. Such ideology will help us understand Mao's dream in the 1950s to surround Tiananmen Square with symbols of China's modernisation, such as factory chimneys. For Mao, that was the most beautiful place Beijing could be. This ideology could also be applied to 'The Scientific Outlook on Development', a concept that was raised by former Chinese leader Hu Jintao in 2007. Today, if you talk about Big Data, people will say 'Oh, let's do it!' Modernisation in China is literally dominated by such uncritical obsessions with technology.

If we want to talk about modernism in China, we cannot overlook the political circumstances in which it is situated. As Professor Zhi pointed out, the 1930s was about the intersection between the influence of the Beaux-Arts and a Sigfried Giedion kind of modern movement. The 1950s was an era dominated by Stalin's influence in the Soviet Union, and was somehow twisted around by Khrushchev's crackdown on Stalin in the mid-1960s. In the 1980s, modern architecture – particularly the international-style white box – was used as a weapon of social reform. It functioned as a symbol of a democratic and open society. Following that, there was the influence of Kenneth Frampton's 'critical regionalism' in China in the late 1980s. In a word, notions of modernism need to be examined within certain political and cultural circumstances.

It is also important to acknowledge the emerging awareness of the negative consequences of modernism in China. For example, Wang Shu has been a very vocal critic, pointing out the unprecedented destruction of China's rural landscape and natural environment. A dialectical understanding of modernity or modernisation is being nurtured among Chinese architectural practitioners and scholars.

**Angelika Schnell:** Yesterday Françoise Fromonot told us that *Criticat* is largely based on an independent position, which means that it actually has economical independence, my specific question to Professor Zhi is how the magazine *Time + Architecture* is financed?

**WZ:** I'd say *Time + Architecture* is not as financially independent as *Criticat* because the majority of the editorial team are PhD candidates and faculty teaching at Tongji University. In other words, the journal is closely related to the academic context as well as partially funded by Tongji University. All activities related to the journal are sponsored by the magazine itself. We have two teams – one focuses on the publication and the other is responsible for activities that can be grouped under the name of 'professional services'. These provide services for small design firms or large design institutes. Therefore, aside from financial support from Tongji University, the main revenue of *Time + Architecture* comes from the services we offer to the design industry. The third major source of financial support comes from advertisements published in our magazine.

**Audience:** This is a question for Chris Brisbin. Thank you for mapping out so many replicas in China. Your presentation reminds me that there was also a replica of Chinese gardens in the US, which was created in the central court of the Metropolitan Museum of Art in New York a while ago. What do you think about these two kinds of replicas: the first type are western-style replicas created in China, whereas the second type are

Chinese-style replicas created outside of China?

**CB:** I think the biggest difference between the replica at the Met and the kinds of replicas I am talking about in China is the object intention. The former has an intention to say something, to be part of a broader curated project, whereas the replicas in China are just modifications. They are intended to sell something at a cheaper rate than the original. They are very different kinds of genres of copy-cat-ness, if you can call them that.

I am trying to make sense of how we can still legibly understand the cultural value of the unintentional copy-cat. Whereas, broadly in the literature, they are dismissed simply because they are not authentic. I think they are incredibly valuable, and so, again, I keep returning to this idea that an informed public can understand the critical purpose of any form of reproduction. I think that should be our fundamental goal. It is not just within an informed, educated academic world or professional practice, but one that is actually more public.

**TZ:** Chris, let me ask another question based on what you have just said. Don't you think it is universal to look for some exotic alternatives to replicate, either in cheap versions or in good versions? Is that not kind of a universal human desire rather than something exclusively common in China?

**CB:** It's absolutely universal. That is exactly what the the the first slide of my talk – Sir John Soane's 'Composite View of Buildings at Kew Gardens' – was trying to show. It is an example in the picturesque tradition of going on a grand tour, mining the ancient classical world of fragments and bits of the past and reproducing them in your English garden so that you can present to others how worldly you are. You can identify and understand what 'taste' is. I absolutely think the biggest conundrum within western discourse is that it tends to heavily denigrate China. In fact, westerners have been doing it for hundreds, if not thousands, of years, but of course on a different kind of scale.

**Nasrin Seraji:** Yesterday we heard Kamran Afshar Naderi talk about the way that the *Memar* magazine has become an environment where you

can be slightly critical. And today, we have heard
that *Time + Architecture* is the place where one
can try to be critical. I think the environments of
criticality in these cultures are very different. In the
west – and Hong Kong fits into that funny place
of western lineage – we still believe that in the
university and among academics we have these
places that we can experiment in our thoughts.
In many countries, this is not only a discussion
about freedom, but also about the environment of
thought. The act of experimentation and making
mistakes has been reduced mainly to magazines.

I think we are going to see that ideas about the
construction of critical thinking could start from
the construction of environments. Also, we might
consider how these ideas can be moved and
shifted into other environments. For example,
knowing some of the universities in Iran as well as in
China, the idea of production and post-production
is much more important than paper production.
This is the same problem we have in this room
right now. Everybody is producing in the studios.
Most of the students – I am not talking about the
ones that are here now – think that production
prevails and is more important than pre-produc-
tion, or even the meaning behind or reason for
production. Also, how much history of Chinese
architecture has been written in the same method-
ical way that western history has been written?
This is something I would like to further discuss.

**TZ**: This idea of history and contextualisation ultimately points to the key issue of writing and history.
After all, history is the common ground for us to
formulate some continuous appearance, or some
cultural norm – for us to measure this contemporary contingency. Otherwise we don't have a site.

# Reading, Writing and Architectural Education

# Reading, Writing and Architectural Education
Sony Devabhaktuni

In her book-length essay from 1958, *The Human Condition*, Hannah Arendt proposes that human activity can be described as comprising three categories: labor, work and action. Using Arendt's classification, architecture as *work* – the leaving behind of a durable trace within the world that mediates human relations– as opposed to *labor* – or the perpetual struggle linked to the maintenance of life, would seem to be an important distinction. For the two panelists who launched the session on architectural education, another aspect of Arendt's triad is also relevant: the tension between work and action: work being, again, the *homo faber* – the craftsman, allying *techné* and *poiesis* to shape nature into a durable object that goes on to comprise the world – and action understood as an engagement with others through processes of discourse, argumentation and exchange that are at once unpredictable and unstoppable.

In their contributions, Angelika Schnell and Jonathan Massey discussed their struggle to reconcile architecture as they initially encountered it as students, with new imperatives for teaching and research that became apparent as they advanced in their careers. What is common to their trajectories as educators and writers is a shift away from the object toward an interest in the production of architecture and the discourses that are implicated in how, by and for whom architecture is made. This shift reflects a broader disciplinary transformation that is not entirely recent; nevertheless, architectural education is still trying to reconcile the implications of what an expanded discipline means for the ways in which architecture is taught and made.

This difficulty is most acutely felt in two areas where the authors are engaged in experimentation: the design studio and the opening of architecture to a broader population of students. One of the questions that came up often during the symposium was the role that architectural education could play in addressing the crisis in criticism, reading and writing. It seemed, in fact, that teaching itself was in a sort of crises, with old models and ways of doing things unable to respond to the world as it has become and to the ways students relate to it.

In questioning 'Who Designs the Design?' Angelika Schnell asks students in her design studio to embody the characters of the architects they are studying. Rather than a formal analysis through models or drawings that operates under the assumption that the object of architecture is itself the cipher of critical meanings, students speculate on the processes and personalities that lead to architecture through a radical occupation and reenactment of bodies and moments. Schnell describes her own disquiet when students encounter the difficulties of performance and she herself confronts the limits of her disciplinary training. As someone educated in the practice and theory of architecture, she had never been prepared for such an acting out. And it is this encounter with risk, and the possibility of failure, that would seem to be a mark of promise in her experimental forms of studio teaching.

Jonathan Massey's contribution charts a broadening set of research concerns for how we describe architecture and its production and also a career in teaching that has brought him into contact with an ever-expanding set of constituencies and interests. If architecture is able to attract and retain a diverse group of students, the opening up of the discipline would seem to demand an interrogation of both the questions we ask and the students we bring to the table to ask them. In the tumult of the contemporary situation, students are eager to find a way through architecture to address the concerns they have for the future. Massey's work as an educator rejects depending solely on our own experiences of education because they inevitably circumscribe architecture's capacities. Massey's more recent efforts as a scholar and educator comprise new modes of collaboration that foreground equity and social justice as a means to expand those limits and ultimately to challenge the discipline itself. Indeed, the most innovative global practices today are not only making exciting buildings; they are questioning architecture's methods and the issues it is able to take on.

Returning to Arendt's formulation, I would argue that Massey and Schnell are searching for an understanding of architecture as a *social* practice that operates *between* work and action, *between* enduring fabrications within the world and the letting loose of processes that create possibilities for exchange and dialogue. Through experiments with teaching and writing, their work seeks, I would argue, to unleash and remake the relations and processes that comprise architecture as a human endeavor.

# Writing a New Discipline

Jonathan Massey

My pursuit of architecture and of its history and theory stems from the pleasure I take in the sensuous qualities of the built world around me, paired with the pleasure of understanding those qualities in relation to abstract realms of meaning: social, cultural, and political. My primary focus is to identify how architecture mediates abstractions such as modernization – how, even as they manifest broader forces in political economy, buildings also realize, shape, and condition those forces.

For much of my career, I developed specialized expertise in architectural history, and I wrote primarily in a scholarly language aimed at other experts. A decade ago, I began chairing the Bachelor of Architecture programme at Syracuse University. My work leading this undergraduate professional degree program included recruiting high school students to commit to five years of intensive architectural study. This challenged me to articulate the value proposition of architectural education. What do we teach our students? What does their learning empower them to do? And what career trajectories does it support? More recently, as dean of architecture at California College of the Arts [CCA] – an independent art, design and architecture college in San Francisco and Oakland, California – I have found myself making the case for architecture and design education to many other constituencies, from provost and president to donors, foundations, and industry partners.

These experiences have helped to shift my thinking about architecture, history and criticism, and architectural education. They have helped me to see what we

[The text is an edited transcript of Jonathan Massey's symposium presentation.]

do from the outside as well as from the inside. They have pushed me to balance the disciplinary perspective I formed as a student and professor with the extra-disciplinary perspective of parents and other non-specialist publics. My scholarship, writing, teaching, and leadership have all changed in response to seeing our field from the diverse perspectives of those both within and beyond. Increasingly, my writing engages these broader audiences, aiming to connect disciplinary expertise with matters of common concern.

This work as a program chair and dean has challenged me to develop a more inclusive set of voices. In parallel, it has also foregrounded for me another dimension of writing about architecture – what we might call its meta function of shaping the field by determining what is legitimate and important, how attention is distributed, whose concerns matter. This constitution of the field as an intellectual territory intersects with the reproduction of the discipline and the profession as sociological domains. What we talk about in schools and journals is one of the factors shaping who decides to pursue this course of study, and who becomes an architect.

This gives architectural history, theory, and criticism a role in moulding the demographics of our schools and profession. In this light, I more and more view the production of architectural discourse as a project of intentionally transforming our discipline to elicit a more diverse and inclusive architectural public.

To anchor this in my own writing trajectory, I'll begin with my dissertation book *Crystal and Arabesque. Claude Bragdon, Ornament, and Modern Architecture*. I'm very proud of this book, and yet it is also a marker registering how much my thinking about architectural scholarship has changed over the past decade. The book is a monographic study of Claude Bragdon, a contemporary of Frank Lloyd Wright, who was engaged in the progressive movement for social reform in the early 20th century and set out to modernize ornament. With a very traditional monographic format, the book is based on close readings of Bragdon's texts, designs and buildings. It pays detailed attention to design artefacts and artworks, teasing out their nuances to articulate shades of architectural meaning that at times became quite esoteric.

Reconstructing the intellectual, social, and historical context of sophisticated architectural works is one of the purposes of specialized expertise, and I value highly the capacity I developed to read the specificities of objects, artefacts and designs. At the same time, I have recognized subsequently that my approach to Bragdon's work was motivated primarily by an architect's desire to recover and legitimate discipline-specific capacities. My sustained attention to the work shed new light on the manifold ways that Progressive Era architects responded to modernization with innovative design practices. But in choosing this project, I didn't think much about the extent to which, by focusing on the work of a leading professional from an era when many women and people of colour were excluded from the formal practice of architecture, I was inherently reinscribing problematic hierarchies of attention and value. In writing a monographic study framed through Bragdon's career and archive, I also highlighted the agency of the individual practitioner – even if I consistently set him in relation to broader networks and publics – over that of systems, institutions, and collectives of many kinds.

Since completing *Crystal & Arabesque*, I have continued to study the work of architects in order to understand the complexity and impact of design. In parallel, though, I have increasingly focused on describing other forms of agency shaping the built environment.

A primary forum for my intellectual development over the past decade and longer has been the Aggregate Architectural History Collaborative – Aggregate, for short. An evolving group of about a dozen architectural historians from universities in the United States and Canada, we approach architecture as an agent of modernisation. Setting aside traditional forms of architectural authorship and individual designers, we reconstruct some of the many other ways that people, institutions, and governments form buildings, cities, and territories: through laws and economic policies, bureaucracies and protocols, ideologies and habits. We shift the conversation from an agonistic paradigm such as that I employed in my Bragdon book – in which the architect either transmits broader social political imperatives or pushes back against them in a kind of critical sparring with normative orders – toward microhistories, Annales School studies of deep structures and slow change, institutional histories, analyses of governmentality. We look for the ways that architecture doesn't just exemplify or resist modernization processes, but instead mediates them. By this I mean that, as an indispensable medium of modernization, architecture both manifests *and* shapes change. Buildings give processes of modernization their specific character and quality as they bring those processes into existence.

To give examples: in our edited volume *Governing by Design: Architecture, Economy, and Politics in the Twentieth Century*, my colleagues showed how cold storage warehouses in the U.S. enabled changes to capitalism by turning perishable produce into financialized commodities (Michael Osman); how home furnishing and decorating practices mediated Islamist ideology in Iran (Pamela Karimi); and how self-help housing brought informal city-dwellers into the formalized economy of developmentalist Pakistan (Ijlal Muzaffar). The book's ten chapters describe twentieth century architecture as a history of multiple forms of biopower and governmentality.

Aggregate meets twice yearly to present ideas and workshop work-in-progress. Participating in this group shifted my work. When I joined, I started a new project that looked at mortgage finance in relation to single family houses in the United States. I set out to understand how something like the Dymaxion House – that I knew as Buckminster Fuller's avant-gardist proposition for transforming housing in the United States in the early twentieth century – was in dialogue with shifting patterns of investment, finance, and consumption for single-family housing.

In this project I redirected my attention from seeing the Dymaxion House as a work in Fuller's oeuvre to seeing it as one of many attempts to redesign consumer participation in a changing capitalist economy. I set it in relation to parallel initiatives such as Everyman's House, a demonstration house built by the Better Homes organisation in Kalamazoo, Michigan in the 1920s to introduce people to the idea of mortgage financing. Everyman's House showed middle-class prospective homeowners how to participate in a new way of financing the purchase of a house that reflected changes in the banking sector, such as the rise of savings and loan organizations. I looked at the emergence of realtors as brokers and mediators who helped teach people to consume housing in new ways and to use their houses as an investment vehicle for retirement, and so as part of managing their household finances. This then led me to look at the intense financialisation of single family houses in the United States from the 1970s up to 2008. These new cultures of housing production and home ownership generated phenomena like tear-down redevelopment, which happened when houses became financially obsolete even if they were still perfectly liveable; or McMansions – which were essentially ways for people to invest larger amounts of money in real estate by taking out larger mortgages. I then connected that back to the homeowner subjectivities and consumption practices that gave rise to the make-over culture that taught people to be real estate entrepreneurs through resale-orientated renovations and transformations. Changes in the design and consumption of houses were linked to macroeconomic changes in part through a vast television and magazine and life-world built around the practice of house-flipping and make-over culture – succeeded today by real estate apps such as Trulia and Zillow teach us to engage our neighbourhoods as intensely financialised territories.

In architectural discourse, we often privilege the unbuilt intention over the built reality, and while there is real value in recovering intentions and unrealized potentialities from the past, this penchant sometimes wards off valuable perspectives and forms of knowledge about the limits and surprising forms of architectural agency. Aggregate has taught me how to look more closely at what actually *is*, and to understand what architects project and imagine and intend by relating it the broader patterns of actually existing architecture.

After publishing *Governing by Design* in 2012, we built a website – we-aggregate.org – where we published scholarship. With Meredith TenHoor of Pratt Institute, I edit a section of the website that looks at architecture's relationship to real estate development and capitalism.

In that stream, I had the pleasure of presenting two years ago here at the University of Hong Kong, a work called 'Risk Design', that looked at the way architecture mediates our relationship to risk and opportunity in neo-liberal economies. I presented a case study of Norman Foster's Gherkin building, 30 St Mary Axe in the City of London. This piece of writing aspires to the mandate of independence, verification, scepticisms and all those criteria that Françoise Fromonot laid out for *Criticat* in her earlier presentation. This project was also my attempt to intervene in the conversation within Aggregate, to re-introduce close reading as a tool for understanding how architecture participates in political economy. I made the argument that the Gherkin actually was pivotal to the restructuring of the City of London's economy because it brokered a renegotiated planning regime permitting redevelopment of the many office towers that followed in its wake. I looked at its architecture as risk management through design.

That was my very intentional attempt to connect the close reading skills that I had developed in architecture school, and then in *Crystal & Arabesque*, with the new prospective that Aggregate had taught me. I still believe this is a sweet spot: connecting big-picture thinking of how architecture participates in modernisation and social transformation, anchored in specific qualities of built object and designed artefacts.

Other Aggregate projects include 'Systems and the South', through which Arindam Dutta, M. Ijlal Muzaffar and Fabiola López-Durán gathered scholars to study the developmental frameworks that shaped and produced architecture at a large scale in the global south. Claire Zimmerman from the University of Michigan published on Albert Kahn Associates, the firm best known for the factory buildings of the Ford Company and other auto makers and military munitions makers in the United States. She describes the new methods it requires to interpret a firm that designed factories around the world by the hundreds, profoundly shaping the course of industrialization in the United States, the Soviet Union, and elsewhere – and leaving behind an archive so large that perhaps only database based 'distant reading' can do it justice. And Aggregate director Pamela Karimi co-edited a collection of essays on the destruction of cultural heritage that takes on iconoclasm and the destruction of buildings in both historical and contemporary perspectives. Our group has been very pleased to have some impact on our field, recognized two years ago when *Metropolis* magazine designated us 'game changers' in the design world.

This work is part of a larger project that aims toward the scholarly reconstruction of the discipline by introducing into architecture schools a greater consciousness of architectural production that goes beyond the intentionality of architects. It challenges our habits in both history courses and design studios, through which we sometimes overestimate the agency of the architect and the impact of the singular work of architecture.

Another 'writing group' has changed my approach to teaching. The Global Architectural History Teaching Collaborative, founded about three years ago by Mark M. Jarzombek and Vikramaditya Prakash, started as a way to leverage their book, *A Global History of Architecture*, into a network of scholars and faculty transforming the ways we teach architecture, especially in high-impact introductory survey courses. It is not often that professors get to talk with one another about teaching, paradoxically. We don't really get trained in teaching, but just throw ourselves into the classroom and emulate the bad habits of our own professors. The GAHTC has convened a great group of scholars to share teaching methods and materials to update introductory architecture teaching to contemporary standards. Moving beyond the 'western plus' approach that dominates in North American architecture schools, this group has helped many of us re-educate ourselves so that we take on truly global and cosmopolitan perspectives in our teaching. By re-granting funds from the Mellon Foundation, the group has supported many groups of scholars in generating shared teaching materials that disseminate best practices in approach and subject matter. The GAHTC website course modules on topics such as 'Armenian Church Architecture', 'Global History of Salvation Architecture', 'Coffee Houses and Tea Houses of Global Architectural History', 'Global History of Rock-cut Architecture. This work connects to and draws from the work of other globally minded networks such as the South of East West group (HKU faculty and scholars Cole Roskam and Max Hirsh are members), which shows how diverse multi-lateral global exchanges of architecture and expertise shaped 20th century architecture.

These different lines of activity are modest approaches to building a discipline that attracts, retains, and promotes a more diverse group of architects and scholars toward building a more equitable and inclusive world. I have heard a lot over the years from colleagues, students, and non-architects from under-represented backgrounds about the challenges they often face at entering the world of architecture and finding their priorities reflected in it. This has focused my attention on one meta-function of architectural writing, which is to shape, indirectly, the demographics and sociology of the field. By celebrating particular achievements and values in particular ways, our criticism and history and theory tilt the field toward certain legacies of privilege that sometimes exclude, and at other times just don't interest, a diversity of talent. One path toward creating the more diverse, equitable, and inclusive world that we all deserve is to refocus our intellectual efforts around a more representative range of histories, epistemologies, and strategies.

In the United States, at least, architecture and architectural education are still very Jeffersonian enterprises. Our curricula still to a great extent reflect the priorities of elite white gentleman of leisure. Elite forms of literacy and cultural heritage are strongly over-represented, while others are neglected or ignored. Let's imagine instead an architectural field that is equitably accessible to everybody--that is not so much a gentleman's game but instead values a wider range of cultural knowledge, priorities, and values. When I was asked to write a 50th anniversary review of *Complexity and Contradiction* for the *Journal of Society of Architectural Historians*, I argued that we have spent too much time studying this amazing, powerful beautiful book, which teaches a mode of architectural discrimination, a way of looking and designing architecture that is wonderful but is vastly overrepresented in our conversation. I suggested that instead we prioritize generating a more representative set of tools for interpreting and generating architecture.

Through Aggregate, with Meredith TenHoor and Sben Korsh, I edited an essay collection in response to the Black Lives Matter movement. We did not see architectural engagements with this movement appearing in our discipline's venues, so we issued a call for short pieces and published a dozen essays looking at the Black Lives Matter movement in relation to architecture and urbanism. Our contributors looked at the United States school and prison system as architectural mediations of the mass incarceration regime known as 'the new Jim Crow': a system of racial segregation akin to that which emerged in the American south to exclude African Americans from full political and economic participation or self-determination. Another essay came from Architects Designers and Planners for Social Responsibility, an activist group that has called upon architects in the United States to refuse to work on prisons on the grounds that to do so means participating in a fundamentally unjust mass incarceration regime. Another group of scholars looked at the ways architects designed for southern, rural black folk moving to northern industrial cities in the Great Migration. Some of the most compelling contributions emphasized the need to address African-American culture, history, and agency not only in regard to state-sponsored violence but also across the full range of creative and professional practices. Let's look at black spaces, some contributors said. What might black formalism look like – a culturally, racially specific formalism? A group of students contributed the piece 'Valuing Black Lives Means Changing Curricula'.

This is one of the major pedagogical projects in the United States right now: to revise the canons we teach, and also our methodologies, so that they attract and empower a diversity of talent. At CCA we translated this into a Black Lives Matter teach-in organised by students and faculty. We took half a day to work through some of these questions together in small groups and also in a large format. What if we started our curriculum with the problem of mass incarceration? How would we understand architecture in a profoundly different way if we considered it a key effect of architectural production? We find examples in collections like those from Toni L. Griffin, who edited – with Ariella Cohen and David Mattox – *The Just City Essays*.

High school pipeline programs teach youth from underrepresented groups about architecture, enhancing a secondary-school curriculum that often doesn't address architecture at all and providing an introduction to the field. The A. Alfred Taubman College of Architecture and Urban Planning at University of Michigan partnered with Detroit Public Schools to create Michigan Architecture Prep, a robust one-semester half-day introduction to architecture aimed at identifying and supporting students who may use architectural knowledge and methods to transform their city and larger worlds.

Reflecting on *Crystal & Arabesque*, when I talk about ornament I now complement Claude Bragdon's approach with others such as those reflected in Miriam Schapiro's *Doll House*, which draws on feminism to consider the gendered language of wallpaper and domestic interiors, or in Kehinde Wiley's paintings, which filter the heraldic qualities of baroque ornamentation through the contemporary codes of hip-hop culture. When we teach classical architecture, we should also teach about the appropriation of neoclassical architecture by suffragettes who used it to advocate for women's rights in the early 20th century, or the alternative classical legacies of Syrian and Egyptian architecture that W.E.B. Du Bois and other African-Americans drew on to challenge the hegemonic whiteness of U.S. neoclassicism.

In sum, the engagement with broader constituencies that has come from teaching and higher education leadership has reshaped my understanding of architectural writing. Documenting and interpreting architectural practice and the corpus of works it has generated is one value that criticism, theory, and history bring to our field. But another is bringing to bear the perspectives of the people and processes that professional structures have excluded from view for architects and architectural scholars. Building a better discipline entails moving back and forth between the specialized expertise of received knowledge and the underrepresented perspectives that help us see the discipline's limits, its distortions, and its unrealized promise.

# Who Designs the Design?

Angelika Schnell

In their ground-breaking empirical study, *The New Spirit of Capitalism,* French sociologists Luc Boltanski and Ève Chiapello demonstrate how capitalism appropriates and incorporates criticism (artistic criticism in particular) and by so doing becomes even more efficient.[1] The study could be understood as a 'sociology of criticism' read through management magazines and books from the 1990s. The authors show that CEOs and other management-level employees appropriate the main features of 'the repertoire of May 1968' such as self-motivation and creativity, as well as 'autonomy, spontaneity, availability, informality, conviviality … originally directed against capitalism'[2] to overcome the bureaucratic hierarchies of traditional companies and encourage employees to work independently – at least seemingly – instead of merely managing the labour of their workers. We all know the results: working at home (nights and weekends) as a form of self-exploitation and a permanent self-evaluation of performance as a practice of criticism. Of course, this has also been the increasingly neoliberal reality of European universities: our daily business, so to say.

Has criticism lost its power?[3] As critics, confronted with this situation, we should continue to reveal and analyse, but we should also look for new paths. For the past several years I have had the opportunity to experiment with 'design-based research' – in other words, mixed methodologies and new questions. This opportunity was made possible by Nasrin Seraji's reorganisation of the

1   Luc Boltanski and Ève Chiapello, *Le Nouvel Esprit du capitalisme* (Paris: Gallimard, 1999).
2   Douglas Spencer, *The Architecture of Neo-Capitalism: How Contemporary Architecture became an Instrument of Control and Compliance* (London: Bloomsbury, 2016) p79.
3   See for example Bruno Latour, 'Why Has Critique Run out of Steam? From Matters of Fact to Matters of Concern', in *Critical Enquiry* no 30 (Winter 2004).

curriculum at the Institute for Art and Architecture in Vienna into five different thematic platforms, one of which is the History, Theory, Criticism course (HTC). This platform opened up the possibility of combining theoretical and historical research *within* a design studio, which is a rare opportunity.

This was the perfect starting point to experiment with design-based research. Together with students, we have been able to discover the benefits of this approach, or at least, to determine which new questions design-based research might open up. Before discussing some examples of student work to come out of this approach and which appear in the recently published *Researching Design*,[4] I would like to make some general remarks on the topic of criticism in architecture. (fig. 1)

Who designs the design? This question already includes a criticism of the *many* debates and theories about 'critical architecture'. Michael Hays propagated this term in 1984[5] to speak about the necessity for architecture to find ways to resist or dialectically contradict the economic basis of our society. Beatriz Colomina proposed that the implication of technically produced images into the design process had fundamentally changed the production of architecture. Following Walter Benjamin, she concludes that the possibility for the 'mechanical reproduction' of any work of art[6] has distinguished 'building' and 'architecture'. Architecture, distinct from the practice of building, has become 'an interpreta-

4    Angelika Schnell, Eva Sommeregger, Waltraud Indrist, eds, *Entwerfen Erforschen. Der 'performative turn' im Architekturstudium* (Basel: Birkhäuser, 2016).
5    K Michael Hays, 'Critical Architecture: Between Culture and Form', in *Perspecta* vol 21 (1984) pp14-21.
6    English translation of Walter Benjamin, 'The Work of Art in the Age of Mechanical Reproduction', *Illuminations*, (New York, NY: Schocken Books, 1969).

1 Cover of *Researching Design*, edited by Angelika Schnell, Eva Sommeregger and Waltraud Indrist, based on three performative and theoretical design studios at the Academy of Fine Arts Vienna, courtesy Angelika Schnell, Eva Sommeregger and Waltraud Indrist.

tive, critical act ... a project in itself, a veritable production'.[7] This intellectualisation has been attacked by proponents of so-called 'projective architecture' or post-criticality (or even non-criticality) who instead argue for an architecture that embraces the innovations of neoliberal society.[8]

Rather than discuss the details of these positions, I would stress how all presuppose that it is architecture *itself* that should or should not be critical. They presuppose, as well, that criticism is miraculously incorporated or inscribed into the body of architecture, seemingly in a permanent way. Michael Hays discusses architectural projects by Ludwig Mies van der Rohe to support his thesis of a 'critical architecture', an architecture able to resist and even contradict common rules and contexts. However, those elegant Mies buildings have since become the *coulisses* for Armani and Mercedes-Benz advertisements. They provide a minimalist design and atmosphere for the global, neoliberal player: a perfect stage for conducting smart business deals – a glass table surrounded by high-finish, onyx walls, slim tablet in hand.

What I want to question therefore is the assumption that architecture *itself* can be critical.[9]

In *Three Critiques,* Immanuel Kant offers a basic – and idealistic – definition of criticism: he proposes that critique is a highly moral standpoint of individuals who are capable of being critical of the reality outside but also, and this is essential to his philosophy, critical of their own ultimate inability to recognise that real world as such. However, for Kant it is this inability that motivates a permanent, self-critical inquiry of the preconditions of observation and judgment.[10] Thus, critical autonomy is a characteristic of human beings and not of forms or objects. Although Kant affirms the role of mathematics and geometry as sciences, which are related to the *a priori* givens such as space and time, he argues that these scientific instruments are the only possible basis and precondition for human beings to recognise reality and make judgments about objects shaped by that geometry. In Kant's philosophy, it is by definition never the object in itself that can be recognised, but only the object 'for us', meaning that autonomy is a critical

7    Beatriz Colomina, introduction to *ARCHITECTUREPRODUCTION* (New York, NY: Princeton Architectural Press, 1988) p7.
8    Robert Somol, Sarah Whiting, 'Notes Around the Doppler Effect and other Moods of Modernism', in *Perspecta,* vol 33 (2002) pp72-77.
9    'The term "Critical Architecture" emerged as a short-hand for critical architectural practice and as a simple way of marking a place between criticism and design in architecture.' – Jane Rendell, 'Introduction. Critical Architecture: Between Criticism and Design', *Critical Architecture,* eds Jane Rendell, Jonathan Hill, Murray Fraser, Mark Dorrian (London: Routledge, 2007) p2.
10   'We have intended, then, to say that all our intuition is nothing but the representation of phenomena; that the things which we intuit, are not in themselves the same as our representations of them in intuition, nor are their relations in themselves so constituted as they appear to us; and that if we take away the subject, or even only the subjective constitution of our senses in general, then not only the nature and relations of objects in space and time, but even space and time themselves disappear; and that these, as phenomena, cannot exist in themselves, but only in us. What may be the nature of objects considered as things in themselves and without reference to the receptivity of our sensibility is quite unknown to us.' Immanuel Kant, The Critique of Pure Reason, translation of the second edition (1787) by J. M. D. Meiklejohn, § 9. General Remarks on Transcendental Aesthetic, http://www.gutenberg.org/files/4280/4280-h/4280-h.htm.

and moral standpoint that makes it possible for subjects to find ways to recognise the world, but it is not a quality of the objects themselves.

However, Hays and Colomina are also right: social, political and cultural issues are implicated in modern architecture just as technically produced images take part in the design process. But the consequence is *first* a transformation of the design process into a critical process and only secondly, architecture. I want to therefore focus on the design process, beginning with Mies – as it is with him that Hays elaborated his famous thesis.

The *Resor House* (1939) series of photocollages are design drawings for an unbuilt, single-family house in Jackson Hole, Wyoming. In his interior perspective of the living room and south glass wall, three black and white photographs of the south-facing view are pasted onto blank paper, creating both the scene outside and establishing the horizontal planes of floor and ceiling. Spare horizontal lines and columnar forms also give structure to the room. In the foreground is an enlarged colour reproduction of Paul Klee's *The Colorful Meal* (1939), and a copy of a wooden veneer serves as a bar. The black and white photographs show mountains with two cowboys in the distance.

Neil Levine has argued that this carefully orchestrated composition provides 'the neutral two-dimensional ground for the free-standing objects in the room'[11] and creates an effect of 'spatial discontinuity and sense of alienation'.[12] Although it is obvious that the minimisation of perspectival depth is caused by the lack of a middle-ground reference, it is due in part to the fact that the relationship between foreground and background is not conveyed by the measurement rules of the drawing, since the enlargement of the Klee painting and the enlargement of the wooden bar are disproportionate. Their size resulted from the technical specifications of the camera-image, which are external to the measurable dimensions of the drawing. The background image, a forced perspective in which the two cowboys in the mountains have been photographed with a telephoto lens, also contradicts the expectation of a panorama view through the large horizontal openings. It is a paradoxical effect.

Each element of the collage – photographs *and* the drawing – has its own logic of spatial and temporal relationships. Distance and proximity cannot be measured in an ordinary way but have to be experienced by assigning the different objects in the picture to one another. The observer is invited to inhabit the picture's own logic of space and time – somewhat hallucinatory, as Vilém Flusser might have put it,[13] but indeed a modern space according to Colomina: a space that has become a superimposition between the physical space outside and the space in our mind, itself increasingly governed by the media and the permanent

---

11  Neil Levine, 'The Significance of Facts: Mies's Collages up Close and Personal', in *Assemblage* 37 (December 1998) p79.
12  Ibid.
13  See Vilém Flusser, *Für eine Philosophie der Fotografie* (Berlin: Edition Flusser, 1983) p10.

pasting and cutting of different images.

What we see here is a new type of *conceptual* design 'drawing' that is not the representation of the measurable reality of a residential house – neither a sketch nor building plan – but the performance of the design idea. This leads me to the title of this paper: Who Designs the Design?

My thesis is that, with modernism, the architectural design process has changed dramatically thanks to the complicated self-referential and self-critical reality it acquired due to the effect of performativity: design drawings and processes have to also be designed in order to make the design idea, the concept and the process transparent, accessible and visible for others.

This thesis is largely based on Manfredo Tafuri's brilliant analysis of modernism (which is also the basis for Hays' writings), which says that the programmes of the avant-garde can be understood as a radical rationalisation process. The irrational fear, or angst, of the often-alarming outgrowths of the modern *Groszstadt* – or megacities – was eased by the anticipatory internalisation of technical, social, political and economic forces into the design process. According to Tafuri, modern architects became 'social ideologists'[14] by trying to foresee the changes and transformations of the modern world and to overcome these accordingly in the design. The design process itself, of course, has become a critical example.

But Tafuri's conclusion was (and this has become a common thesis) pessimistic: the contradictory avant-garde search for autonomous forms that pervade and at the same time transcend reality has failed. The architect–ideologists have been unmasked as carriers of a 'false consciousness'.

However, we should not overlook the new possibilities that 'rationalised design methods' have opened up. With such methods, the design process has to be conceived and designed exactly like the building itself. Designing acquires a political and social agenda. The design method becomes a social and a critical passport, which in turn becomes a driving force for the increasing and ongoing differentiation of design methods.

There are consequences for architecture theory and architecture criticism.

First, we need an alternative historiography – namely a history of design techniques and methods – that is related to the traditional history of architecture (the history of buildings) but is not exactly the same. From the perspective of this alternative historiography, there is perhaps no real difference between modernist and postmodernist or post-postmodernist design methods, although these methods would seem to multiply and increase in diversity at those moments when architecture was trying to be most critical (towards modernity). And maybe this history has yet to be told.

Second there are seemingly no coherent or common aesthetic, technical or media characteristics, that make it possible to borrow familiar '-isms' – or any

14    Manfredo Tafuri, *Progetto e utopia. Architettura e sviluppo capitalistico* (Rome: Editori Laterza, 2007/1973) p7.

other theories – from art history. How then should we analyse and interpret the heterogeneity and quantity of design processes? How many architects started a critical practice?

This leads me to the second section of this lecture. As described earlier, I started to experiment with design-based research because I wanted to figure out whether this might be an instrument to look more precisely at these design processes and their 'tacit knowing'.[15] From the beginning, I did not want to do design-based research in the usual way: namely, to do research *about* design methods and techniques. I wanted instead to test this new category methodologically, meaning that I wanted to find out whether architectural design processes might lead to specific knowledge not only about architecture, but also about the world in which architecture appears. Is it a kind of knowledge production? Does it have an epistemological value as such? I encouraged students to do theoretical research *with* design methods. After several years running the studio, I can say that design-based research opens up new questions; I would like to now discuss several examples to come out of the design studios at the Institute for Art and Architecture at the Academy of Fine Arts Vienna.

Students were asked to investigate certain architectural design methods from the twentieth and twenty-first centuries. Their task was to research the case studies using the same design methods that were used to create them. The premise underlying this brief was that since modernism, the design process has already become a 'social and a critical practice' and a production of knowledge whose outcomes only become clear when it is both the object and the tool of the research. Consequently, the studios consisted of specific 'case studies' in which the employed techniques and media of the design process were reused and re-designed experimentally in order to re-evaluate and assess their methodological potential.

In one studio, fifth-semester students had the choice of 'conceptual design images' by twentieth and twenty-first century architects.[16] Those by Kasimir Malewitsch, Theo van Doesburg, Le Corbusier, Ludwig Mies van der Rohe, Frederick Kiesler, Alison and Peter Smithson, Superstudio, Aldo Rossi, Peter Eisenman, Rem Koolhaas, Neil Spiller and Lebbeus Woods were quite different. Nevertheless, they were neither traditional design sketches nor premade design drawings. The students were required to 'research by design', by using the same visual media used by the case study.

They noticed that the visual media of the 'conceptual design images' were often borrowed from other disciplines with an intrinsic time factor, such as film and photography, theatre, dance and performance, as well as literature, comics or

---

15  The term 'tacit knowing' was introduced by Michael Polanyi, meaning that with many bodily practices we know more than we can tell. See: Michael Polanyi, *The Tacit Dimension* (Chicago: University of Chicago Press, 1966).
16  Led by Angelika Schnell and Eva Sommeregger (2012–13). See: http://www.designparadigm.net/portfolio/building-the-design/.

sheet music. We asked them to reconstruct the design drawings at a larger scale, and they began to re-tell or re-enact them in different ways.

For example, Desislava Petkova and Paula Strunden re-enacted drawings and sketches by Le Corbusier that draw their style from comic strips. Le Corbusier often used these drawings for lectures and publications, and their communicative and flexible capacities were impressively simulated by the students. They split the architect into a drawing body and a voice, and they embodied the entire interactive process of drawing, reflecting and designing. In this process of embodied re-drawing, the students began to recognise the complexity of the original sketches and to understand how thinking and drawing go hand in hand. (fig. 2)

Similarly, but in quite a different way, Nadja Götze and Jasmin Schienegger simulated Alison and Peter Smithson's 'Patio & Pavilion' concept from 1956. They reconstructed the pavilion and performed the 'as found' principle using contemporary means, chaotically overlapping images and sounds. Avin Fathulla and David Rasner reconstructed Kasimir Malevich's supremacist and two-dimensional architecture drawings using three-dimensional analytical and suspended models. And one final example is the performance of Aldo Rossi's theatre as a memory model with a front and a rear side by Kay Sallier and Doris Scheicher. (figs. 3, 4)

The result was an exhibition of 12 different 're-enactments'. These works are not conventional analytical research: rather, they add new levels of understanding. They revive the procedural and conceptual character of the designs in a way that makes them visible once again, with new aspects that make it possible

2 Desislava Petkova and Paula Strunden re-enact Le Corbusier's sketch from *La ville radieuse*, courtesy Angelika Schnell, Eva Sommeregger and Waltraud Indrist.

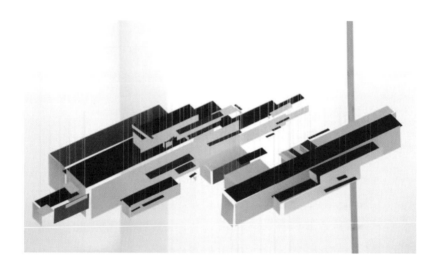

3  A 3d-model by Avin Fathulla and David Rasner in order to demonstrate the flatness
of Kasimir Malevich's *Architektons*, courtesy Angelika Schnell.

4  *Palimpsest of Memories* is the title of Kay Sallier's and Doris Scheicher's Aldo-Rossi-theatre,
courtesy Angelika Schnell

to even touch or listen to the works. By doing this, they reveal and emphasise something: their processual and conceptual character, the 'tacit knowing' of the architectural design process.

One year later, in the studio 'Play Architecture',[17] we continued the results of the previous studio by focusing more on the media techniques of the design process. Undergraduate students were asked to investigate film and animation design techniques in order to visualise the spatial *and* social character of living. Working with well-known works of literature or scientific studies, they were asked to show architecture's role in constructing the interrelationship between the social and the spatial. Not architecture as *coulisse* but as an actor itself. **(figs. 5, 6)**

For example, in a reprogramming of Norbert Elias's structural analysis of the rational spatialisation of etiquette in baroque court society, students Fabian Puttinger, Julian Raffetseder and Jiri Tomicek wrote a computer game program for moving through rooms based on the regulated behaviour of members of the court. In another project by Eva Herunter and Roxy Rieder, a camera literally penetrated the wall of a nineteenth-century Gründerzeit building as a response to Vilém Flusser's statement that the new media blur any kind of inside and outside – that we all become nomadic again. Even though you don't see any people in the video, the visual perception of an almost irreal quality of architecture might only be possible through the perspective of a human being.

In one final example, a student from Hong Kong, Ka Man Lam, visualised Heidegger's famous description of shaping space by building a bridge (in this case the bridge of the river Neckar in Heidelberg) in *Building Dwelling Thinking*. She also critically reconstructed the role of Heidegger's wife in his black forest hut. **(fig. 7)**

Another studio[18] looked at performative character from a teaching perspective. In teaching, 'tacit knowing' has to become 'explicit knowledge'. The studio, 'Design the World – Keeping Up With the Bauhaus', was based on the recognition that despite the huge amount of literature the concrete teaching processes of the different Bauhaus masters is hardly documented. Fragments of letters and notices of former students allowed for a (speculative) reconstruction of their education practice. Based on Oskar Schlemmer's stage and theatre design (and his mechanical ballet) – bringing everyone and everything at the Bauhaus together – they sometimes literally played the Bauhaus masters' roles and by doing so inverted the roles of teacher/jury and student, which was fantastically performed by Svetlana Starygina, who alternately played the master Mies van der Rohe and one of his students. **(figs. 8 - 10)**

17  Taught by Angelika Schnell and Eva Sommeregger (2013–14). See: http://www.designparadigm.net/portfolio/teaching-201314-play-architecture/.
18  Studio led by Angelika Schnell and Achim Reese (2015–14). See: http://www.designparadigm.net/portfolio/design-the-world-keeping-up-with-the-bauhaus/.

5 Fabian Puttinger, Julian Raffetseder and Jiri Tomicek programmed a game based on Norbert Elias'
*The Court Society*, courtesy Fabian Puttinger, Julian Raffetseder, Jiri Tomicek.

6 Vilém Flusser's writings were the blueprint for Eva Herunter's and Roxi Rieder's animation of constantly
penetrated walls and windows in a Viennese Gründerzeit building block, courtesy Eva Herunter, Roxi Rieder.

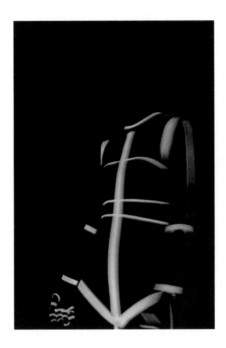

A student, Lea Pflüger performing Paul Klee, asked the audience/jury to do exercises from his famous *Pedagogical Sketchbook*, which convincingly demonstrated the difficulties understanding and even executing Klee's somewhat confusing writing. Meanwhile, students Nadja Krause and Lisa Ungerhofer, disguised as 'mechanical figures', guided the audience to a place where they should do a short yoga course. Physical exercises and embodiment of artistic processes were an essential part of Johannes Itten's teaching programme. Hence, his famous 'Vorkurs' foundation course might be seen as an immediate introduction into 'tacit knowing'. Maximilian Klammer and Duha Samir even visited the last surviving students of the Bauhaus pedagogy in Geneva. (figs 11, 12)

Additionally the audience listened to a reading by Ludwig Hilberseimer (Ella Felber), saw an electronic light show inspired by László Moholy-Nagy (Lukas Strigl) and followed a press conference of a (fictive) detective performed by Jakob Grabher, who desperately wanted to investigate the disappearance of Theo van Doesburg, who secretly established a counter-Bauhaus in Weimar. (fig. 13)

Even the jury tried to understand – and unsuccessfully master – the confusing colour and form theories of Kandinsky. Which of course opens up the question: what are our own limitations as professionals? How often do we cheat our-

7  Nadja Krause as a mechanical figure à la Oskar Schlemmer, guiding the audience/jury through the play: Design the World – *Keeping Up With the Bauhaus*, courtesy Angelika Schnell.

selves or others when we are referring to those masters, without ever looking so precisely at the material? Also important here is the fact that the students dared to face authority – that monument of famous names. They learned to criticise them in a way that, at the same time, maintained a certain respect and curiosity. Through design-based research, and in particular through performative methods, former passive sources become active objects of knowing. This not only allows the next generation to take a more independent approach to new questions and paths, but it also challenges the normativity of 'a rigidly logocentric view of the world',[19] which always doubted the equality of bodily experience for theoretical construction.

19   Gesa Ziemer, *Verletzbare Orte. Entwurf einer praktischen* Ästhetik (Zürich: Diaphanes, 2008)

**8  Svetlana Starygina explains the authoritarian didactics of Ludwig Mies van der Rohe, courtesy Angelika Schnell.**

9  One of the many enigmatic drawing exercises in Paul Klee's *Pädagogisches Skizzenbuch*, performed by Lea Pflüger, courtesy Angelika Schnell.

10  The audience/jury was asked to do some yoga exercises before the show started with director Walter Gropius' (Florian Betat) complaints about the many inner and outer conflicts at the Bauhaus, courtesy Angelika Schnell.

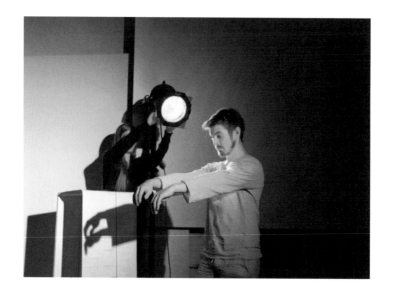

11 Maximilian Klammer performs the esoteric education of Gertrud Grunow,
a lesser known teacher at the Bauhaus, courtesy Angelika Schnell.

12 An electronic light-show by Lukas Strigl, inspired by László Moholy-Nagy,
courtesy Angelika Schnell.

13  Jakob Grabher as a fictive detective, who is searching for traces of Theo van Doesburg in Weimar, who never became a master at the Bauhaus, courtesy Angelika Schnell.

# Debate
# Reading, Writing and Architectural Education

Sony Devabhaktuni (Moderator),
Jonathan Massey, Angelika Schnell

**Sony Devabhaktuni**: I want to start with a point Angelika Schnell made, about making students the actors in the construction of their knowledge and giving them the opportunity to have their own understanding of architectural history. In the last few slides you showed, it seemed that the experiments were not only about a design process, but also experiments in teaching – in how we transmit ideas to students so that they develop an awareness. Jonathan, how do you think this notion of students constructing their knowledge in a design studio could operate: for example, in the studios that take place at the California College of Arts & Crafts?

**Jonathan Massey**: The first thing I would say is that the projects Angelika showed epitomise the ideal of experimental history teaching that my former colleagues Irene Cheng and David Gissen pursue at CCA. By using multiple media and multiple practices, you have created an interaction with the historical archive and an active exploration and testing of ideas rather than a receiving and repeating back of predetermined interpretations. I felt that was a beautiful activation of innovative pedagogy.

I have two thoughts in the context of today's conversations. First, active pedagogy – that is very much discussed, at least in the US – seems

to conform exactly to the Luc Boltanski–Laurent Thévenot thesis that we are training students to be effective producers in the creative economy. This is the explicit measure at CCA much of the time. That is maybe a self-reflection on active pedagogy, which has become fashionable but is also, I find, very compelling. Second: one of the big conversations in higher education in the US right now is about the different learning culture brought by students from China. That is very different from active pedagogy. So, I wonder what all this looks like from here. What does active pedagogy mean in the context of different Asian cultures?

**Angelika Schnell**: Maybe I should answer this double question: first, to the Boltanski work. Of course, for me, it might lead to a quite depressing conclusion that criticism makes no sense at all since finally it is capitalism that is always able to absorb it in a way. But of course, this is also not the position of Boltanski. This doesn't mean that we should no longer be critical or creative. I also think this kind of criticism, in particular this topic, has been investigated based on that typical, old bohemian model of artists of the late nineteenth century – where you try to become a misfit or exist outside of society by being completely autonomous and out of the mainstream. But this type of artist does not exist today. It doesn't matter whether we are designers or critics or theoreticians. We are designers, critics, theoreticians, historians – sometimes all together – and we try to find our position within that mix of situations. And I don't think we should stop being creative or critical, but we should be also be critical about the fact that the others could use our arguments in different ways. Similar to what happens with Mies van der Rohe's buildings in advertisements – something Mies probably would not have liked. But this is how it works. Maybe in 20 years Mies van der Rohe's buildings are completely dated for another reason.

**SD**: I have another question about the idea that architecture at some point stops being critical. When you are talking about methods, you showed a series of drawings of architecture and discussed methods of criticality that engaged new ways of representation. I am wondering if those drawings also at some point lose their criticality and become absorbed into a kind of a normative culture of representation, and if it means that you are always having to re-question those forms: that they no longer work as models. Is this what you are trying to do by having your students re-use them as a way to kind of break them apart?

**AS**: I see them less as representations and more as a performance of the design idea, which makes them different. These design drawings produce not only architecture, but also produce the architects. And they also produce the audience. Therefore, as a historian or a theoretician, I do not want to see them or interpret them as representations alone. At least this is another way to look at them: re-performing them in order to visualise their process-like character.

**JM**: I love that you showed those BMW advertisements. I was schooled in the Manfredo Tafuri lineage, which now has revived the rhetoric of Mies as critical architect. But at least in the work he did subsequent to his immigration to the United States, I have never seen any empirical evidence that the work had any critical impact. In fact, the Seagram building came to epitomise corporate authority. The Barcelona Pavilion as you showed us came to epitomise a certain kind of luxury. And

IIT represents a model of urban redevelopment that devastated African American communities. I do not think that Mies, at least post-immigration to the United States, is a critical architect in any way.

**Françoise Fromonot**: Angelika, from what you showed of your amazing teaching work – which I was not aware of and is really quite incredible – I understand that contrary to Luc Boltanski's analysis, some of the key moments of conceptual design that you are studying and re-enacting still have an active critical power: they still can destabilise accepted thinking, intellectual evaluation and even teaching itself. However, most date back from the inter-war period of the twentieth century – the most creative, sort of idealistic, optimism of the century, as already discussed yesterday – up to the Ville Nouvelle Melun-Senart project by OMA, which was a seminal project for urbanism. We could say that *this* twentieth century – between, let's say, 1920 and 1995 – is somehow closed: with globalisation we have entered another historical period altogether. So today, which ideas and projects do you see taking over that role, and who produces them? Which contemporary production do you foresee having such an active power tomorrow?

**AS**: My first intention was for the students to feel so engaged that they would become aware of the richness of ideas and concepts in architecture of both the twentieth and twenty-first centuries. There is a reservoir of ideas, activities and concepts that have not even been really understood and explored. When I started, I wanted to show that this kind of critical potential is part of modernism itself. It actually started in the late eighteenth century. There were some predecessors, which I now have omitted. Tafuri has brilliantly analysed this involvement of *non*-architectural forces – technical, social, political and so on – into the design process, which makes it critical per definition. And this is what I call the 'designing of the design process'. But it also makes this process so complex that we first have to understand this paradigm. And it really is a paradigm shift. But there are also several continuities between pre-modernist and modernist periods. And this challenges conventional historiography.

What also makes contemporary production quite difficult is the fact that digitalisation changed design production. At first glance, everything looks the same because they all use the same software. I felt that in order to understand what was going on with digitalisation I had to understand more about these digital tools, since I am myself pre-digital. Just a couple of weeks ago, I had my first Rhino workshop to be more aware of these processes. The next step in order to investigate is to really learn how it works.

**Nasrin Seraji:** It is like learning Mandarin. I would just like to interject. I am very glad to see how this platform has sustained itself and has gone beyond what it was to be at the beginning. I think it is also very important to use history as a bridge for projects. When you use history and historical models – such as what we understand as the brief – it forces students to come up with another type of device for design. Therefore, the platform of history and theory and criticism as a design platform was created in order to experiment with how we can actually leave our clothes off and begin to march into the process of design as naked as possible.

I think what is happening is that – of course we are looking at a very specific part of the twentieth century, and also modernism – when it becomes the design brief, then it immediately destabilises thoughts of process and forces you to come up with new ways of designing. I am looking forward to seeing how might change our relationship with the design. It is the beginning of a total paradigm shift as I see it.

**Cole Roskam:** Thank you both for the very stimulating talks. I have a reflection and also a question as someone who has taught here and teaches a discourse class to our year-one MArch students. The idea of history as being a general static idea is challenging. It is challenging to teach history as a design tool, and I will reference comments that both of you made in your papers. Angelika, you began by talking about 1968 in Europe. The way I teach is that you can't understand 1968 in Europe without referencing the Cultural Revolution and the influence of Maoism. For example, you said 'I am sure all of you are aware of the Mies

van der Rohe's collage.' I don't teach it. I teach Arata Isozaki's *Re-ruined Hiroshima* collage from the 1960s to talk about Japanese architectural culture. I wonder if you can talk a little bit about whether you tried to internationalise the discourse you use in the history and design interactions.

And for Jonathan, I applaud your effort to challenge the legacy of Robert Venturi and Denise Scott Brown and *Learning from Las Vegas*, but I use it in my class. I use *Complexity and Contradiction* in architecture. For example, we talk about *Learning from Las Vegas* in my class in part because of the new book *Learning from Shenzhen*. There is a certain kind of canonical value to *Las Vegas,* at least in terms of understanding that reference. Understanding how *Learning From Shenzhen* is organised and contextualised requires at least some awareness of Venturi and Scott Brown. Maybe one way to frame the question is like this: in relation to the international students, which I assume are involved in both of your programmes, how do you see your pedagogy engaging with them or interacting with them and the potential backgrounds they are coming from?

**JM:** Great question. As I am not teaching this days, I don't have much of a granular sense of how this is operating with CCA students. But I do remember a colleague saying she would like to start her urbanism course by asking each student to draw the path that they take to buy a carton of milk or whatever is the corresponding daily food stuff. And then starting the conversation with that kind of reflection on their life-world. This conveys to the students that they can draw on first-hand experiences to open up comparative conversations about how housing and dwelling are organised in different contexts. It was a way to bring out cultural, geographical and socio-economic differences as well as to activate the student not only as a learner but also a holder of knowledge.

**AS:** This is certainly an important question. In particular when experimenting with so many teaching levels and research methods, I always limit myself to topics that I know well: mostly European and North American architecture. But it also goes the other way: At the moment, I teach a Master's studio where the students 'simply' have to write an essay, which is a technique that is familiar to them and familiar to me. And in this studio, there is no specific focus or a specific topic. At the Academy of Fine Arts Vienna there are a lot of students from Eastern Europe or Russia, who often want to address the critical, mostly political, issues of their countries. Here, the students decide on the content.

**Cecilia Chu**: My question relates especially to Jonathan's presentation and the nature of the agency of architecture – agency not confined in the figure of the architect, but involving other agents including those who consume, those who are not just the ones to be educated. These days we talk about architects and expertise. Experts can learn from the everyday and people who consume these problems. That also brings up the question about the theme of the conference: on crisis. The description of the conference itself brings up the neoliberal political economy and the question of how architecture can engage with the neoliberal. I would be interested to hear how, in your teaching and pedagogical practices, you specifically engage with these questions. How do we teach students to understand these complexities? How have design processes been shaped by what has changed in the last 20 or 30 years? Would the neoliberal economy affect different parts of the world in different ways? And in relation to this, if we want students to understand these questions, what other disciplines outside architecture can we engage with? And how do we teach theories associated with that to students who are unlike other students in the social sciences or humanities. Design students may not have a very solid grounding in critical theory or social theory. How do you let them engage with these questions. Do you have any insights on enabling students to gain a criticality for design practice, without the burden of going through all these very heavy, loaded, often European works. That again also address Jonathan's questions about Chinese students coming to America, trying to gain some critical perspectives of design practices. How do you teach them? Are there challenges that you might share with us?

**JM**: That is a big question. I certainly don't have a lot answers but two things come to mind. One is Andrés Jaque's 'Phantom. Mies as Rendered Society' from 2012, which is an amazing pedagogical device. Jaque curated a show at the Barcelona Pavilion of the material in the basement. The podium of Mies van der Rohe's building contains a storage space that is also where the maintenance workers leave their stuff and make their coffee. And it is where the cat that is allowed to roam in the pavilion at night to catch mice, lives during the day. As a result, the cat has lost its vision because it is never in the light. The project therefore pulls up all the repressed elements that are necessary to the functioning of the pavilion up into the curatorial space and embraces them. It is essentially a Latourian exercise of reassembling Miesian architecture. It intersects with disability studies and with non-human theory. It intersects with class questions, taste cultures. There is a pin-up calendar in the basement; many other artifacts introduced by those whose labour sustains the building. It is one example of a pedagogical practice that is very close the kind of work you are doing.

I think also of the feminist art and architecture collaborative project Contested Spaces from the Global Architectural History Teaching Collaborative, which looks in part at the kitchen and the closet. Every culture has some kind of food-preparation space. The kitchen is the most obvious way to open up questions of class, gender, labour and culture. This is a pedagogy that teases out concepts from the objects and relationships – concepts that might be difficult to access just by reading texts but which are manifest very concretely in buildings.

**AS**: For me, as for Jonathan, that is a big question and not so easy to answer. However, seen from the specific context at the Institute for Art and Architecture at the Academy of Fine Arts Vienna, the answer is quite simple. As a teacher I can combine theoretical work with design work. But I find it generally important to read the different theoretical works. For example, we have other departments – fine arts, restoration but also the institute for art and art theory where many lectures and courses are given and where students can learn about this particular field of cultural studies and all these political and cultural contexts in which architecture is embedded.

What your question asks is how we do this with Chinese students. We have an exchange with students from Hong Kong. My impression, as I mentioned, is that these students are extremely engaged and eager to learn. And they very often want to read and study the most difficult texts – for example the writings by Martin Heidegger, even though he is a troubled figure. I am impressed by this engagement, and I do not think that it is necessary to change the teaching programme. And besides this: we, of course, want to learn something from them.

**Audience**: I am interested in the student's point of view because no one has opened up that perspective. I would like to know your point of view on the student workload in architecture because you are talking about studio, but architecture is not just studio. It is one of the most demanding programmes and one that demands the most hours. And I have this feeling that students are conditioned to do more and more and more. And this follows us in the professional field where we end up working for free – for example, competition work. Who else wants to work for free? But we do it because we are conditioned to do more with less. You would never see an engineer say, 'I will do more and not ask to be paid more.'

**JM**: This is one of the biggest topics for architectural educators: the way we socialise students in school into undervaluing their labour and their time and distorting their life priorities. The first thing this does is weed out a lot of people who need to work to earn money in order to study. They are not going to study architecture. It weeds out people in firms when they have to choose between career advancement or family life. It raises profound questions for architectural education. Currently, the average time from starting an architecture degree to becoming licensed in the US is 12 and a half years. And architecture school, at least in the US, requires more contact hours per credit than do other fields of study. So, the way we teach architecture distorts the field in systematic ways.

Sometimes, the worst offenders are actually the avant-garde design practices, including those run by professors. The corporate firms usually at least pay workers for their overtime. Faculty members, whose practices are not necessarily revenue-generating, sometimes just transmit the underpayment and exploitation to their student employees within their practices. The design studio is a good place to start testing alternative pedagogies, because it is where students learn the architectural culture of overwork for under-compensation. You effectively raise the question: can design only be learned in this particular way? Or are there less all-consuming ways to become an effective architect?

**AS**: There are several levels to address there. Personally, I do not have an office. I am not a practising architect. Instead I can give students the opportunity to publish something: a book, for example. My goal with these studios is also to challenge the very rigid curriculum, which has become reality as a consequence of the so-called Bologna process. First of all, it is a didactical goal. But teaching students to experiment with new methods of research and to encourage them to explore their own ideas, their own ways to elaborate and also to develop their personalities, shifts to pedagogy, which is not the same as didactics, but is related to it.

To give you one example from the Bauhaus design studio I showed you, which became somewhat frightening to me: one of the students (she came from Moscow) performed Ludwig Mies van der Rohe. She played the role not only of Mies but also of the student of Mies. So, she constantly changed the sides of the desk. First, she was very authoritarian as Mies who was actually working as a traditional architect: one who lets his students work in his office without paying them. And then she was playing the very devoted student, afraid of the judgment from the god-like master. She was so convincing, and after a while we had the impression that her personality had really changed – in a very positive way, since she has become more self-confident. However, I suddenly found myself in a role for which I never was taught. I have certain didactic goals, but I am not a pedagogue. Experimentation with research and even with teaching methods implies that my own position is challenged.

**Audience**: I want to come back to the question of critique, or criticism, and what it is good for. Because I hear some assumptions in the room: saying critique is to destabilise, or critique is to challenge capitalism, or criticism is a very modernist project. So why should architecture be critical? I think it is more fundamental. Vitruvius places criticism and critique at the beginning of architecture. He talks about people making buildings and discussing his buildings and based on these discussions making improvements and improving buildings, and so coming to architecture.

In the Vitruvian sense, critique plays a fundamental role in the making of architecture. Of course, it can also have very different functions in society. It can be an archetype of political systems, economic systems. It is a problem to mix them. So, why should critique, as a political act, be able to challenge capitalism? Capitalism is an economic system, which is at odds with political systems like democracy or communism. You have to understand that these are different ways of organising society.

When we do critique as architects, it can be a means of social attack: destroying people, destroying students. But it also can be constructive, such as when when we try to improve something in the Vitruvian sense – like discussing and discovering differences. In learning from these differences, we make improvements. But what is criticism? Is it a political act or is it a creative act?

**AS**: Of course, there are many ways to address criticism. We can find many roots of criticism – and as Françoise Fromonot also said, it stems from Greek. But I think the way we use it usually goes back to the enlightenment, as professional critique is a production of enlightenment. We did not have this before. But these people were not defined as critics. We called them thinkers, philosophers, authors, politicians. Cicero was also critical, but we do not call him a critic. It goes back to the French enlightenment and also, I think, in particu-

lar to Kant. He gave a definition of criticism – as I tried to summarise – which is still at the centre of our understanding of criticism. But of course, Luc Boltanski, as I said, has made a study that he calls the 'sociology of criticism', where he has investigated what kind of role criticism plays in society. And one of his outcomes is the 'criticism of criticism' as it is organised along a vertical axis. This establishes hierarchy: there is always one who criticises, who is above, and the other one who is criticised always located below. Maybe this is what you also mentioned as a destructive way of criticism.

**Nasrin Seraji**: I would like to go back to the question of teaching load and learning load. Everything that you say is the perception within every architecture school. It may seem like I'm complaining, but I am looking at the lecture hall and less than one-third of our students are actually here. You can call this discussion a time not of relaxation, but of learning very differently, because as soon as you start engaging the way that you do with the discourse – which then moves your mind to another question, which then brings you back into the core of what you are doing, which is the discipline of architecture – it is in itself a form of critical thinking.

This sort of teaching and learning displaces the concentration that one has in the studio in terms of production. In order to make that understood, we really need to work for it to become a culture, so that we don't have to get you to have this distance between the thing that you are producing and the thing that you think you should produce. One of the biggest problems that most schools of architecture have is the fact that the relationship between collective production and singular production has not been addressed. Architects still think they are the singular producers of architecture. We are not the singular producers of architecture. We have never been. However, we have constantly studied the capacity of the architect to have a singular voice and a singular authority. Since we are not, we need to redesign the collective.

Relating to your point about engineers who don't do work for free – engineers don't accept this condition because one engineer is working on five projects at the same time one architect is working on one project. We are still – fortunately or unfortunately – seen as the people who synthesise the totality of the work itself, even though we don't. It is BIM that is doing it, and it is going to do it more and more whether we like it or not. I am a dinosaur. I am from another part of architecture. I still believe in the capacity of architecture to transform not only the way we live, but also the way we think about world.

But your generation needs to re-evaluate the way that you want to make a change. That change could be working like engineers: you could work on five projects at the same time, and you get paid only for the sections that you do. You can still look at architecture as something that is more social and political, which then has a direct relationship to the economy, whatever that economy is. Or you can be exactly like engineers that work with five projects and only do two hours on each project. And only get paid for those two hours. I usually call those guys corporate architects. Perhaps for you 'corporate' is not a bad, nasty word. It is for me, but not for a lot of other people. I think it is very important to see what kind of architect you want to be.

Because you can also be an architect like those who are in this room: actually contributing to the world of architecture through the written word, the blog, history. I think it is a fantastic time for asking this question. A different curriculum allows for the relationship of those hours to be looked at differently.

I had a fantastic opportunity in a very small institution – only 100 students (75 when I arrived at the Academy, in 2006, and they became 120) – to experiment with a platform system. It did not reduce the amount of work the students were doing, but it changed the impression and the perception of the way they were working. We were not going from one class to another. We were instead part of a research platform where you had a direction, and you wanted to make that amount of work to be what you were bringing to the table. It meant being challenged not by your teachers but by yourself.

# Closing Debate

## Lost in Translation: The Dilemma of Esperanto
Xiaoxuan Lu

I first heard about Esperanto from my grandfather, a Chinese ammunition engineer who worked for nearly ten years in Moscow during the 1950s. While he spoke fluent Russian, my grandfather started learning Esperanto as soon as he arrived in the capital. At that time, the surge of interest in the language was not unique to the Soviet Union, where many young scientists from other socialist countries came for short- and long-term research exchange programmes. Esperanto was also very popular among intellectuals in both China and Japan after the First World War, and my grandfather recalled how his elder brother in Beijing studied the language in the 1920s.

Designed in 1887 by LL Zamenhof, a Polish medical doctor, Esperanto became one of the most widely known artificial languages, one that is still alive today after more than 125 years since its first grammar was published. Zamenhof grew up in Białystok, a multi-ethnic city with people who spoke a wide variety of languages and dialects. In his early years, he witnessed cultural misunderstanding, prejudice and even hatred that resulted from language barriers and miscommunication. The phonology, grammar, vocabulary and semantics of Esperanto are based on the Indo-European languages spoken in Europe. With these roots, it sought to become a global *lingua franca* for the promotion of peace and understanding between people regardless of their distinct geographical locales and native languages.[1]

While this symposium is not focused on linguistic research, the words 'language' and 'translation' have come up often – in part because of the diversity of native tongues that are spoken by participants. On occasions such as this, attendees use English to communicate, even though many may think or articulate ideas for themselves in a different, more familiar language. When speaking about bilingual or multilingual platforms for design criticism, such as websites or magazines, Françoise Fromonot emphasises the tremendous effort that translators make to project themselves into the frameworks and linguistic cultures of their authors. Oftentimes, however, we read texts that are reduced to domesticated

1 Gotelind Müller and Gregor Benton, 'Esperanto and Chinese anarchism in the 1920s and 1930s', *Language Problems & Language Planning* vol 30, no 2 (2006) pp173–192.

paraphrasing that carelessly erases the nuanced expressions and distinct cultural context of the original.

I find that my grandfather's Esperanto story resonates with this discussion. While advocates of Esperanto once praised it as the key to unlocking a door to cultures of the world, critics dismiss the language as 'a-cultural' because of its origin as a standardised technological system and its ascendant adoption during an early wave of globalisation. Indeed, the dilemma of Esperanto mirrors the crisis of the internationalisation of criticism and the crisis of language and translation that we encounter. But perhaps here, we could use the Chinese word for crisis: *Wéijī* (危机), which Chris Brisbin highlights in his contribution: rather than a harbinger of pain and suffering, through *Wéijī* we acknowledge the coexistence of 'danger' and 'opportunity'. This dualism is also reflected as in the dilemma of Esperanto.

Because language and translation are situated at the core of debates about design criticism in our global market, perhaps the best way to mediate the neoliberal drive toward standardisation is not to decry the existence of a global language such as English or Esperanto, but to rethink translation as a critical act. Rather than merely a conduit for works of foreign literature, translators serve as cultural ambassadors who reveal the customs of the authors they are working with: their particular ways of expressing themselves, their sensibilities and their humanity.

The influence of the market on translation is one of many ways in which the hegemony of neoliberal ideas is shaping the critique and discussion of architecture. The final panel touches on others as well: the role of expertise in architectural debate and the siloing of knowledge in academic institutions; the image and its capacity to outrace words in a techno-economic ecology that promotes optimisation and efficiency. Indeed, commercial media platforms render words invisible, and inquiry is degraded into a de-worded process of image-making. All of these issues are imbricated in their causes and results into the larger 'crisis' in which we find ourselves.

By foregrounding the processes of translation and communication in architecture, by being conscious and critical, of and through language, we might be able to take advantage of the opportunity embedded in this crisis. The panel makes an argument that such an effort is essential if we are to enable trans-, multi-, inter-, cross-disciplinary research as well as creative teaching strategies that inspire curiosity and inquisitiveness. The 'opportunity' embedded in such a crisis, the possibility that lies in language, is central to the construction of new bridges between design professions and the public.

We see this in *Criticat*'s publication of critically *re-presented* drawings of architecture – in place of mainstream photos – as a means to reveal under-discussed aspects of buildings and the built environment; or, in *Manifest* journal's experimental para-tours, where objects, buildings and landscapes reveal narratives, fictions and socio-political issues as they are played out in architecture. These decisions and initiatives enable the public to interrogate and validate the information they encounter, and also to access the non-visual qualities and properties of architecture.

The highlight of my grandfather's Esperanto story was that in the early twentieth century a group of Chinese intellectuals who first introduced Esperanto to China, including the linguists Wu Zhihui and Qian Xuantong, advocated the abandonment of Chinese and its replacement with Esperanto; they saw this radical act as essential to accelerating the opening of China to the world, and to the construction of 'a road toward great harmony'.[2] While Esperanto never replaced Chinese as these intellectuals envisioned, similar efforts to standardise and universalise have accompanied neoliberal agendas around the world. The reading of language and translation might help us identify not only danger but also opportunity in the internationalisation of criticism. The crisis could be the possibility for every freethinking individual – architect, writer, critic – to be conscious of his or her capacity to shape language and practice translation as a critical act.

2  Binghui Song, 'The ideal of Esperanto and the translation of the literatures of minor nationalities into Chinese', *Frontiers of Literary Studies in China* vol 1, no 2 (2007) pp 300–313.

# Closing Debate

Cecilia Chu, Xiaoxuan Lu, Eunice Seng (moderators)
Anthony Acciavatti, Chris Brisbin,
Françoise Fromonot, Seng Kuan, Jonathan Massey,
Graham Brenton McKay, Kamran Afshar Naderi,
Angelika Schnell, Nasrin Seraji, Wenjun Zhi

**Cecilia Chu**: In this final session of the symposium, with my colleagues, Lu Xiaoxuan and Eunice Seng, I will post a series of questions for our panellists to respond and debate. This debate will be followed by questions and responses from the floor.

Before we post the first set of questions, I would like to revisit a couple of key phrases that framed the symposium itself, using these to point to several issues that I think we could dwell on a little more to create an opening for the discussion.

The first is that the symposium is supposed to, 'situate architectural criticism today in a global neoliberal market'. We have already heard extremely stimulating discussions on the indispensable role of writing and criticism and how both have helped encourage critical thinking that challenges the status quo. We have also seen inspiring experimental projects in both teaching and practice that deliberately engage with larger social issues arising out of the new liberal marketisation that affects all of us. I have, however, found myself hoping to hear more about the changing relationship between architecture and the neoliberal political economy, which accounts for the forms of crisis we are facing: environmental, ecological, social and so forth.

For instance, it might be interesting to interrogate how neoliberal financialisation has been fundamentally reshaping the processes, criteria, conceptions and values of design in specific ways. And to ask what kinds of new knowledge architects need to acquire – perhaps from outside of the realm of their disciplines – to engage in such processes. How do we achieve this systematically? What are the inherent difficulties for architects to do so? And how might they be compared with those in other built environment professions such as planning, urban design, landscape architecture and real estate? These questions highlight the other key phrase in the symposium brief, which has not been discussed as much as other issues, and that is to consider the 'recurring struggle of universities around the world to place architectural design in a "research" context'. This is an especially urgent question in this part of the world, where the design discipline faces tremendous difficulty legitimising itself in a context in which funding tends to prioritise science-based research that relies on quantification and calculable impacts. This constitutes a huge crisis not only for architecture, but also for humanities-based research. The problem is institutional and operates at a level that shapes teaching, research and practice. Given this crisis, I wonder if more needs to be said and done not just to challenge and critique the capitalist system *per* se, but also to engage with the complex processes that govern research and design production today, where architects operate as labour within particular institutions in the new knowledge economy. How can we reflect on our own arguably subordinate positions within an increasingly neoliberal academia?

The first question is more general and relates the nature and forms of criticism. Are the traditional critiques of capitalism from the left, of commodity fetishisms and of the ideology of institutions still effective weapons in the age of neoliberalism? Are there any blind spots or omissions – silences even – in the progressive architectural theory that emerges from the 1970s onward? Could it happen that the form of critiques themselves actually prevented certain kinds of discussions about the actual forces that have been fundamentally shaping the urban environment and the profession?

The second set of questions is concerned with architectural research. How is it possible for architects to effectively engage with the requirements of today's neo-liberal academy, considering how much we criticise the bureaucrats who decide research funding for not understanding the nature of design practice? What are the best strategies for dealing with this situation? What in your view are the specific knowledges an architect might need to acquire from other disciplines? And what are the challenges of doing so?

This question inevitably requires a degree of reflection on our own institutional and cultural context. Please discuss your position on these issues and how your own institutions and educational training might shape it. Are there any forms of struggle to try to engage with? Conversations with other professions and disciplines?

**Kamran Afshar Naderi:** The situation in Iran is a bit different compared to the other countries. Every country is different. As I have explained, we created our magazine 20 years ago we were working at the state magazine *Abadi*, which was published by the Ministry of Housing and Urban Development. At that time, there were only two magazines in Iran. One was half-government, and the other was a completely governmental magazine. My articles that criticised the architecture establishment or the establishment

of the academy were always rejected because the Ministry of Housing and Urban Development would not accept their publication. We decided we could not continue in this way, so we created our magazine.

Of course, it was not easy in the beginning because we had no funding, but there was a market. We could sell what, for us, was a great number of issues – about 10,00 copies. And then we were obliged to reduce the size of our publication because the price of paper was increasing. Now we sell fewer magazines, even if we could potentially sell double, because paper is so expensive. But we also have a number of sponsors for our activities.

So, there was a shift over two decades from financial control by the state to sponsorship and private funding of our various programmes and publications. This is also the case for universities. When I entered university, before the revolution, there were only four faculties of architecture in Tehran. In Iran there were really very few. Now there are 800. Many are half-private. The effect of this liberal market on magazines was maybe positive, but in the universities, it has not been so positive. For the magazines and the organisations – for example in Sharif and Isfahan, which are freer – it was possible to have symposia and other cultural activities that could be privately funded or organised. But for the state universities, which before the market had few students, big budgets and few well-trained professors, now have too many students. We have tens of thousands of professors in the field of architecture, which means that quality decreases. You cannot have that many good people in teaching. And what has happened is that the magazines and the private organisations are replacing the universities. For example, the Iranian Architectural Centre organises private courses attended by many university students who take part because they feel they lack knowledge in some specific issues: criticism, design, computer skills – issues that are supposed to be university subjects. These private organisations replace what is lacking in not only state university teaching but also in publishing and translation. These are things a university should be doing.

**Chris Brisbin:** I think these questions are clearly interrelated. I don't think we should necessarily be surprised in a globalised neoliberal economy that higher education is getting to a stage where any form of authority or expertise becomes marginalised to a point that the value of what we do and what we say is contradicted effectively by the supposed democratisation of critique and criticism. In fact, everyone has an opinion in terms of the internet and other forms of media.

When we have these kinds of systematic conversations about how we affect change, to me they run contrary to the neoliberal system itself, which demands, systematically, an optimisation: an on-going making of things more efficient to a point where expertise is siloed.

We keep talking about universities trying to transcend the silo, but actually neoliberalism reinforces a silo of knowledge. The kind of rhetoric that I hear in the universities where I have been in the world ('trans-multi-inter-cross-disciplinary research'), which I believe we need in order to ask the right, run contrary to neoliberalism. It wants to silo expertise. We need instead to desegregate knowledge in order to invest in collaborative and collective responses to world's greatest challenges. It is a wicked problem and it requires a fundamental systemic challenge in order for all of us to address this crisis of faith in criticality.

**CC**: Do you have any ideas or strategies for dealing with this situation?

**CB**: A revolution.

**Graham Brenton McKay**: I have mapped all the players in this particular crisis. We have academia, research and academic publishing, which is not widely influencing the global architectural design practices who are themselves the major players in this crisis. Global architectural design practices are interacting directly with commercial media. The commercial media interacts directly back. There is a split: academia and research have been cut off, and this is a big problem that is going to get worse because global architectural design practices are interacting with the commercial media in platforms that don't require words. They have social media managers.

**CB**: This kind of relevance is highly contestable. I think we are just as relevant as we ever have been. I actually fundamentally agree with you that the

media and the way we disseminate our critique is changing and slow to recognise that we do probably need to get more engaged with our public, whoever they might actually be. You need to find other ways to get engaged. I would be more provocative in this final roundtable forum and argue that it is our audience that is lazy. I think we are getting to a stage where our broad public is so disenfranchised with the shear saturation of information in the world that they don't spend the necessary time to search out, interrogate and validate information put in front of them. These are broad cultural concerns.

Architecture and the kinds of questions we are asking about criticism are part of that. We should not be surprised that we have a broad public, and indeed a profession, who do not value what we have to say. Because they actually do not see that it has any impact on what they do. In the Australian context, I have seen a kind of separation between the industry, the public we serve, the clients or even the public that operates within cities, the architectural profession and the academy. Unfortunately, there is an ongoing blame game: that pointing a figure is your fault and a lack of an open, optimistic engagement that you might find in a symposium like this. But we are preaching to the converted in some way. You give your time on a Saturday morning to come here listening to us talk about things you already value. It is something like when I complain about students who are not showing up to lectures to the students who are there.

**Françoise Fromonot**: Maybe we should not have this debate in this amphitheatre. Maybe we should have it outside the university, in Central or in the lobby of the New World Tower. To continue to talk among academics only with the few students and teachers who are already interested is not going to take us far enough. However, this symposium has initiated some debate and, in that respect, these two days were incredibly generative: we mutually discovered what we do and where we eventually differ or disagree. However, it seems that our paths can intersect when it comes to reflecting on the impact on architecture of neoliberalism as a global regime and to thinking about how to question its values: consumption, the obsession with so-called innovation, the way regulations and standards – in an apparent contradiction with liberal economy – are actually crucial for its development. In my view, these kinds of issues are what we have to question, with architecture as a basis. What can we do to reconstruct a political culture from architecture, and more broadly 'environmental arts'? Certainly, rehabilitating editorial activity is one thing. Like Kamran said, what we write *is* read by students and sometimes matters beyond architectural schools, because architecture is somehow of interest to everyone.

**CC**: I wish colleagues from other departments within this Faculty of Architecture could be here to listen because they all participate in the neoliberal economy, planning and real estate especially.

**Seng Kuan**: I am rather intrigued by the term 'neoliberal academy'. I want to get a better sense from the panellists on what exactly you mean by that. I can think of three scenarios where we associate the values of neoliberalism with universities or academies. One is obviously the wealthiest of American private universities – Stanford and Harvard – for which a campaign is measured in the billions of dollars. The second situation applies to the privatisation of universities, especially public ones in the European context or here in Hong Kong at this university where the department of physics and astronomy was essentially cancelled – the concentration was cancelled. And the third dimension is the bureaucratisation of the university structure. These are three dimensions of what I think you mean when using the term neoliberal. But these need to be unpacked carefully. Also, I want to caution that perhaps we are yearning for a golden age of universities and academies that actually never existed.

**CC**: One thing that I have been thinking about is how research within the university context increasingly follows a business model. This definitely affects our research funding and expectations related to architects do research, with terms like 'calculable impact' that are borrowed directly from business models.

**Angelika Schnell**: The difference between academia and architecture is that architecture is always involved in economy more or less. In the past, academia in certain European countries was not hugely affected by the rules of the economy since universities are largely financed by the state. However, this situation has changed and is changing. Neoliberal thoughts and instruments are increasingly penetrating this system.

Seen from my own position within academia as someone who is doing research, and also trying to find funding for research, I would argue that to me it is quite obvious how criticism has become a part of the neoliberal system in academia. I constantly have to evaluate myself. I have to evaluate others, and others are constantly evaluating my work. We are seemingly in a trap because every time you try to protest about the amount of work of evaluating and being evaluated, everybody tells you that this is how research works – that it is intellectual, critical work. However, within the neoliberal logic this work is mainly bureaucratic work, which is constantly growing and leads to an absurd situation, which we really have to question. Because all this bureaucratic evaluation has almost nothing to do with intellectual freedom, which to me is the basis for critical work.

This leads automatically to another aspect of neoliberalism, which makes the situation more complex. Freedom is actually at the centre of liberalism. But, in particular, leftist criticism, which is against the neo-liberal capitalist society, has to be more precise about this criticism, since historically there are intersections. We even have to rethink what Françoise said: what part of neo-liberalism do we agree with? Where are the intersections? It is not as easy as saying 'the neoliberal economy is always against us', or 'we are on the other side'.

We can't escape the common roots of this thinking, but we have to reflect on these roots and on the parts of our thinking that are liberal – which is also part criticism, of course. At the moment, this leftist thinking is also quite weak. It is really a complex situation. If we look at what is going on in the world – in particular the right-wing positions that are becoming increasingly powerful at least in Europe and in the US – we should become even more precise and rethink our position in a more global perspective. Maybe we should come together and write a manifesto. Maybe we can publish in *Manifest*'s next issue.

**CC**: I think probably the other panellists have something to say but I would like to collect a few questions and then we can engage in further discussions.

**FF**: As a response to Seng's question about what is wrong with neoliberal regime in academia, France is one of the last European countries where universities are completely free. A lot of public – taxpayer – money is put into architectural education by top down, state-driven policies. Yet, the anecdote about the end of free entry for people from outside of my architecture school is telling: under the twin pressures of the financing model of private universities and of the type of social control attached to it, such experiments based on the idea of architecture knowledge as a kind of public service become moot. This is a real problem.

**Wenjun Zhi**: In terms of the relationship between the university and the state in China, the state certainly funds universities to be a kind of social service: research as a form of social service. In that sense, it is very meaningful. Universities can utilise that mission to fully engage with the problems of society and to serve society. That's the benefit.

**Anthony Acciavatti**: Given the title of the symposium and the kind of conversation we have been having, I think we can take both solace and be quite scared, that this is not something that only affects architecture and criticism. It is something that many disciplines struggle with. And I think about some of the comments made about getting more people to read what we do, but I tend to think that – because I am trained as an architect but also as a historian of science – what I am supposed to do is to contextualise science: to show that there is a great deal more to weigh about it than just the quantifiable. That it has also been shaped by its own political and cultural contexts. And I think there are a lot of parallels between what I do and what historians of architecture do. When I teach history of science, we look at Charles Darwin, who was terrible at math, and yet the theory of evolution is very much based on a simple arithmetic model. Or we think about Alexander von Humboldt, who transformed the way we think about the environment and planted the seeds of ecology, which is an incredibly powerful science today.

So that is to say, we are working in the dark. And I think we don't necessarily know how things are going to go out into the world. When you look at the way science today is conducted, a great deal of research goes absolutely nowhere but gets transformed into various things. For example, propecia – which we all know of as Rogaine, which makes your hair grow if you have male pattern baldness – was originally developed as a blood thinner. Or Playdoh, which was originally used as a wallpaper cleaner is one of the most popular children's toys. There are many ways of putting things out in the world, and then they get appropriated, used and abused in very different ways. Part of what we are doing here is trying to look around the bend of history. But I think has something to do with not how we reach larger audiences, but how we create an audience for the work we do. This is a challenging task, but there are a few ways we can do it.

For us at *Manifest*, one way was a journal that created a kind of experience economy, and to use neoliberal jargon, developed a base of inside supporters. I also think that at the university level it becomes increasingly important that students outside of architecture take the history of architecture so that they get a better sense of why the built environment is an incredible place to understand and look at politics, society and the sciences at very different angle.

There are a number of ways that we can cut through that layer cake. And part of being an architect and a critic is as much about being omnivorous as it is about being promiscuous. I would say polyandrous as well. I really think we are working in the dark and we have to take a little bit of comfort in that.

**Nasrin Seraji**: Let me just ask something not representative of anybody but representing the practice of architecture. One of the issues that is extremely thorny in schools of architecture around the world is the relationship of practice and research. For most of us practising in various ways at something a bit marginal there a real sort of knuckle fight in terms of this relationship. I don't want to go back to make a history of architecture – going back to the Beaux Arts and traversing the whole history of architectural teaching in academia. However, I think one of the biggest problems we have today is how we situate ourselves within this economic and political condition.

Neoliberal, liberal, liberalism, leftism, not leftism, right, extreme right. They are all extremes and, as Angelika said, complex political situations. Each have different economies, and the architect works with all of them – from fascists to the left to the centre to the radicals to the absolute dictators.

Isn't it time we completely threw out the baby and the bath water – I'm talking about studio teaching – and instead looked at different ways of connecting a set of networks and possibilities into the experience of what you learn in order to create new practices? We know that when an architect goes through five years of school, there a chance that he or she will go out and have a marginal practice. We know them. There are assemblages. Rural Studio was there for 25 years. Everybody tries to be a little bit marginal because we like it. Or as one of the students said the other day, architects are still trying to show that *I am original*.

Where are the cracks for us to move into? How can we open them to create different relationships with the public and the ways in which the public views architecture? How can we work with the public – not only our clients, and not only the users? I have some answers myself, but I am not going to answer my own questions because I have been dealing with this for the past 15 years. However, I would like us to talk about them because they are important. We are here in Hong Kong, and we have a fantastic representation of different places, different schools and different types of teaching gathered here. However, I bet you anything that your relationship to studio and theoretical teaching and criticism is almost exactly the same. So, can we talk a little bit about this relationship of practice and academia?

**Jonathan Massey**: Most academies don't do themselves a great service by emphasising their distance from practice – by teaching modes of practice only in one programme and course that in the US is tightly scripted by the American Institute of Architects protocols and the licensing and registration processes. I agree with Nasrin that my ideal architectural school would constantly discuss questions of what it means to practice. What are the modalities of effectiveness of architecture? And for a school like this, it seems to me that critical finance and critical real estate are the path to success. Hong Kong is the

world's centre of innovation in real estate development. If this school can't harness that and become not marginal but central to the discussion and find agency in tweaking the algorithms rather than in separating from them and proclaiming the autonomy of architecture, then where is it going to happen?

**FF**: Two very important things were said. First, Anthony said we should bring other students to architecture and open up our fortified castle to other disciplines so they can come to us and listen to what we have to say. I would go even further. I would say open the castle up to lay people. We tried to do that in Paris-Belleville, a state run, public school. We opened history and theoretical courses to anybody who wanted to come. And for a time in my amphitheatre, I had up to 20 people who didn't belong in school. One of them was a former bookseller who had retired. There was someone from the municipal planning authority who wanted to become more conversant with the history of architecture. There were students from other schools, such as design schools, and even a couple of college kids. Then suddenly the school administration decided, under the pretext of security or insurance, that these people should register and pay a fee, which would make extra money, like private universities do: this was part of the argument. From one day to the next the experiment collapsed. It is a pity because the presence of older people so eager to learn improved the atmosphere in the amphitheatre, and they were often asking the best questions at the end of the courses. All of it was wonderful for everyone and freely decided by all parts. So that is an example of something that for me is worth fighting for. It may seem small but it is a start.

And the second important thing is that of the studio. It is funny because *Criticat* is thinking of organising a conference in France that could be provocatively called 'Let's Get Rid of the Studio?'. The issue is how we teach studio on the one hand, and other courses on the other. How this increasing balkanisation is splitting what perhaps, in a not so distant past, was more easily linked between things, and what should be a more dynamic and mutually interactive relation between history, theory, construction, studio and so on. Instead we have an archipelago that does not really communicate and this contributes to student workload. They get a series of things that really do not connect into something more dynamic and whole with all the interactions that could be generated in terms critical thinking. So rethinking the studio: maybe not calling it 'studio'.

I am thinking about this example I always have in mind – maybe I fantasise a little bit about it. It is the way Ian McHarg in the 1960s at the University of Pennsylvania Department of Landscape instituted his famous holistic teaching of ecology-based landscape design. There were not only people teaching students, but people learning together about what at a time was a science – ecology – starting to infuse the landscape. Learning alongside these invited guests – from poets to farmers, biologists, engineers and planners – to think together. Architecture also encompasses many fields. For me, academia is that: not just for the reproduction of knowledge, but for learning, thinking and creating collectively.

Finally, my last point: I am always a little bit sceptical talking about *practice*, as a generic term. We should talk about practice-s because there is not just one way to be an architect, and we all testify to that. As almost all of us stated in their presentations, we consider ourselves to act as architects whether we direct an architecture school, we write or we teach architecture. We are the living examples that there are multiple practice-s of architecture and perhaps this fact should be retroactively embedded into academia.

**CC**: Pondering on the question about practice and considering that you brought up the idea of landscape, I think that connecting it with the second set of questions that Lu Xiaoxuan will moderate is a good idea.

**Xiaoxuan Lu**: Cecilia and I are from the Division of Landscape Architecture, which may partially explain why we are talking about landscape and the role of interdisciplinary thinking as a broader critical act. The topic of landscape and interdisciplinary thinking has something to do with my own academic trajectory: a bachelor degree in architecture, a master degree in landscape architecture, and more recently, a doctoral degree in human geography. The spatial and temporal issues that I have been focusing on in the past decade keep changing and, in most cases, expanding from the architectural scale to the landscape and

ecological scale and then to the geographical and geopolitical scale. Each of these transition periods was truly an identity crisis in a positive and rewarding way. It was like the process of learning different languages. Each of the transition periods enables a process of self-criticism, a chance for reflecting on what I did in the previous years. I have two questions for our panelists today, each specifically related to the identity crisis I experienced over the past decade each time I moved from one discipline to another.

The first question is about the duality of inclusion–exclusion. Architects are professionals who are commonly expected to draw boundaries, borders and edges that define a limit within our environment. I wonder how you draw a line in a given project, either within practice or research? What do you include and exclude when you have to make decisions on the scale and scope of your investigation or intervention? Second, how do you respond to a geographical turn in the field of design? Several of our panelists spoke about the act of construction as a tool of political propaganda. We can speak about a shift of scale from building-scale projects such as the $800 million CCTV Headquarters in Beijing by OMA to national-scale projects such as Donald Trump's $15 billion wall that is approximately 3,100km long and then to the transnational- or continental-scale projects such as Xi Jinping's trillion-dollar development strategy, the Belt and Road Initiative, which comprises the involvement of 60 plus countries in Asia and Europe. What is the role of architectural criticism in this expanded field of architecture, and how can you take advantage of the propagandistic nature of these projects to expand either the methods or the tools of criticism?

**JM**: This has been a big part of Aggregate's (Aggregate Architectural History Collaborative) objective: to recognise the modes of agency that happen in the tweaking of bureaucratic regulation and that ripple through a large system. These ripples end up producing shifts in ways that don't map on the conventional scale and scope of architectural practice in the terms that we learn in our professional degree training programmes. I tend to believe in working multiple angles. Take for example the One Belt One Road project. There might be modes of effectiveness and agencies in some of the seemingly arcane protocols that the project will have to go through to get realised. But at the same time, I am thinking of the project that Ron Rael at Berkeley completed – Borderwall as Architecture – that deploys architecture's projective, representational and imaginary capacities to reframe the conversation about Donald Trump's wall. Delving into the systems that will have to be activated to produce these transformations is one mode of architectural effectiveness. Another is the summative, powerful, polemical, visual intervention that architects are trained to create.

**NS**: Before you go further, you have to contextualise the two lines: the theoretical lines. One of them is the line that divides, and the other one is a line to reunite. It would be interesting to talk about these two. Why? Because they are not the same. The line in Mexico is supposed to *not* allow. The line that is One Belt One Road is supposed to reunite a series of cultures and a series of economies. And maybe you can talk about these two.

**JM**: They are both trying to secure a nationalist vision.

**NS**: Sure, but they are also both imagined. They are both propaganda. Let's contextualise both of them. Maybe Lu Xiaoxuan can contextualise it a little for those who don't know. Mexico: it has been tweeted so many times that we know what it is. But One Belt One Road has not been tweeted as much as the other one.

**XL**: In late 2013, China launched the Belt and Road Initiative to strengthen the country's connectivity with the world. 'Belt', refers to the overland routes for road and rail transportation, whereas 'road' refers to the sea routes. Oftentimes referred to as 'China's Marshall Plan' by media and analysts, the BRI is known for accelerating the expansion of large-scale transnational infrastructural projects. I remember Françoise talked about the importance of visiting the project before you start to write about it. The emergence of these transnational- or continental-scale projects definitely challenges the definitions of project and site, and the methods of visiting and writing about them. For example, it took me more than two weeks to drive along the Central Asia–China gas pipeline, which runs from Turkmenistan via Kazakhstan to China.

**Audience**: Where is the best base to conduct

comprehensive research? Without a doubt, the university. And then the highlight of university service is that it has increasing autonomy: like the division and separation of each discipline. When I talk about inter-disciplinarity, we are facing a situation where everyone just wants to protect themselves within their own territory. For example, within our faculty, we barely talk to urban planning and real estate faculties. It is difficult to integrate common research and projects. I would say we have to think about a new form of teaching research and also a new form of practice that can cross boundaries and scales.

This is also the fundamental problem of our trained students. They go out – no matter how well we train them – to work for corporate architects. No matter how many staff members are hired by the corporate sector, they always work on extremely fragmented development projects. There is no way for them to think about anything larger. As a university that aims to conduct innovate practice and education and research, this has to really go across disciplinary scales.

The state is still the ultimate client that the university needs to confront. We cannot say that in a neoliberal economy the state completely disappears – it plays an active role: on the one hand, centralising some land resources, and on the other, abandoning its own responsibilities. But sometimes the state does have good intentions, and sometimes it needs an expert to give good consultation. But the university is not prepared for making that consultation because the university cares about autonomy. Refereed journals and publications are trivial things that do not really lead to this kind of holistic knowledge. I would say that the practice needs to look for a very active engagement with the government, especially the Hong Kong Chinese government.

**SK**: Going back to the lines of architecture and landscape architecture, I just had one quick note. The two institutions I am personally most familiar with – Washington University where I taught for six years, and the Harvard Graduate School of Design where I was a student for many years – both have three-and-a-half-year professional degree programmes, one in architecture and one in landscape architecture. A couple of years ago, I was on a search committee for the new programme director for the MLA programme at Washington University, and one question I had for each of the candidates was whether or not it is possible to institute a one-year diploma programme to embellish the three-and-a-half-year MArch programme to expose them to fundamental courses and to the technical considerations of landscape architecture. The MArch three-and-a-half-year programme in the US is very rigid because of professional requirements. And one question for each of the candidates was whether or not they would even consider this idea of a one-year embellishment.

For them, the sense I got was that in reality it would be very complex. They think that if the integrity of a substantial three-and-a-half-year professional degree in MLA, is somehow reducible to a set of basic skills that you can perhaps acquire in one year, that it is in fact the de-professionalisation of the vocation.

The problem is that the MLA/ MArch joint degree programme at both the GSD and Washington University are exceedingly popular, and to do a joint degree and dual degree that adds two years to what is already a very expensive, highly consuming programme would be difficult. I think it's debatable whether you actually need two professional or just one professional degree along with another package of skills, you can acquire from the school.

**CB**: I think the answer requires a whole new structure and not just folding into one another. We have construction management come to us asking to do a similar thing wanting to create a one-year ad-hoc certificate to allow their graduates to have some kind of written architecture qualification. And we get equally prickly because you end up with a kind of territorialisation of knowledge. I think the only way to transcend that is to really form a new conception of architecture: whether as a cultural practice or as an entrepreneurial set of skills and a knowledge system that we think graduates are going to need.

**AA**: At the Rhode Island School of Design, where I did my undergraduate education, I was taught half by landscape architects and half by architects, and I never realised that they were separated until I went to the GSD, which reminded me of a stereotype of Indian villages separated by caste – the closer the caste, the less they talk to one another across caste.

And the further away they are, the more they talk to one another. That's the kind of typical stereotype.

I really got scared when I went to Princeton and left after a year because it was absolutely terrifying to me to think that architecture had such hard boundaries. But I do think that as a kind of analogy, the boundary can then split it open. This is also where the Andy Warhol analogy comes in, where basically you say: we are the centre. You create a whole culture around it and then kind of transform it. That is why we have the Kardashians today too. You can really draw a clear line between them and Andy Warhol.

I do think that there are a whole other set of issues. I do a lot of research on the National Institute of Design in India, which was set up in the 1950s and which was the first school of design in the developing world. Charles Eames was brought over to actually set it up. The idea was not about training designers to be professionalised, but about training designers at this school of design to go back and forth between the village and the studio to fully infiltrate consumer goods in India. It was meant as a kind of generic model in terms of authoring handmade and industrialised products. Conceptually, it was actually a service-cum-research institute for that state.

The school of design was not in the Bureau of Education, but Commerce and Industry, and it was a complete failure. What happened was that the people who were going to these institutes were often wealthier urban Indians who had absolutely no interest in going out and staying in a village with no running water. There was a whole set of cultural issues to overcome. So, I think there are also limits to what pedagogy can really do for us. But I like the idea of building upon what Jonathan was mentioning, and a number of others as well. That is, thinking of architecture as both a kind of lab science and field science – going back and forth between studio and the greater outdoors like a sinusoidal wave that brings explicit and tacit knowledge into play. This works to privilege amateur knowledge as much as professional, which to me is something unique about architectural education: it is as much about the amateur as it is about the professional mandates and boards that you have to go through.

**Audience**: I agree with Françoise that there is already a crack in academia when you think about the teachers and the seminars, and then the workload itself in the studio. They do not relate to each other. And I have to talk about the example of Vienna, where all the seminars and all the lectures are still – even though they have their own programme and way of teaching – somehow related to the studio, with teachers engaging and questioning that studio. In the end it becomes one project, and this is how it should be. Finally, one decides where to teach and hopefully to enjoy talking about the studio and discussing studio topics, which is kind of rare I would argue at HKU.

**AS**: What is always very important to me is intellectual freedom and encouraging intellectual freedom. This is what makes architecture design studios exciting. You can combine intellectual practice with creative practice and can therefore experiment methodologically with a combination of different disciplines (whose own backgrounds you should be aware of and, which should be taught as well). To me academia has to provide both studio and seminar as an opportunity.

**Audience**: I am a MArch student who graduated from the bachelor programme and experienced the rigid structure that was spoken of earlier. Before my undergraduate work, I went to a local school with a rigid local system and with a regular rate of student suicides due to the academic pressures of both the school and parents. When I came here I experienced the structure of the whole curriculum: a studio with a support spine made up of building technology, visual communication and history and theory.

I also spent a semester at Paris Malaquais when Nasrin Seraji was dean. I was surprised by the student gap in ability. In a way, some were really brilliant, and with others I wondered how they got to that step. But in the end, I found that the gap was a freedom that the school provided for them to experience and engage so that the good ones could explore on their own with the support of the school, and I found that to be absolutely good. At HKU I found instead a rigid system where students were following step-by-step so that in the end they were all were producing at the level of students with the least average ability. I keep thinking that perhaps we have to get rid of the spine and allow for free space to accommodate new topics. What do you think we can get rid of, or what can become optional?

**JM**: I think this is why Nasrin focused us on the question of studio. Because we all recognise, certainly in the US and also here, that this extreme number of credits within the degree dedicated to design is not necessarily what all architects learn from as they make their own paths. Ultimately, their practice might not really draw from their design skills. It might be about negotiating with the contractor. It might be about integrating building technology into the process. The design studio is not only a huge number of credits, but the number of contact hours per credit is extreme. Add to that the number of expected hours outside of class for students to complete the work. We could be smarter about design education. We don't make the smartest use of our students' time. The culture of pin-up reviews leaves a lot of students dozing or facebooking on their phones behind a row of critics engaged in a one-by-one discussion of student projects. And in terms of generating design work: the work that students do at three in the morning is generally not their best work. I think many of us believe that by becoming smarter about the role of design in our degrees, and about how we teach it and how students learn it, then we could do lots of new stuff like what you are talking about.

**CB**: I am in the exact opposite position. I think studio should be the centre of our education. I think we should get rid of everything else.

**NS**: It has been this way for the past two centuries.

**CB**: It is, and I think we should get rid of everything else. Or rather at least fold those into studio. What we should be doing is actually looking into the modalities and pedagogies that occurred within different kinds of learning environments. I would be very hesitant about an architectural education that does not actually design or that does not put the vocation of a practitioner front and centre in what we actually do. But as for the expectations and the tools we expose students to – here I think we are still caught in the nineteenth century.

**AS**: The study of architecture is one of the very rare studies where you have a variety of different cultures of curricula. There have been more technically oriented schools: technical universities, the art academies, the Bauhaus tradition. In the US, there is a different culture of teaching architecture than in western Europe or here in Asia. Of course, I know you can't actually judge all of them. In itself it is interesting that there are so many models for teaching architecture. This already says that there is not one *via regia,* or royal path and says a lot about the discipline itself. And even though – and at least you had the opportunity to study at Malaquais, which already gave you the opportunity to compare two completely different systems – you can't take all of them, to see and experience and test and reflect on two systems is already useful. There are not so many studies where you have this kind of opportunity. I would not say one is better than the other. Maybe you will find your way because you have already started to compare and to reflect.

**Audience**: The topic that has not yet been addressed is even if you try to create these innovative programmes, you are still not looking at the core of the university structure where we still review and evaluate the work with a critique, which is quite an old idea that is not working. Yet this is still in every university and every subject. It gives you an attitude to devalue your work because you know you present two months of work in two minutes to a group of strangers who don't know you. We can be really innovative in what we say and how we teach, but ultimately the system is the same one that has been here for years.

**AS**: My proposal is to strike for a better education. I once did it when I was student. This was the best semester in the whole of my studies. It was the only semester where I spent every single day at the university because we had so much work to organise: the strike and a variety of events, lectures, panel discussions, writings, etc. The strike was the beginning of my career as an architecture theoretician.

**Eunice Seng**: I want to pick that up because I think what the audience member has touched on, is how critique is dished up and how critique is performed. For the most part we have discussing criticism in writing, but we have not talked about the process whereby critique happens.

**CB**: We are obviously talking about the pedagogical role of critique within the academy. We often believe that critical thinking – at least idealistically – occurs within the critique. But in my upcoming co-edited book, *The Routledge Companion to Criticality in Art, Architecture, and Design*, one of the contributors, Michael Newall from the University of Kent, is writing a history of the critique within the art academy, and it struck me that there is no parallel history within architectural discourse from the Bauhaus to now, either in terms of the different ways in which the critique enables or destabilises student thinking, or in terms of how we assess measured learning, which is starting to affect critique. The kinds of derivative documents I see filter down from 'teaching and learning' bureaucrats within certain universities, turn the critique into a kind of matrix: a box-ticking exercise rather than a mutual obligation through which tutor and student search for value, and in which criticality itself seeks to answer concrete questions that are being explored through projects. This suggests that student works are themselves less and less engaged in asking questions and more in answering and being constructed by these derivative checklists. Within the visual arts there is a whole series of other critiques that we just don't use within architecture. I still feel very wary whenever I am involved within my own visual arts school. For 40 minutes, we as a panel sit in the room, absorbing a work before any kind of discussion. It has become about interpretative modes of operation. For architecture academies it becomes about minimum compliancy standards because they are predicated on being vocational institutions to generate graduates.

**NS**: We are talking about different things here: criticism, criticality, critique and criticism in architecture schools. But criticism in architecture school has become evaluation, and it is no longer criticism. In the 1980s, when you were in a critique at the Architectural Association School of Architecture, there were plenty of discussions that would turn into debates. Each project was the perfect example or the perfect sort of articulation between a series of thoughts that would trigger a series of discussions and debate. The question here leads us to believe that the student basically thinks they are pinning up their project in order to be evaluated. We are in the twenty-first century – the spreadsheet-evaluation century. It is going to be very difficult to bring this past culture back, but we need to build another culture that asks what does this former sort of debate and collective discussion allow for? How does it fit into teaching and how does it fit into learning? I think one of the biggest desires that we have in most of the schools – and I always say this to the teachers on the panels with me – is let's not do another desk crit! Let's have a discussion. We are not talking about what is correct or what is wrong, but students get into an automatic situation of 'What do I do to please you?', and 'What do I do to please them?', and 'How can this be evaluated?'

**FF:** But it is exactly the same in architectural criticism. Architects provide critics with stuff they they want them to write about. Then critics evaluate more or less and say it's a good building. That's exactly what happens. In my work as a critic and studio teacher I judge the buildings and the work of the students by the quality of debate they are able to initiate. I think that is a different criterion for criticism.

**Audience:** What I found here was that in the first few weeks, I tried to engage in questioning during the review and it felt completely foreign, with everyone looking at me as if to say 'what are you doing'. I had a feeling that I was going nuts. The general discussion felt like the reviewers in the front with the professors and all the students at the back.

**Audience:** It's very hierarchical

**Audience:** Yes, exactly. It is also just a matter of how the professors situate themselves in the classroom. It is also maybe a sense not exactly of sympathy but of relating to the students as well. Some professors say 'I did the same thing and now it's your turn.' There is never a reckoning, as if to say 'maybe it was wrong, and it should be changed'. Even though students can revolt, it comes down to where the professors situate themselves.

**ES:** In this case I was the professor.

**Audience:** A lot of us are situated between ideology and practice. Ideologically we are on the same ground – a kind of openness where knowledge production is valued over simply knowledge transmission. But at a fundamental level, when we think about architecture as a practice or as a

discipline, we in the room are part of the discursive community. We also have to go back to reflect on how we position ourselves in the larger society. This student hits the nail on the head by talking about the context. As educators, we all are fundamentally transmitting knowledge and producing knowledge. We hope that in ten or 20 years you are also part of it. We hope that this community is also as diverse and that it has opened and that it is not as hierarchical. In all this talk of crisis, it is hopeful that all of us who are teaching in schools are transmitting and producing knowledge. That is now our only obligation or responsibility to the future of the discipline.

**NS:** I am not interested in transmitting knowledge. I maybe transmitting interest and creating a site, whereby those of us who are on it, around it and in it can began to understand our own coordinates within the discipline of architecture. I am not interested in transmitting knowledge because I don't know the channels of transmission, and every time I want to transmit something I fall into a radio programme. It is a big problem that we are not being more radical about the ways we position ourselves within the universities.

Architecture has come to the universities only recently. Our models have been inherited. Now architecture has the capacity of being as wide as possible. However, when it goes into the university, it becomes restricted. Why? Architecture has windows, but when it goes to the university it becomes a bunker. It becomes something that nobody comes into except two students from Sciences-Po that are on exchange at HKU. They come into this horrible looking amphitheatre that we have made only slightly better by painting 'architecture' grey and putting white plexiglass on the table so it looks a little bit sunnier. Why is that we don't interest more people on a Saturday morning? Have they all gone shopping? This is a problem. We have to face it that we no longer interest anyone. How can we? Are we going to strip naked and run around streets? How are we going to interest people in architecture and show them that it is much greater than what everybody thinks it is? By greater I mean its importance in terms of its relationship to society and politics.

**AA:** There are ways in which architecture indirectly

reaches out to the world. I think about the way in which many people I know in the movie and film industry look to student work to shape their set designs. They look at what is happening in architecture studios. That is an interesting and indirect way in which architecture goes out to the world and becomes a kind of set upon which any number of narratives, fictions and political or social issues are played out.

**CB**: But do we need more stuff out there? That is not a transmission of knowledge. It certainly does not answer the call for a different kind of engagement. How do you bring together and unfold different kinds of disciplinary approaches and methodologies? How do you also create the link between the field work, as you were suggesting, Anthony, and the laboratory work. What does it look like?

**NS**: I want to bring up two or three issues. I think that in the west, and in those countries that have eaily adopted western models, we are extremely saturated. I remember exactly 12 years ago in Iran being invited for the *Memar* Prize and talking to a younger architect who asked, 'You are the head of this. You are the chair of that – why don't you come back to Iran after all these years and do something here?' And cowardly – or being afraid of what I would do in my home country where I can't speak my own language – I said: 'No I can't, but why don't I begin to engage with the place in a different way?'

I proposed a school that would be site-less and start each year with a conference series that the students could actually use as a way of hearing other voices beyond the university lectures they were involved in. I opened the first one myself and gave two days of three types of lectures with workshops that followed. This became something that was replicated and a variety of people came and gave lectures. There were 2,000–3,000 students every time. You could not find a place to sit. There was a fee, and students in Iran couldn't pay that much (of course, there was a discount for students). However, some travelled 3,000km to hear these lectures. Perhaps they came because there were not enough lectures at their own universities. In the west and places like Hong Kong, we have too many of these lectures. So, I'm thinking now of abolishing the studio, cancelling the lectures

and only having this symposium once a year. Maybe next year this auditorium will be full because everybody would love to go to a lecture if there hasn't been anything else all year. We really need to get radical. Revolution happens from creating, There is no more bread. There's no more water. In schools of architecture there are no more lectures. You are going to have more time to do nothing. So perhaps doing nothing is going to be a way of interesting our students.

**ES**: Because I have the pleasure of wrapping up, I would like to bring us back to the question of crisis. Last night I sent a call to 25 students asking for questions because some are too shy and some cannot make it today even though they had attended earlier sessions. I wanted segue with their question submitted by the representative for the final fourth year of the undergraduate BAAS programme. 'What tools or suggestions or advice do you have for someone who has to graduate and then deal with the world of capitalism and bureaucracy? How do we think critically and how should we position ourselves? What are the tools for struggling' – struggle is repeated multiple times in this question – 'with clients, with the capitalist agenda and the government's bureaucracy?' And so, before I give it back to you, we have been talking about crisis so much, perhaps we can talk about *what* crisis.

We are in a very affluent of town, and we were talking about the presence of the studio. I think, 'What crisis? Whose crisis?' Is it the academy's crisis or the students' crisis? In the conversation with the studio, I constantly feel I am the only one in crisis. We can start the conversation about platforms and tools and our roles as facilitators. Do we join the revolution? Another thing that came out was the space for contemplation, which goes back to this notion of production. A lot of us here are engaging in writing and thinking and the nature of producing a design. The inherent paradox between making and thinking is one that we all struggle with. How to produce crisis?

**GBM**: Only until about 200 years ago, many people knew about architecture by etchings of architecture: illustrations of buildings, often commissioned by their owners. But photography changed all that in the early twentieth century. Now we are in a situation where architecture is comprehended as image.

So maybe we could just roll over and think about what an Instagram-able architecture could be. I'm sure someone somewhere is already perfecting it.

**CB**: I don't think we have to see it pejoratively, which is part of what I was suggesting yesterday. I think it is an opportunity. Certainly, many of us are trying to flesh out how we can see that as a specific kind of opportunity. One of the most disturbing things that I ever heard in studio was a unit-coordinator who a year ago in his briefing to his students at another university in a final year studio had suggested that they should start planning what image they were going to post on Instagram in graduation. He was not much older than those students, and I found that incredibly destabilising towards our own sense of disciplinarity – that you can reduce an entire education to a singular image. That is incredibly disturbing. Perhaps the crisis is something that we hold more dear than others. But in terms of the student's question I don't think it is an issue of the tools we are providing.

**CB**: It does go back to what Nasrin suggested. It might surprise many of you that I actually I spent ten years in the Australian defence forces as a soldier before I had a career in architecture. Straight out of high school I didn't have the grades to go to architecture school. It seemed like the right idea at that time and I found that in training we had our hands held. Everything we asked were do was constantly framed and reframed. There is no way you can fail any form of the system. In the defence force, you would just be retrained and reassessed. If you failed, you'd be re-trained, reassessed. It created a servient environment and an environment where no one asked questions and everyone was just simply a Fordian outcome of a system. I see this happening with the kinds of learning or teaching mechanisms we have been discussing.

When the student asks those kinds of questions, I also find it uncomfortable because it suggests that they expect us to have the answers. We are not the gatekeepers of knowledge. Some of the pedagogical shifts we are talking about are engaging in a kind of collaborative knowledge that starts to fold multiple modalities together in order to generate new ways of thinking about and operating in the world. Students actually have to see that their role in practice is no longer vocational

but perhaps about advocacy – advocating for the city, advocating cultural values. They need to have a strong ethical and moral compass about who they are and why they operate in particular ways.

**ES**: Why do you advocate for only studio and why does Jonathan say no studio?

**CB**: It might be about terminology. Maybe we are actually talking about the same thing. I am talking about a centralised kind of design, rather than studio-based. Design can then fold other different kinds of disciplinary practices together. That is the kind of model I prefer.

**ES**: Do history and other things that haven't been folded into design fall in that model?

**CB**: I find part of this conversation very interesting because it's how we teach right now at my university. There are studios centred around particular agendas, not just in terms of a thematic but there are multidisciplinary staff who deliberately juxtapose against each other in order to explore important problems. We do this not to provide answers, but to see studio as a way to flesh out a knowledge system that grounds students so that they can engage that system over the next ten years after they graduate.

**Audience**: I think this is also relevant to the comment about how architecture is becoming visual. It is also a question of the type of work expected – because you would never hand in an essay for a studio for submission. Professors would not accept it. You have to produce and you are taught to produce. So maybe the struggle is that you want to, on your own, try a multidisciplinary way of thinking but you remain stuck in the same structure of what you are expected to hand in. How could the system be more accepting to different forms of thinking?

**Audience**: I am a full-time international masters student at HKU and did my undergraduate degree at the University of Melbourne. I just had a comment about crisis or about how do you produce crisis. What I wonder is whether there is really crisis within the students and in the environment in Hong Kong. I've found that students don't speak to tutors. They are not necessarily honest with their tutors. I am an outspoken and honest person, and so this is a completely different environment than in Melbourne. I often feel I am the only one speaking. I do wonder what crisis is really happening – is it a crisis with the teachers, or is it happening between the students? Or is it suppressed by a kind of overarching bureaucracy or hierarchy? Or does it go back to the previous point: where does the professor put themselves in the classroom? I am lucky enough to have a studio teacher who puts herself within the students, and our critiques have been run in discussion type formats. This was fantastic because you learn how to pose questions to other students, which teaches you a lot more than learning how to make a good plan.

**NS**: I don't know if I want to answer immediately or not, but I just want to make a point here: there are teachers who believe in architecture. There are teachers in architecture and also in landscape architecture who believe that their disciplines can still save the world. And there are teachers who think that we can maybe save the world, we have to ask ourselves questions and know the world. There is a big difference between the way they relate to their students and the people they are working with.

I think the question that you bring up is extremely important in terms of how an institution can enable its students, first of all, not to be afraid of anything, and secondly, to teach them that being afraid of something is actually stopping them from being the architects they want to be. And thirdly an institution can teach students to ask questions in such a way that they never need to ask the question of 'what tools can they have'.

I don't want to go back to the 1970s and 1980s because as soon as you start doing that you sound some like old fart. I think that what has become apparent is that the crisis is different for different cultures. At Malaquais there were some students who couldn't even run a cold bath, while others could actually become very important debating architects – maybe not producing architecture – in places where they could actually change things.

The most radical thing today has to be for us to search and find out how our students can be more inquisitive about the world around them.

They don't need to be told what to do. One of the biggest problems we have in architectural education today is how we allow that curiosity and inquisitiveness to come back. How not to be in a position of being laid back. Our teachers do it and do it with every ounce of energy they have and there are teachers that are not doing it.

As heads of programmes, as deans, as leaders or simply as people interested in the progress of the discipline of architecture in these discursive ways, we need to think about how to actually change the status quo and encourage students who are interested in, or think they are interested in, architecture to branch out to other things. To allow architectural education to widen the range of possibilities. No matter how much building in the street booms because of economy, it is not going to allow us to make a dent in society. Architects are only good when they can make dents in societies – not to rip society apart but actually to make changes, or at the very least visions, of these changes. It is really problematic when a student is desperately asking about why he continues to be an architect while hating to be the kind of architect everybody wants him to be. This is what the discipline of the building architect demands of everyone.

I would be for abolishing accreditation and no regulation by any practising body. The only thing the practising body is interested in is creating labour for themselves. As soon as you create – as Ian McHarg would have said – a relationship of labour to therefore master labour in architecture, architecture disappears. The more that students – those of you who are present – think that you are going to become the future labour of the building industry, the less you are going to do architecture. The more you think you are not going to be part of that labour, and the more you think you are going to deal with the crisis of architecture today, and the more you think of how you are going to actually create these new practices for yourselves, the less you are going to ask what tools there are because whatever there is you are going to *make a tool out of it*. You are going to create your own tools. That is why I say I cannot prescribe your tools for drinking. I can drink out of my own hands.

**ES**: One of the few things that come up in terms

of the language of criticism is maybe the language of asking the question – learning how to formulate the question. I don't think it is unique to HKU that the programme doesn't exactly give you the tools to formulate the question. And the best of the students could do that efficiently, verbally. But that doesn't mean that there is a lack of curiosity, but there are other issues in terms of platforms, exposures. I would like to bring it back to the table to see if there are any closing comments and particularly any reflections on the last two days.

**GBM**: It's about reading and writing criticism as the only way we can show the value of the non-visual qualities of architecture.

**CB**: I think it is important to have a better understanding of the neoliberal economy. I think we need to make that front and centre in what we do. We are fundamentally part of that system, so I think we need to become more versed in it. And we need to become the agency of change within that system, and recognise the opportunities that education provides.

**FF**: I would like to say that I am very puzzled in a good way by the turn of this morning. Usually these closing sessions are a reiteration of what we have already said. We haven't had time to digest it. We need time to think about it. We are tired and we go for an easy ending. But then your questions as students came in, and those of you who spoke have exercised what we constantly advocate, which is criticism and questioning. I think you have succeeded in doing what we are advocating, which is to destabilise the debate because you ask questions. As much as we say we should be critical, we are all in our own bubbles, in our own sort of trained selves and in things we have spoken on, exhibited, talked about during these past two days. Suddenly you come in to the picture. The questions you asked are important because you asked them to yourselves. I feel that I have really learned something I did not know. The other thing I noticed is the only students who talked were women. I wonder if there should be an equal opportunity for criticism from men at this school. Yes, there was Thomas – in the form of a sort of SMS. So, think about that. If the university hopes to become a mirror of society, this state of things to be questioned is also part of the picture.

**AA**: I think it is important the way in which writing criticism is tied to reflection and to thinking critically. When I teach urban history at Colombia University I always begin by asking 'Who in this country do you think you have a fiduciary responsibility to as architects?' And these are students from all over the world. The majority come from China. Many of the students say their responsibility is to the client. And who is the client? The person who is paying for the work. And I tell them, 'No, in the context of the US at least, your fiduciary responsibility is actually to society.' Whatever that means. We don't go into great detail about what constitutes society, but it makes architectural history unique in that it is very important at a very pragmatic level – in the context of the US – to know the history of architecture because you can be liable if you do something that maybe has been done before that clearly doesn't work or that creates harm or injury. That is a base or platform on which to talk about the importance and relevance of history and to get students involved in critiquing projects and thinking about their own work. This creates a reflexive atmosphere for discussion. The questions they have in studio and the questions they encounter in their history and theory courses start to form a larger and more productive cycle and discourse. The relationship of thinking, drawing and also writing is also critical to architects and to the imparting and the cultivation of architectural knowledge.

**JM**: I would like to thank our hosts here at HKU for inviting us into what seems to be a rich process of figuring out how your own mission and practices might evolve in a context of rapid transformation in China, in Hong Kong's relationship to China. Those macro changes are triggering all kinds of questions for architecture, culture practice and pedagogy. I think the primary outcome of this symposium will take place here, in the department, but those of us from outside are taking away some very different perceptions and perspectives on what we are doing as well.

**ZW**: It is an international symposium but architecture is a discipline facing different crises, so it is interesting for me to learn different opinions from different areas.

**KAN**: In Iran, you never put all critics in one room. It is impossible. Maybe because we are very critical and obsessed, but maybe also because such gathering involves discussions about politics and about other things. Somebody says that in Iran there is freedom of speech, but there is not freedom after. It is the reason that the symposium has been very fruitful for me. The experience of being together as critics always happens to me in other countries and it has been very interesting.

**AS**: You mentioned something important: – that there might be consequences, and sometimes very unpleasant consequences, of criticism. Every kind of criticism does have a political dimension in it, which means that I wasn't joking when I said just organise a strike. Of course, it is not necessarily a strike. Maybe you can find other ways of protest. What is the next step after criticism? You have to identify the kind of political message or political issue within it. You then have to talk about that message and position yourself. You have to fight your own ways, to argue through issues in order to improve your situation.

**SK**: I think doing away with accred- itation is a wonderful idea.

**NS**: As a practising architect, who has probably spent more time in schools then in my office, I can say that this is the way I like to do a project. You come into a place, you have a site. The site for me now is HKU. You have material in there. You have intelligence. You have people that have made the place. You have students. You have fantastic, excru- ciatingly beautiful geography. You also have politics and an immense amount of money circulating in the city, the third most important finance centre in the world. Of course, I am not alone in this. I am here with my colleagues and we have you the students and you this panel that gets together to discuss that burning question I have, which is: how do we react to the question of teaching and learning architecture differently here than in other schools such as Cornell, Princeton, the Academy of Fine Arts, Malaquais? How do we make something that becomes specific to this place, to this geography, to this context and to this culture? I have noted many things. You have been the ingredients of many ideas, which could see the end of the day or could be lost as they go along.

I am delighted that we have been able to go through these two days of intense positioning, debate and also disagreeing. Because I really believe that

disagreement in architecture is the fuel of radical thinking. When we came together and when I asked Lu and Sony to help me put this symposium together, it wasn't that we wanted to present our situation of architecture as a crisis. We were thinking of how architecture critic Ada Louise Huxtable responded to a reporter who asked her, 'And Madame, what are you doing in criticism?' She said, 'I am go- ing from crisis to crisis.' This was the 1980s and whe was talking about postmodernism, and when modernism was at the crossroads of confusion.

We have talked about magazines as forms of new schools; critical thinking as a new way of desta- bilising schools; words, if we want to be tough, and difficult like myself, as new guns – and it is very difficult for an Iranian to say 'guns'. Maybe the salon of the eighteenth century has been long been destabilised, even though we are in the situation of a salon here because we are among ourselves. But as Françoise said, maybe we should go to the public space. Maybe we should occupy Central and beyond. Maybe we should occupy everything in order to not make ourselves more relevant be- cause we are, but to make others understand that architecture is their business and not only ours.

Perhaps if *open* universities are the things of the twentieth century, we now have to go to the moving universities. Would we do revolutions or resis- tance? I don't know. These are all words of the twentieth century. Perhaps we do need to make a common language so that our real estate and urban planning colleagues come into this room.

**Nasrin Seraji** (AA dipl FRIBA- ONM, OAL) has pursued a path constantly enriched by her simultaneous engagement in architectural practice, teaching and research. After studying at the Architectural Association and practicing in London, she moved to Paris in 1989 to establish her studio where architecture is treated as both a cultural debate and a critical practice. After studying at the Architectural Association and practicing in London, Nasrin Seraji (AA dipl FRIBA- ONM, OAL) moved to Paris in 1989 to establish her studio where architecture is treated as both a cultural debate and a critical practice. She has pursued a path constantly enriched by her simultaneous engagement in architectural practice, teaching and research. She has lectured and exhibited her work in Europe and North America, as well as China and South East Asia. She has taught at the Architectural Association in London and taken on leadership roles in several schools of architecture. She was, notably, Professor and Chair of the Department of Architecture at Cornell University, head of the Institute of art and architecture at the Academy of Fine Arts in Vienna and, for ten years, Dean of the École *Nationale Supérieure d'Architecture Paris-Malaquais* before being appointed head and professor of architecture at the University of Hong Kong.

Architect of the award-winning Temporary American Centre in Paris, Seraji has completed several significant buildings, notably a 30,000sqm complex for the Transport Authority of Paris comprised of 213 housing units, a bus depot, a kindergarten and shops. She has authored numerous competitions for student and affordable housing as well as urban plans in Southeast Asia, Europe and the French cities of Le Rheu, Marseilles, Lyon, Montpelier, Caen and Pau. Recently a private and social housing complex brought the prestigious *Mention de l'Équerre d'Argent* to her practice. Seraji has received recognition from the French government for her contributions to architecture. She is a *Chevalier de l'Ordre National de la Légion d'Honneur,* as well as *Officier de l'Ordre Nationale du Mérite* and *Officier de l'Ordre des Arts et des Lettres.*

**Eunice M. F. Seng** is Associate Professor and Chair of the Departmental Research Postgraduate Committee in Architecture at the University of Hong Kong; and Founding Principal of SKEW Collaborative Shanghai-Hong Kong. She is founding member of Docomomo HK, member of Asia Urban Lab, Singapore, and co-director of the Singapore Institute of Architects Archifest 2017. Trained as an architect and architectural historian, her work explores various disciplinary intersections and questions of agency in architecture. Her research interests include the histories and theories of modernity, modern domesticity, housing and the metropolis, politics of power, utopias, artefacts and their cultural representations.

**Françoise Fromonot** is an architect and critic based in Paris. She has taught and lectured worldwide on contemporary architecture and urban design, and is currently Professor (design, history and theory) at the Ecole nationale supérieure d'architecture de Paris-Belleville and William Wayne Caudill Visiting Professor of Architecture, Rice University, Houston, TX. A contributing editor to *l'Architecture d'Aujourd'hui* (Paris), joint editor of *le visiteur* (Paris), columnist for *A+* (Brussels), she is the author of numerous monographs and essays, including *Glenn Murcutt: Buildings and Projects* (Electa, 1995 and 2003), *Jørn Utzon and the Sydney Opera House* (Electa, 1998) – both recipients of the 'Architecture book of the year' award from the French Architecture Academy, Paris – and *La Campagne des Halles* (La Fabrique, 2005), a critical account of the latest urban competition for the renovation of central Paris. She is a founding member of and contributing editor to the Paris-based architecture journal *Criticat* (www.criticat.fr); a selection of articles from the first ten issues, entitled *Yours Critically*, appeared in English in 2016.

**Kamran Afshar Naderi,** freelance architect, Branch Manager of Artelia Engineering Company (based in Paris), architecture critic and co-founder of the *Memar Magazine*, began his professional career in 1986 in Italy. Until 1993 he collaborated with several well-known Italian and international companies such as Renzo Piano Building Workshop. As a design team member, he was involved in Kansai Airport (Osaka) and Lingotto rehabilitation projects (Turin). In 1993, he established his own office in Tehran. He has completed several projects for international organizations and companies in Tehran: projects for the embassies of Italy, Denmark, Austria, the Netherlands, Japan and Norway, the Italian School, the UNDP, the World Bank, Nuovo Pignone, Shell, MAN Ferrostaal, Bayer, Festo, Ebara and Roche. Since 1993, Afshar Naderi has taught non-continuously at Azad and Soureh Universities of Tehran. He has published around 180 articles and three books: *Istituzioni colletive nelle citta' Islamiche* (Electa, 1987), *Iranian Architecture* (Tehran, 2003), *The Gardens of Paradise* (Rome, 2007). His essays and interviews are published in Iran, Italy, England, Switzerland, Kuwait, Turkey, Cyprus, China and Germany. In 1998, Afshar Naderi and Soheila Beski, founded *Memar Magazine*. He continues to be a partner of the magazine and member of the editorial board.

**Graham Brenton McKay** is an independent architecture writer, critic, blogger, and lecturer currently living in Dubai. His blog, Misfits' Architecture, links an informal network of practitioners, instructors and students around the world. McKay deals with universal themes such as architecture's relationship with art, nature, technology, society and education. Refusing to let the idea of social responsibility in architecture die, McKay highlights the foibles and dissects the statements of architecture media stars and the self-styled avant-garde. With equal regularity, he celebrates those misfit architects whose contribution to better performing buildings has never been fully appreciated, Josef Frank being his most recent honoree. McKay is currently a lecturer at Department of Architectural Engineering at the University of Sharjah.

**Cole Roskam** is Associate Professor of Architectural History in the Department of Architecture at The University of Hong Kong. His research examines architecture's role in mediating moments of transnational interaction and exchange between China and other parts of the world. He holds master's and doctoral degrees in art and architectural history from Harvard University. His research has been supported by the Graham Foundation for Advanced Studies in the Fine Arts, the Fulbright-Hays Program, the Mellon Foundation/American Council of Learned Societies (ACLS), the Society of Architectural Historians, the Center for Advanced Study in the Visual Arts (CASVA), and the University Grants Committee of the Hong Kong Special Administrative Region, among others. His articles and essays have appeared in *AD* (*Architectural Design*), *Architectural History*, *Artforum International*, *Grey Room*, the *Journal of Architectural Education*, and the *Journal of the Society of Architectural Historians*. His first book, *Improvised City: Architecture and Governance in Shanghai, 1843-1937*, will be published by the University of Washington Press in early 2019. He is currently at work on his second book-length project, *Designing Reform: Architecture in the People's Republic of China, 1972-1989*, which is under contract with Yale University Press.

**Seng Kuan** is an architectural historian with teaching appointments at the University of Tokyo and the Harvard Graduate School of Design. He previously taught at Washington University in St. Louis and the Chinese University of Hong Kong. He has written extensively on Japan's postwar architectural culture, especially on the Metabolists and on collaborations between structural engineering and architecture. He is completing books on Tange Kenzō, Shinohara Kazuo, and Maki Fumihiko. Among the exhibitions he has curated are 'Utopia Across Scales: Highlights from the Kenzō Tange Archive' (Harvard Graduate School of Design, 2009) and 'On the Thresholds of Space-Making: Shinohara Kazuo' (Kemper Art Museum, 2014; ETHZ 2016). He holds a PhD in architectural history from Harvard University.

**Anthony Acciavatti** teaches at Columbia University in New York and is a founding partner in Somatic Collaborative. Trained as both an architect and a historian of science and technology, he is the author of the award-winning book, *Ganges Water Machine: Designing New India's Ancient River* (2015), and an editor of *Manifest: A Journal of American Architecture and Urbanism*. He is currently completing a book on the connections between the sciences and design in Asia and the Americas.

**Tao Zhu** is Associate Professor in Architecture and Co-director of the Centre for Chinese Architecture and Urban Design at the University of Hong Kong and Founding Principal of Tao Zhu Architecture Studio. He received his Master of Architecture and PhD in Architecture History and Theory from Columbia University. He practices in China and his research focuses on contemporary Chinese architecture and urbanism. He has published essays in *AA Files*, *AD* (*Architectural Design*), *a+u* (*Architecture and Urbanism Magazine)*, *Bauwelt*, *Domus,* and *Time + Architecture*. His recent writings include *Liang Sicheng and His Times* (Imaginist, 2014), a monograph examines Chinese architectural development in relation to Mao Zedong's socio-political campaigns during the 1950s, and a book chapter entitled 'Architecture in China in the Reform Era 1978-2010' for *A Critical History of Contemporary Architecture 1960-2010* (Ashgate, 2014). In 2010, he received the first Architectural Critics Award from the China Architecture Media Awards organized by China's mass media *Southern Metropolis Daily* in collaboration with eight major Chinese architectural magazines.

**Chris Brisbin** is Senior Lecturer in Architecture History, Theory, and Design at the University of South Australia and is Program Director of Architecture. He holds a PhD from The University of Queensland in art and architectural history. His research interests focus on the critical functioning of vernacular and contemporary architecture across the Australasian region. His work explores the interwoven relationship between signification, sign systems, and aesthetics applied in the public faces and threshold spaces of architecture. He publishes widely and has been an invited speaker and visiting professor in architectural design and counterfeit culture. He has co-convened symposia and conferences exploring the inter-disciplinary structures of critique, criticism, and criticality across Art, Architecture and Design. His most recent publications include *The Routledge Companion to Criticality in Art, Architecture and Design* (co-editor, Routledge, 2018); 'Horse horse tiger tiger: the critical functioning of Chinese copying and assemblage aesthetics', in *The Routledge Companion to Criticality in Art, Architecture and Design* (2018); 'Lost in translation: a critique of copyright and the aesthetics of re-production in China', in *Law Culture and the Humanities* (2017); and '"I hate cheap knock-offs!" Morphogenetic transformations of the Chinese "culture of the copy"', in *Disegno* (2016).

**Wenjun Zhi** is Professor in the College of Architecture and Urban Planning at Tongji University, Shanghai, China. He was a visiting scholar at the University of Hong Kong in 1996 and at Princeton University in 2009. He has authored and edited over 20 books, including *Contemporary Architecture in China, 2008-2012* and *Mario Botta, 1960-2015*, both published by Tongji University Press. Since 2001, he has been editor-in-chief of *Time + Architecture*, which, in its search for profound insights into contemporary urbanism and architecture, is one of the most influential academic journals in China. Zhi was a jury member for international architectural awards such as the BSI Architecture Award (Switzerland 2008) and exhibition curator of *M8 in China: Exhibition of Contemporary Young Chinese Architects* (Frankfurt and Berlin 2009).

**Guanghui Ding** is Associate Professor in Architecture at Beijing University of Civil Engineering and Architecture, China. He had worked as a Postdoctoral Research Fellow at City University of Hong Kong after receiving a PhD from the University of Nottingham, UK. His scholarly writings on the history of modern Chinese architecture appeared in *Architectural Research Quarterly*, *Habitat International*, *Journal of the Society of Architectural Historians* and other edited volumes. He is the author of *Constructing a Place of Critical Architecture in China: Intermediate Criticality in the Journal* Time + Architecture (Routledge, 2016) and co-author with Charlie Xue of *A History of Design Institutes in China: From Mao to Market* (Routledge, 2018).

**Sony Devabhaktuni** is Assistant Professor in the department of architecture at the University of Hong Kong. His research focuses on the capacity of architectural representation to address cultural, socio-political and economic issues. With his colleague, John Lin, he is currently studying informal transformations to vernacular housing typologies in Chinese villages. With Raffael Baur and Patricia Guaita from the Swiss Federal Institute of Technology (Lausanne), he founded The Open City Research Platform, an ongoing building workshop in partnership with David Jolly Monge from the School of Architecture and Design in Valparaiso (Chile) that explores collaborative design processes and open-ended construction. His work has been supported by grants from the Graham Foundation for Advanced Studies in the Fine Arts, the Fulbright Scholar Program and the General Research Fund of the Hong Kong SAR government. He studied architecture at the Cooper Union for the Advancement of Science and Art and literature at Stanford University.

**Jonathan Massey** is Dean and Professor at the Taubman College of Architecture and Urban Planning at the University of Michigan. In his previous position as dean of architecture at California College of Arts, his primary responsibility was for the vision, leadership, and administration of the CCA Architecture Division, which includes three accredited programs in architecture and interior design. At Syracuse University, he was the Laura J. and L. Douglas Meredith Professor for Teaching Excellence, where he chaired the Bachelor of Architecture program and the University Senate. Massey holds undergraduate and doctoral degrees from Princeton University as well as a Master of Architecture degree from UCLA. He was a co-founder of the Transdisciplinary Media Studio and the Aggregate Architectural History Collaborative, which focus on the ways that history and practice of architecture and urbanism are understood and taught. His ongoing research explores how architecture mediates power by forming civil society, shaping social relationships, and regulating consumption. His work on topics ranging from ornament and organicism to risk management and sustainable design has appeared in many journals and essay collections, including Aggregate's essay collection *Governing by Design: Architecture, Economy, and Politics in the 20th Century* (University of Pittsburgh Press, 2012).

**Angelika Schnell** is Professor of Architecture Theory and Architecture History at the Academy of Fine Arts Vienna. She studied Theatre Science and Architecture in Munich, Berlin and Delft. From 1993–2001, she was the editor of the Berlin-based architectural theory magazine *ARCH+*. Since 1999, she has held teaching positions in architectural history and architectural theory at several international universities. She is a permanent member of the editorial board of *ARCH+* and of *Candide*, journal for architectural knowledge. Her book, *Aldo Rossis Konstruktion des Wirklichen. Eine widersprüchliche Architekturtheorie*, will be published in 2019 under the renowned theoretical book series *Bauwelt Fundamente*, for which she has recently been named co-editor. Her numerous essays in international magazines and journals look at the history and theory of modernism, modern architecture and urban planning in the twentieth and twenty-first century, media and architecture, design methods, and the relationship of postmodern architecture and theory to the arts, to literature and to psychoanalysis.

**Xiaoxuan Lu** is Assistant Professor in the Division of Landscape Architecture at the University of Hong Kong, where she teaches landscape history and theory, and design studios. Before joining the Division of Landscape Architecture, she practiced in the fields of architecture and landscape architecture at Turenscape in Beijing, West 8 in Rotterdam, Bjarke Ingels Group in Copenhagen, and SWA in Los Angeles. Her research focuses on the cultural landscape and geography of conflict, particularly in transboundary regions. Applying analytical cartography, photography and videography in her research, she aims to reveal the hidden layers of landscape where multiple tensions converge. Her articles have been published in *LEAP, Calvert Journal, ON SITE Review, Journal of Natural Resources, Human Geography,* and *Acta Ecologica Sinica.* She received her Bachelor of Architecture from Southern California Institute of Architecture, and Master in Landscape Architecture from Harvard University. She was a PhD Fellow at Harvard University during the academic years of 2014-2016, and received her PhD in Human Geography from Peking University in early 2017.

**Cecilia L. Chu** is Assistant Professor in the Division of Landscape Architecture at the University of Hong Kong, where she teaches urban theory, urban design and architectural and landscape history. Prior to her academic career, she worked as a professional designer in Canada and Hong Kong and research consultant for several NGOs focusing on urban renewal and conservation strategies. She is a founding member and current president of DOCOMOMO Hong Kong Chapter, an executive board member of the International Association for the Study of Traditional Environments (IASTE), and an editorial board member of *Journal for the Royal Asiatic Society Hong Kong, Traditional Dwellings and Settlements Review*, and *Surveying and the Built Environment*. Dr. Chu is a recipient of two major research grants awarded by the Hong Kong Research Grants Council. Her articles have been published in leading academic journals, including *Journal of Architecture, Journal of Historical Geography, Urban Studies, Habitat International, Planning Perspectives, Geoforum, Design Issues,* and *Architectural Theory Review*. She is currently completing a monograph, entitled *Colonial Urban Development in Hong Kong: Speculative Housing and Segregation in the City* (under contract with Routledge, to be published in its Planning, History and Environment Series in 2019). She is also co-editing a book that examines emergent forms and norms of the built environment amidst escalating property speculation around the world in the 21st century.

**From Crisis to Crisis: debates on why architecture criticism matters today**
This publication was supported by a design publishing grant from The University of Hong Kong.

**Editors**
Nasrin Seraji, Sony Devabhaktuni and Xiaoxuan Lu

**Authors**
Anthony Acciavatti, Chris Brisbin, Cecilia Chu, Sony Devabhaktuni, Guanghui Ding, Françoise Fromonot, Xiaoxuan Lu, Jonathan Massey, Graham Brenton McKay, Seng Kuan, Kamran Afshar Naderi, Cole Roskam, Angelika Schnell, Eunice Seng, Nasrin Seraji, Wenjun Zhi and Tao Zhu

**Design**
Actar

**Cover**
The cover design is adapted from the symposium poster by Klaus Stille.

**Copy editing**
Sarah Handelman

**Transcription**
Stephanie Veanca Ho

**Proofreading**
Joy Zhu

**Acknowledgements**
The editors would like to thank the administrative staff in the department of architecture for their assistance. We are particularly grateful to Esther Siu, who helped to ensure that the symposium ran smoothly for both speakers and attendees and to Olivia Lai who navigated various institutional and administrative hoops to make this publication possible.

**Printing and binding**
Tiger Printing, Hong Kong

All rights reserved
© edition: Actar Publishers
© texts: Their authors
© Designs, drawings, illustrations, and photographs: Their authors

This work is subject to copyright. All rights are reserved, on all or part of the material, specifically translation rights, reprinting, re-use of illustrations, recitation, broadcasting, reproduction on microfilm or other media, and storage in databases. For use of any kind, permission of the copyright owner must be obtained.

**Distribution**
Actar D, Inc. New York, Barcelona.

New York
440 Park Avenue South, 17th Floor
New York, NY 10016, USA
T +1 2129662207
salesnewyork@actar-d.com

Barcelona
Roca i Batlle 2-4
08023 Barcelona, Spain
T +34 933 282 183
eurosales@actar-d.com

**Indexing**
ISBN: 9781948765053
PCN: Library of Congress Control Number: 2018942826

Printed in China

Publication date: January 2019